Advar...

Another Chance at Life

"Who better to tell the story of the prodigal in fresh, insightful, convicting and instructive ways than Warren Wiersbe? If you think you're familiar with this story, think again. This is vintage Wiersbe!"

Dr. Joseph Stowell
President, Cornerstone University
Grand Rapids, Michigan

"Warren Wiersbe's new book *Another Chance at Life* gives us another chance of learning valuable lessons from the most memorable parable that came from the lips of Jesus. You will be reminded again of God's incredible love and grace as you see yourself in this story of the son who was given another chance at life. This masterful Bible teacher has produced a masterpiece that gives us fresh hope for the future."

Pastor Jim Cymbala
The Brooklyn Tabernacle
Brooklyn, New York

ANOTHER CHANCE at LIFE

WARREN W. WIERSBE

CLC
PUBLICATIONS

Fort Washington, PA 19034

Another Chance at Life
ISBN: 978-0-87508-996-6

© 2009 by Dr. Warren W. Wiersbe
This printing 2009
Published by CLC Publications

U.S.A.
P.O. Box 1449, Fort Washington, PA 19034

GREAT BRITAIN
51 The Dean, Alresford, Hants SO24 9BJ

AUSTRALIA
P.O. Box 2299, Strathpine QLD 4500

NEW ZEALAND
10 MacArthur Street, Feilding

The Story of the Prodigal Son

Now the tax collectors and sinners were all gathering around to hear Jesus. But the Pharisees and the teachers of the law muttered, "This man welcomes sinners and eats with them."

(Luke 15:1–2)

Table of Contents/Cast of Characters

Prologue

The most successful people are those who enjoy satisfying relationships, give useful service to others and know how to make new beginnings, even after what looks like failure. They're concerned about making a life and not just making a living.

When successful people fail, they don't make excuses. They get up and start over again. They realize that failure doesn't have to be permanent. And when they succeed, they don't relax and start bragging. They find new challenges and start tackling them. They find people who need help, and they help them.

It's a great way to live, but we can't do it alone. We need divine help. We need Jesus.

This book is based on an ancient story Jesus told, the parable of the prodigal (or wasteful) son. It's found in the New Testament in the fifteenth chapter of Luke's Gospel. The story is so simple that a child can understand it, and yet it's so profound that we can study it over and over and still learn new truths from it.

The story has a Jewish setting, but the characters and events in it belong to every generation of every nation. They belong to you and to me, and so do the lessons they teach.

Each of us is somewhere in this story. Therefore, we need

to read it carefully, learn from it and act on the lessons we learn. By doing this, we take steps toward the new beginnings that will help us turn failure into success.

It's always the right time for a new beginning—to start living a new life.

Warren W. Wiersbe

One

The Wonderful Teacher

(Luke 15:1–10)

When was the last time you listened to what Jesus had to say about life?

Many people have written and spoken about life, but nobody ever did it better than He did.

"No one ever spoke the way this man does!" That's what people said about Jesus when they heard Him in the temple courts in Jerusalem (John 7:46). Matthew wrote that "the crowds were amazed at his teaching, because he taught as one who had authority, and not as their teachers of the law" (Matt. 7:28–29). Luke the physician wrote that the people "were amazed at the gracious words that came from his lips" (Luke 4:22).

Luke introduced the story of the prodigal son with, "Now the tax collectors and sinners were all gathering around to hear Jesus" (15:1). That's the setting of the story. Now let's get acquainted with the members of the cast, because each of us is in the cast—somewhere.

*   *   *   *   *

The tax collectors, or publicans, were Jewish men who had purchased from the Romans the authority to collect taxes from their own people, and for this "treachery" they were disowned by just about everybody. When tax collectors came to be baptized by John the Baptist, he warned them, "Don't collect any more than you are required to" (Luke 3:13), which suggests that their dealings weren't always honest. For robbing the Jewish people and fraternizing with the godless Romans, the publicans were a hated class. According to the rabbis, if a tax collector entered a Jewish house, he defiled it, and the house had to be cleansed.

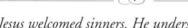

Jesus welcomed sinners. He understood them and taught them what they needed to know.

The people Luke called "sinners" were Jews in name only. They had abandoned religious practices and lived more like Gentiles than Jews. They didn't honor the feast days or the Sabbaths, nor did they attend the synagogue or temple services. They didn't hide the fact that they cared little about dietary laws or ceremonial traditions.

Instead of trying to win them, the teachers of the law (scribes) and the Pharisees condemned them and gave them a wide berth. However, Jesus welcomed them. He understood them and taught them what they needed to know. He also died for them, just as he died for you and me.

The Pharisees and scribes were the religious leaders of that day, and Jesus didn't have much good to say about them.

The word "Pharisee" means "separated one." They felt that they were better than other people and prayed, "God, I thank you that I am not like other people—robbers, evildoers, adulterers—or even like this tax collector" (Luke 18:11).

In Matthew 23, Jesus called them hypocrites—"play actors"—and compared them to cups that looked clean on the outside but were filthy on the inside. He said they were like whitewashed tombs filled with unclean bones, and anyone who touched them would be defiled.

To Jesus, these men were blind guides who didn't know the Scriptures and were leading people astray. "You snakes!" He said to them. "You brood of vipers! How will you escape being condemned to hell?" (Matt. 23:33). Jesus rejected their egotistical religious legalism, and most of them rejected Him.

There were a few Pharisees like Nicodemus and Joseph of Arimathea who trusted the Lord and followed Him (John 3:1–21; 19:38–42). But for the most part, the Pharisees rejected Him and opposed His ministry. However, Jesus loved the Pharisees and died for them, too.

The religious leaders were shocked when they saw large numbers of tax collectors and sinners gathered about Jesus. They kept muttering, "This man welcomes sinners and eats with them" (Luke 15:2). That critical statement is one of the keys to this story: *Jesus attracted sinners.* He welcomed the outcasts and the rejects and even sat down and ate with them. Why? *Because He loved them and wanted to give them another chance at life.* He said, "I have come that they may have life, and have it to the full" (John 10:10).

Jesus didn't attract the tax collectors and sinners by catering to them, entertaining them, agreeing with their lifestyle or compromising His message. If you read Luke 14:25–

35, you will discover that Jesus had just preached a stern message on discipleship and three times had used the phrase "cannot be my disciple." He never adjusted His message just to get a crowd. He told the multitudes that to follow Him meant carrying a cross.

The publicans and sinners heard Him say this, and yet they wanted to hear more. Jesus said to the chief priests and elders, "Truly I tell you, the tax collectors and the prostitutes are entering the kingdom of God ahead of you" (Matt. 21:31). It takes more than "religion" to experience real life.

Success that is aware of itself can easily lead to failure. "Pride goes before destruction, a haughty spirit before a fall" (Prov. 16:18). But when we know we've failed and we admit it, we take the first step toward success. Those tax collectors and irreligious Jews were taking that step by listening to Jesus and taking His message seriously. They wanted to begin again, and He alone was the one who could help them.

*   *   *   *   *

How did Jesus deal with these critical scribes and Pharisees? After all, He loved the outcasts the Pharisees were attacking, and He was even enjoying a meal with them; so why interrupt His ministry by starting an argument? Why turn the dining room into a courtroom? Jesus did a very wise thing: He started telling stories.

Often in His ministry Jesus defused a potential crisis situation by telling stories called "parables." The word comes from the ancient Greek language and means "to cast alongside."[1] A parable begins as a picture of something familiar in life. This picture is "cast alongside" the situation we are in so we can better understand it. As we look at the picture, it gradually becomes a mirror and we see ourselves. We are in the story!

If we accept what we see and admit our needs, the mirror then becomes a window through which we see God and His life-changing grace. If we reject what we see in the mirror, the parable does us no good. Often during Jesus' ministry, when the religious leaders grasped the true meaning of one of His parables, they became angry and wanted to silence Him (Luke 20:19).

Jesus told them three stories focused on the same theme: finding something that's been lost and giving it a new beginning.

"Then Jesus told them this parable" (Luke 15:3). Actually, He told them three stories focused on the same theme: *finding something that's been lost and giving it a new beginning.* His words were like a beautiful jewel of three facets: a lost sheep, a lost coin and a lost son. With this triptych parable Jesus captured their attention, convicted their hearts and encouraged their faith.

When He spoke about the sheep and the coin, He began with the word "suppose" as if to say, "Surely you won't disagree with this scenario." Even though the Pharisees personally thought that women and shepherds were inferior people, they would still agree that a shepherd would rescue a lost sheep and a woman would scour the house to find a lost coin.

However, the Pharisees might not agree with Jesus that a father would welcome and forgive a wasteful, disobedient son. Jehovah the God of Israel was made of much sterner stuff than that. There was no place in Pharisaic theology for merciful new beginnings.

*　　*　　*　　*　　*

Let's pause to consider the sheep, the coin and the son.

Why was the sheep lost? Because that's the nature of the beast. Sheep have poor eyesight and no built-in compass to direct them. While eating in a grassy field, they can easily wander far from the flock, make a wrong turn and end up lost. Sheep get lost because of *heedlessness*. Many people are just like them. "We all, like sheep, have gone astray, each of us has turned to our own way" (Isa. 53:6). Lost people go through life giving no thought to God or to their own destiny, and they wander into failure because they don't have a shepherd.

The coin was lost because of *carelessness*. The drachma was a silver coin that, oddly enough, was worth the price of one sheep. Perhaps the coin was part of the woman's wedding necklace. She certainly wouldn't want to mar such an important piece of jewelry, so she searched diligently for the coin. More than one son or daughter has been lost because of carelessness on the part of parents or siblings *right at home*.

But the boy is our main interest, the lad we call "the prodigal son." He wasn't lost because of heedlessness, because he sinned with his eyes wide open. Nor was there carelessness on the part of his father, who loved him dearly. He was lost because of *willfulness*.

Granted, his older brother may not have been the easiest person to get along with, but that was still no reason for the boy to leave home. The young man had a hidden agenda and was determined to follow it. He wanted to be free, but he didn't really know what freedom was. He wanted to do things his way, and he felt his only option was to leave the family and go it alone.

God "wants all people to be saved and to come to a knowledge of the truth" (1 Tim. 2:4), but not all people are willing to hear the truth and believe it. Jesus said, "These are the very Scriptures that testify about me, yet you refuse to come to me to have life" (John 5:39–40). This is the sin of willfulness.

*   *   *   *   *

The sheep and the coin were found again and experienced a new beginning, and the son was welcomed back home and forgiven. But it's a good thing the people who found them weren't motivated by mathematics; otherwise, they might have deserted them. Why worry about one sheep out of a hundred or one coin out of ten? The percentage keeps getting higher until we have one son out of two.

It wasn't a matter of percentages, but of values, because to God each individual soul is precious. The shepherd searched for the sheep because it was *his* sheep and was valuable to him. (Jewish shepherds would call each sheep by name.) The woman searched for the coin because it was valuable and stood for something precious to her. The father waited and watched for the younger son and welcomed him home with forgiveness because the lad was valuable, a human made in the image of God.

In this day of widely publicized church statistics, we wonder if measuring crowds hasn't made us forget the importance of loving individuals. Jesus took time for individuals and even interrupted His public ministry to the crowds to heal one sick woman or help one grieving father.

The word "pastor" means "shepherd," but some of today's shepherds don't even know the names of their sheep, let alone the battles they face and the burdens they carry. Some don't even want to be called "shepherds," and this may be a good thing, because they are more like CEOs of a business or ringmasters of a circus than like shepherds of God's flock.

*   *   *   *   *

We've looked at the cast. Now let's examine the vocabulary. We'll begin with the question, "What does it mean to be lost?"

God didn't create us to be out of place, in danger,
useless and unhappy.

From the viewpoint of these parables, being lost means being out of place, useless, unhappy and in danger. The sheep belonged in the flock, under the shepherd's loving care, and was useless wandering in the wilderness. Any hungry predator could have killed and eaten it. The coin belonged on the necklace. It still had the same value when it was lost, but that value couldn't be put to work. You can't buy anything with a lost coin. If it had not been found, it might have been carelessly swept up and dropped in the trash.

As for the son, because he was out of place, he lost the enjoyment of home and the experience of his father's love. All he could do in the far country was live on memories. He was useless to his father and brother, and not much help to his Gentile pig farmer. Day by day, he went from bad to worse, asking for food and never receiving it. God didn't create us to be out of place, in danger, useless and unhappy.

What, then, does it mean to be found? It means to be back in the place of safety, service and enjoyment, being and doing what God ordained for us. It means we are no longer in danger. Instead of wasting our lives and our resources, we are investing ourselves in others and producing good to the glory of God.

But notice the new element introduced when the lost are found—*rejoicing.*

The shepherd rejoiced at finding the sheep, put it on his shoulders (note the plural—the animal couldn't escape), took it home and invited the neighbors to rejoice with him. The woman rejoiced to find her coin and invited the neighborhood women to celebrate with her. The father rejoiced at his son's return and invited the whole village to make merry with him. Jesus said that when the lost are found and experience a new beginning, there is even joy in heaven.

Nobody denies that there is pleasure in sin. But that pleasure is temporary and costly. There's no lasting joy in sin, nothing that reaches up to heaven and moves the angels to praise God. Lost people don't like to admit it, but they are miserable as they spend time and money searching for relief from their boredom and their aimless way of life.

We can never find satisfaction and fulfillment in that which doesn't last—"the fleeting pleasures of sin" (Heb. 11:25).

Happiness usually depends on happenings—and most happenings are not in our control. But joy is a gift from the Lord, a "fruit" that grows in our hearts and produces more fruit (Gal. 5:22–23). The message of Jesus is "good news of great joy" (Luke 2:10).

Why would the angels in heaven rejoice when people repent, trust Jesus and experience a new beginning? Because they know what we were saved *for* in the wonderful plan of God—to serve Him on earth and to one day share in His glorious home in heaven (John 14:1–6). They also know what we were saved *from*, the terrible judgment "prepared for the devil and his angels" (Matt. 25:41).

The angels have never experienced God's saving grace personally. But as they have watched God's plan unfolding on earth, they have understood something of what it means to become a new creation in Jesus Christ and to share the very life of God. Living as a child of God isn't punishment; it's the highest form of enjoyment and enrichment, *and it lasts forever.*

*   *   *   *   *

Perhaps you think these ancient stories really have no significance for enlightened people in today's world. You may see them only as interesting literary museum pieces and nothing more. Then let me tell you a story of my own.

Back in the turbulent sixties, I was invited to address a group of college and university students in upstate New York. I began by asking them this question: "If you had to name three men whose ideas about humanity have most impacted our world this past century, who would they be?"

I gave them three minutes to make up their minds. They pondered a moment and then began huddling and discussing until I signaled that the time was up.

A hand immediately went up. "Charles Darwin!" Another hand went up. "Karl Marx!" Then there was a brief silence until a student called out, "Freud!"

I congratulated them on their choices and asked a second question: "What view of human beings did each of these men hold? Let's start with Darwin. When he looked at a man or a woman, what did he see?"

"A highly developed animal," replied a young lady.

"Excellent—an animal. And what did Karl Marx see?"

"A worker, an economic factor in a capitalistic society," said a young man.

"Very good. An economic factor." Before I could say another word, a student called out, "And Freud saw us as children who never really grew up, spoiled brats with all kinds of weird hang-ups."

I congratulated the students on their answers and said, "Did you know that Jesus would have agreed with all of your choices? Open your Bibles to Luke, chapter fifteen, and see for yourselves. In these three stories, Jesus says we are animals—lost sheep; we are economic factors—lost coins; and we are mixed up kids—lost children, sons and daughters who want our own way. Students, Jesus was centuries ahead of His time."

But I'm not the only writer who has linked Darwin, Marx and Freud. William Golding in his book *A Moving Target* called these three men "the most crashing bores of the Western world."[2] A courageous statement indeed! Psychiatrist Erik H. Erickson also connected these men: "And chances they took, the revolutionary minds of the middle class of the nineteenth century: Darwin by making man's very humanity relative to his animal ancestry; Marx, by exposing the middle-class mind as class bound; and Freud by making our ideals and our very consciousness relative to an unconscious mental life."[3] Finally, one of my favorite historians, Barbara Tuchman, called Darwin, Marx and Freud "the three great makers of the modern mind."[4]

I rest my case.

Two

The Wasteful Son

(Luke 15:11–16)

" There was a man who had two sons" (Luke 15:11).
The people in this parable are nameless, but we have
no problem identifying them. The father represents God in
the person of Jesus Christ. ("Anyone who has seen me has
seen the Father," said Jesus in John 14:9.) The younger son
represents the publicans and sinners who had wandered from
their spiritual home and were seeking a new start in life. The
older brother pictures the self-righteous Pharisees and the
scribes who criticized Jesus and His friends and who would
not repent. Like the sheep, the younger son wandered away
from home, and like the coin, the elder brother was lost *at*
home even as he faithfully obeyed his father.

When Jesus said, "There was a man who had two sons,"
He immediately awakened their interest, because the image
of two sons runs through the book of Genesis and forms a
foundation for the history of Israel.

Adam had two sons, Cain and Abel (Gen. 4). Abel was a
true believer who brought a proper sacrifice and was accepted

by the Lord, while Cain, a counterfeit, was rejected. The apostle John wrote that Cain "belonged to the evil one," which explains why Cain killed Abel and then tried to cover his sin (see 1 John 3:11–15). Satan is a liar and a murderer (John 8:44), and Cain imitated him. God rejected Cain the firstborn and accepted Abel the second born.

Abraham had two sons, Ishmael and Isaac. God had promised Abraham and Sarah a son, but as the years went by and they grew older, no son was given. Sarah suggested that Abraham father a son by her maid Hagar, and that's how Ishmael was born. Fourteen years later, Isaac, the promised son, was born. Here's how Paul distinguished between the two boys: "His son by the slave woman was born as the result of human effort, but his son by the free woman was born as the result of a divine promise" (Gal. 4:23). God rejected Ishmael the firstborn and accepted Isaac the second born.

God still rejects our first birth and offers us a second birth—a "new birth" through faith in Jesus Christ.

Isaac was the father of twin sons, Esau and Jacob. Before they were born, God announced that the older son (Esau) would serve the younger, so Jacob was considered the "first-born" by God (Gen. 25:21–26). Again, the Lord rejected the firstborn and chose the second born, and Jacob became the father of twelve sons who founded the twelve tribes of Israel.

Jacob's son Joseph had two sons, Manasseh and Ephraim (Gen. 41:50–52). When their grandfather blessed the boys, he crossed his arms and put his right hand on the head of Ephraim, the younger son, and gave him the blessing of the firstborn (Gen. 48). From then on, people said "Ephraim and Manasseh." Once again, it was the second born who received the blessing, not the firstborn.

God still rejects our first birth and offers us a second birth—a "new birth" through faith in Jesus Christ (John 3:1–18). God didn't "cross His arms" to give us this blessing. Instead, He sent his Son to a cross to die for our sins, making the way for us to be born into the family of God and receive a new beginning in life. "Therefore, if anyone is in Christ, the new creation has come: The old has gone, the new is here!" (2 Cor. 5:17).

*   *   *   *   *

The younger son's heart was in the far country long before he went to live there. In his imagination he secretly enjoyed the pleasures he planned to find once he got away from home.

The imagination is like a womb that can give birth to ideas that are either creative or destructive. "Then, after desire has conceived, it gives birth to sin; and sin, when it is full-grown, gives birth to death" (James 1:15). David gives a similar description in Psalm 7:14: "Those who are pregnant with evil conceive trouble and give birth to disillusionment."

The longer the boy dreamed of the far country, the more he sowed the seeds that would eventually produce trouble and disappointment. Dean William R. Inge expressed it well in his *Outspoken Essays, Second Series*: "We are always sowing our future; we are always reaping our past."[1]

It wasn't unusual for Jewish young men to leave home and join their relatives or friends in other parts of the Mediterranean world. Historians estimate that there were at least four million Jews in the *diaspora*[2] in contrast to only half a million living in the Holy Land.

But the younger son wasn't planning to visit relatives. He wanted to remain a successful stranger in the far country so he could "do his own thing."

The quotation from the French mathematician Blaise Pascal comes to mind: "All the unhappiness of men arises from one single fact, that they cannot stay quietly in their own chamber." The lad didn't realize that if he couldn't find satisfaction at home, he would never find it anywhere else. "I have learned the secret of being content in any and every situation," wrote the apostle Paul, and his secret was, "I can do all this through him [Christ] who gives me strength" (Phil. 4:12–13).

*   *   *   *   *

"Everybody's always talking about people breaking into houses . . . but there are more people in the world who want to break out of houses." Playwright Thornton Wilder makes this statement in *The Matchmaker*, and it applies to the prodigal son. What the younger son wanted was freedom—freedom from the authority of his father as well as from the critical watchful eye of his big brother. But he had no idea what freedom really meant.

James Boswell in his *Life of Samuel Johnson* reports that on Thursday April 8, 1779, Johnson was dining with some noblemen, and one of them mentioned a man who "had a great love of liberty." Dr. Johnson smiled and said, "He is *young*, my Lord; all *boys* love liberty, till experience convinces them they are not so fit to govern themselves as they imagined." In his play *Man and Superman*, George Bernard Shaw stated a similar truth in another way: "Liberty means responsibility. That is why most men dread it."

But our young man had no fears. All he needed was freedom from the family and some money in his pocket, and he was sure he would be happy and successful. But if you had asked him to define *freedom*, *happiness* and *success*, he would have failed the test.

When the far country is more inviting than home, and when having our own way is more important than developing discipline and obedience, we're truly heading for trouble.

The American philosopher William James wrote in *The Will to Believe*, "The first act of freedom is to choose it." He might have added, "The second act of freedom is to pay for it," because freedom is not free. It's very costly. *Freedom is life controlled by truth and motivated by love.* "If you hold to my teaching," said Jesus, "you are really my disciples. Then you will know the truth, and the truth will set you free" (John 8:31–32).

The person whose life is motivated by pride, selfishness or hatred is in terrible bondage. If that life is controlled by lies, it only makes matters worse. Until he returned home, the younger son lived reprehensibly because he was under the illusion that money, independence and distance would provide the freedom he longed for.

It's sad when a person loves things more than people and uses and abuses people just to get those things. Consider the way the boy treated his father. According to Jewish law, when the father died, the older son was to receive a double portion of the estate and the younger sons a single portion (Deut. 21:15–17). In asking to receive his inheritance, the younger son was telling his family—and everybody in the village— that *he wished his father were dead!* When the far country is more inviting than home, and when having our own way is more important than developing discipline and obedience, we're truly heading for trouble.

"A man's worse difficulties begin," said Thomas H. Huxley, "when he is able to do as he likes." The most painful discipline God can send people is to allow them to have their own way and suffer the consequences.

Three times in the first chapter of Romans we read "God gave them over" (1:24, 26, 28), which means He permitted them to have their own way. In *The Great Divorce* C.S. Lewis writes, "There are only two kinds of people in the end: those who say to God, 'Thy will be done,' and those to whom God says, in the end, '*Thy* will be done.'"

"Freedom to enjoy" is not the same as "the enjoyment of freedom." We can't really enjoy freedom unless we're doing the will of God and being accountable to others. True freedom involves commitment and community. The younger son wanted to be free *from* his father and brother, and also free to *do* his own will. But freedom without responsibility and accountability leads to license, and license leads to anarchy. This is how dictators rise to power.

As novelist George MacDonald wrote, "In whatever man does without God, he must fail miserably, or succeed more miserably." The boy eventually experienced miserable success, as will everybody who follows his bad example.

*   *   *   *   *

We must not ignore the phrase in Luke 15:13, "Not long after that . . ." Indulgence and impatience usually go together. Patience is a mark of maturity (James 1:2–4), while impatience is something we expect in little children. Almost every family has at least one child who, while on a vacation, asks every five minutes, "Are we there yet?"

Once the boy had money in hand, he was ready to leave home, and he took his whole inheritance with him. That way he wouldn't have to return home. He didn't save or invest any of it for future use, nor did he ask his father or brother for advice on how to spend it. After all, he was a big boy now! Or was he?

We all need to respect the discipline of delay if we're going to become mature people. The importance of "postponed pleasures" for the building of character can't be overrated, for character is the foundation of a successful life. A man and his girlfriend were employed in the same office and eventually ended up sleeping in the same bed. When they finally got married, a fellow employee sent them a telegram on their honeymoon that read, "So what's new?"

Nothing was new, but apparently the couple didn't care. We don't hear as much about the "Now Generation" today as we did years ago, but the malady is still rampant. Sex isn't a toy to play with; it's a precious gift to protect and enjoy in the sanctity of marriage. According to the apostle Paul, even married people need discipline in this area of life (1 Cor. 7:1–7).

But sex isn't the only thing that's defiled by immature and undisciplined people who can't wait. There's also the matter of money. The ease of obtaining and using credit cards has created a generation of passionate consumers who kite checks and apply for new cards to help pay off old ones.

When children and teens go too far, too fast and are handed adult experiences, they get just enough to keep them from getting the real thing.

Their appetites aroused by clever promotion, these "shop-a-holics" are as out of control as the alcoholics and are doing almost as much damage. They must have new versions of every electronic device, not because they need them, but because they want them—and don't want to be laughed at for being without.

It's sad when children and teens have opportunities to waste wealth before they're ready to appreciate and enjoy God's gifts. Childhood and adolescence are rapidly vanishing as entire industries devote themselves to making young people grow up as quickly as possible so they can become trapped and trained consumers.

Don't these promoters know that it takes some maturity to really enjoy the great experiences of life? When children and teens go too far, too fast and are handed adult experiences, this premature exposure acts as a vaccination: The young people get just enough *to keep them from getting the real thing.* Many victims become pseudo-adults who spend their lives enjoying pseudo-events and living on substitutes.

*   *   *   *   *

Perhaps the greatest modern delusion is that money and the things it can buy are keys to freedom. In themselves, things aren't evil, because God made them and pronounced them "very good" (Gen. 1:31). God knows that we need things (Matt. 6:31–34), and He wants us to enjoy them (1 Tim. 6:17). God also knows that we need money to purchase things, so He "gives [us] the ability to produce wealth" (Deut. 8:18).

However, He warns us not to put wealth ahead of the Giver, because that's idolatry. God sees "things" as "fringe benefits" in the lives of those who willingly submit to Him. "But seek first his kingdom and his righteousness, and all these things will be given to you as well" (Matt. 6:33). "Watch out! Be on your guard against all kinds of greed; life does not consist in an abundance of possessions" (Luke 12:15).

And yet, when a man dies, somebody is sure to ask, "How much did he leave?" The answer, of course, is always the same—*everything*. "For we brought nothing into the world, and we can take nothing out of it" (1 Tim. 6:7).

It's good to have the things money can buy if we don't lose what money can't buy. The young man left more behind at home than he gained in the far country: fellowship with his father and growth in wisdom; productivity alongside his brother and the servants; promoting good fellowship among the neighbors; and maturing in soul, mind and body to the glory of God. Money can buy knowledge but not wisdom. It can purchase lust but not love, physical pleasure but not spiritual enrichment.

The younger son didn't realize his folly until he had spent

his inheritance and was begging for food. While living at home, he had decided that luxuries were necessities, but when living on the pig farm, he discovered that necessities were really luxuries. The young man's prayer, "Father, give me," led to disaster, but his later prayer, "Father, make me," led to another chance at life.

While he was still at home, he was a son with the potential of becoming a success; in the far country, he was a slave with a very dim future. His "freedom" was actually indulgence that enabled his new friends to drag him into bondage. "They promise them freedom, while they themselves are slaves of depravity—for 'people are slaves to whatever has mastered them'" (2 Pet. 2:19).

Sin promises life but brings death; it promises freedom but produces slavery; and it promises success but generates failure. The young man wanted to find himself, but, alas, he lost himself! He also lost his new friends, for as soon as the boy's money was gone, his friends were too. The German poet and dramatist Goethe wrote, "Whatever liberates our spirit without giving us self-control is disastrous." Bondage and bankruptcy aren't a happy combination.

The younger son definitely had "I" trouble: idolatry, indifference, impatience, ignorance, independence, indulgence . . . On it goes.

What did he need? British theologian P.T. Forsyth said it best: "The first duty of every soul is to find not its freedom but its Master."[3]

That Master is Jesus Christ, and the boy finally met Him.

Three

The Grateful Son

(Luke 15:17–20a)

The statement "no one gave him anything" (Luke 15:16) pulls at your heart. But he was a stranger in town, an inexperienced youth among crafty adults, a Jew among Gentiles and, even worse, a destitute pig tender, so it's no wonder people ignored him. He had wasted his inheritance buying friends, but now that his money was gone, the so-called friends had forsaken him. "Look and see, there is no one at my right hand; no one is concerned for me. I have no refuge; no one cares for my life" (Ps. 142:4).

He was alone. But enforced times of solitude can become turning points that lead us to another chance at life.

If while still at home the boy had spent quality time alone—meditating on God's truth, pondering the lessons of life his father taught him—he might not have acted so foolishly. But some people can't stand solitude, probably because they always need someone or something to entertain them and distract them from themselves. I find solitude refreshing, but perhaps in Jesus' day, as in ours, any solitary youth was branded odd. Most young people today are ardent groupies.

"What a commentary on our civilization," wrote Anne Morrow Lindbergh in *Gift from the Sea*, "when being alone is considered suspect; when one has to apologize for it, make excuses, hide the fact that one practices it—like a secret vice!"

Whenever my wife was away from home helping one of our children with a newborn baby, or perhaps attending a women's retreat, it bothered me the way some of my friends pitied me and offered to entertain me. They didn't seem to understand that, no matter how much married couples love each other, they can't live in each other's hip pocket seven days a week. They need breathing space, margins in their lives, room for growth. Solitude rightly used can do that for us. I was always glad to see my wife back home, but the days she was away weren't wasted.

Enforced times of solitude can become turning points that lead us to another chance at life.

Jesus used the first hours of the day for private communion with the Father. "Very early in the morning, while it was still dark, Jesus got up, left the house and went off to a solitary place, where he prayed" (Mark 1:35). "He wakens me morning by morning, wakens my ear to listen like one being taught" (Isa. 50:4).

But just as it's possible to be lonely in a big crowd, so it's possible to experience solitude in a big crowd, if we've practiced true solitude away from the crowd. On more than one occasion in an airport or a crowded doctor's waiting room, I've "crept into myself" and communed with the Lord. There are times when this is the only way to keep life from falling apart. One of the best things that happened to the young man in the far country was this opportunity to be alone and think.

*   *   *   *   *

The second best thing he did was talk to himself.

Unless you're old and senile, you can't easily get away with it—but he did it just the same, taking brave steps toward his new life. A friend of mind used to call this "putting your heads together," and I recommend the practice when you're alone. When the young man "came to himself" (Luke 15:17, KJV) and then talked to himself, he got better acquainted with himself—and things began to change.

Hunger pangs had something to do with it, of course. They awakened memories of ample meals at home where even the lowest servants—the day laborers—were eating better than he was in the far country.

Jesus compared the heavenly Father's will to food. "My food . . . is to do the will of him who sent me and to finish his work" (John 4:34). The young man had asked for his father's wealth but not for his father's will, so what should have been nourishment became punishment. When we pray the Lord's Prayer (Matt. 6:9–13), we ask for the Father's will *before* we ask for daily bread, lest we waste what He gives us.

An ungrateful heart and a bad memory often lead the way to disobedience. When people forget God's goodness and stop thanking Him, they become fools, and they start worshiping idols. "For although they knew God, they neither glorified him as God nor gave thanks to him, but their thinking became futile and their foolish hearts were darkened" (Rom. 1:21–25).

The English words "thank" and "think" are related not only etymologically but also experientially. Once the younger son started being thankful, he started thinking straight, and he began to make much wiser decisions.

Too many people have the idea that sinners repent because they're crushed by their own "badness," when actually it's the overwhelming kindness of God that leads sinners to repentance (Rom. 2:4). Once we acknowledge His goodness to us, we have a better view of our own sin, and then we can appreciate and experience God's grace.

In theological language, the young man was experiencing *repentance*, which simply means he was changing his mind. For weeks he had been "beside himself" and unable to get the right perspective on life, but now he "came to himself" (KJV) and began to think clearly. Weighing the situation in the far country against the generosity of his father at home, he realized that the best thing to do was to go back home.

True repentance isn't shallow regret or temporary remorse. It's a profound awareness of sin in the heart, a vivid memory of the past blessings of God and a strong determination in the will that moves us to do the right thing.

A Sunday school teacher told her class that repentance meant "being sorry for your sins," and a pupil corrected her and said, "It means being sorry enough to quit sinning." The younger son finally had it right: "I will set out and go back to my father" (Luke 15:18). It was time to make a new beginning.

*   *   *   *   *

As he trudged along the road, he started planning what he would say when he arrived home, starting with, "Father, I have sinned. . . ." (15:21).

This was a wise plan. Perhaps he recalled hearing Hosea 14:1–2 read in a synagogue service and adapted it to his own situation: "Return, Israel, to the LORD your God. Your sins have been your downfall! Take words with you and return to the LORD. Say to him: 'Forgive all our sins and receive us graciously.'"

> *It's quite a paradox that a broken heart*
> *is the first step to a mended life.*

Like David, he knew that no amount of sacrifice could atone for what he had done, because what God wants from us is "a broken and contrite heart" (Ps. 51:17). It's quite a paradox that a broken heart is the first step to a mended life.

"I have sinned" is a confession that came from the lips of at least eight persons in Scripture, some of whom were insincere when they spoke those words. The first is Pharaoh who spoke them twice as God's judgments were devastating Egypt (Exod. 9:27; 10:16). The covetous prophet Balaam is the second speaker (Num. 22:34), and the disobedient soldier Achan is the third (Josh. 7:20).

King Saul spoke the words three times, but his conduct proved he didn't mean what he said (1 Sam. 15:24, 30; 26:21).

David said "I have sinned" four times (2 Sam. 12:13; 24:10, 17 [1 Chron. 21:8, 17]; Ps. 51:4), and each time the words came from a broken heart. Shimei's confession is suspect (2 Sam. 19:20) as is that of the apostle Judas (Matt. 27:4), who confessed his sins to the religious leaders and not to the Lord.

The young prodigal admitted he was a sinner, but he planned to bargain his way back into the family circle instead of trusting his father's mercy. He didn't know his father well enough to realize that he would welcome him and forgive him. "Make me like one of your hired servants" (Luke 15:19) indicates that he wanted to *earn* forgiveness and love.

There were three levels of servants in those days. The bondsman (*doulos*) was of the highest worth, treated almost like one of the family. Of secondary value was the young manservant or maidservant (*paides*), and in the lowest position was the hired servant (*misthios*) who came and went and was paid by the day. Hired servants didn't live with the family, and they received no fringe benefits.

The younger son was willing to take the lowest place if only he could start over again. It would take time, but perhaps he could earn enough money to repay his father and improve his reputation in the village.

His future was frightening, but that's what happens when we reject the Father's will and go it alone. The future is your friend when Jesus is your Lord. Turn your back on Him, and life goes on—but there comes a point at which everything seems to conspire against you.

Take the prophet Jonah, for example. Even though he was disobeying God, he still found a ship going where he wanted to go. He had money to pay the fare, and he was even able to sleep during a violent storm. But eventually, everything began to fall apart. He was tossed overboard like excess baggage—then he became fish food, and finally he ended up vomit! It was hardly a picture of success.

Remember: The future is your friend when Jesus is your Lord.

*   *   *   *   *

In one of the *Peanuts* comic strips, Lucy is in her psychiatry booth, and her star patient Charlie Brown shows up. As usual, he is depressed because he sees himself as a total failure. "Look at it this way, Charlie Brown," says Lucy. "We learn more from our mistakes than we do from our successes." To which Charlie Brown replies, "Then that makes me the smartest man in the world!"

It's tragic that a son could live at home all those years and not know his own father's heart. But the boy was not unlike many Christians today who have no idea what God's character is like.

Charlie Brown's personal problems were light years away from the problems the younger son faced as he plodded home in his dirty, ragged, smelly clothes, wondering what his father would say and do when he saw him.

Would he reject him? The fear of rejection is a powerful emotion that paralyzes some people. Would his father lecture him and put him on probation? Would the family servants abuse him now that he was the lowest of the low? Would the neighbors even allow him to enter the village? How much did they know about his life in the far country? He had sown the seeds of sin, but now he was hoping for a crop failure.

It's tragic that a son could live at home all those years and not know his own father's heart. But the boy was not unlike many people today who go to church, perhaps even read the Bible, yet have no idea what God's character is like. They don't know what pleases God or what angers Him. They don't know what to expect when they disobey.

Will God punish them or forgive? How can they receive His forgiveness? "The essence of idolatry," said A. W. Tozer, "is the entertainment of thoughts about God that are un-worthy of Him."[1] This means that many professed believers are really idolaters.

After teaching a lesson about the fatherhood of God, I was approached by a university student who said, "You say God is like a father. If God's like my father, I'm not inter-ested!" And he turned and left the room.

But the hungry Jewish boy kept going, because he re-membered his father's generosity and hoped he would for-give him. "As a father has compassion on his children, so the LORD has compassion on those who fear him; for he knows how we are formed, he remembers that we are dust" (Ps. 103:13–14).

During the boy's absence, his father had been waiting and watching, ready to welcome him home, just as the heav-enly Father today is watching for sinners. He is waiting for people who are weary of the far country, tired of earning the wages of sin—people who are seeking another chance at life.

There's more we could learn about the young man and the far country, but it's time for us meet this merciful father.

Four

The Merciful Father

(Luke 15:20b–24)

If we were reading this parable for the first time, we wouldn't be surprised at the words and actions of the two brothers, because we've met people who are foolishly wasteful or arrogantly critical. (At times, we've probably acted like these two sons ourselves.)

But we would be surprised at the father, because he's a most unusual person. It's the father who is the key actor in this drama, because he demonstrates God's attitude toward people who are seeking another chance at life. The parable of the prodigal son is really the parable of the merciful father.

Surprise number one is that *he gave the younger son exactly what he asked for*. It's doubtful that the other fathers in the community would have done that. They would have lectured their sons about the follies of youth, told them to grow up and then sent them to the fields to work. Nothing cures a sick youthful imagination like pulling weeds or digging out rocks.

It surely grieved the father's heart that his son treated him so cruelly and wanted to leave home, but he set aside his own feelings and complied with his son's wishes. He knew the boy didn't know how to handle his wealth, but he freely gave him what he himself had worked so hard to get.

However, this scene isn't all that new; it's been repeated millions of times since our first parents wanted their own way and rebelled against God. The Lord made a beautiful, bountiful world and turned it over to them as His co-regents, knowing full well that their disobedience would bring sin and death into the world (see Rom. 5:12).

It's the father who is the key actor in this drama, because he demonstrates God's attitude toward people who are seeking another chance at life.

Ever since their fall, the human race has been selfishly wasting the riches the Lord has so freely given us. The Lord "gives everyone life and breath and everything else," Paul told the Greek philosophers. "For in him we live and move and have our being" (Acts 17:25, 28). He "richly provides us with everything for our enjoyment" (1 Tim. 6:17).

The frightening alterations in nature today that we calmly call "an ecological crisis" are basically the result of selfishness and sin in the human heart. In mankind's constant quest for money and pleasure, God's laws are ignored and His wealth is wasted.

So, millions of people are "prodigals" in one way or another.

*   *   *   *   *

The second surprise is that *the father didn't go looking for the son and beg him to come home.* The shepherd searched for his lost sheep, and the woman for her lost coin, but the father didn't run after his lost son. If sons and daughters don't learn their lessons the easy way at home, they must learn them the hard way far from home. Parents hope and pray that their children won't learn these lessons too late. It's painful to see people abuse and waste their opportunities.

Like us, the boy was created in the image of God—he had a mind, a heart and a will by which he could think, feel and decide. Unfortunately, these wonderful abilities have been infected by sin, and we are all desperately in need of divine help.

As with all lost humans, the boy's heart was "deceitful above all things and beyond cure" (Jer. 17:9). His mind was sinful and hostile to God (Rom. 8:7). His will was rebellious and disobedient (Eph. 2:2, 5:6). It wasn't until the boy made a mess of his life and admitted his real needs that things began to change.

The younger son probably said to his father, "Father, I must leave home. I want to find myself." This is youth's usual excuse for planned disobedience. Over the years, whenever I've heard that excuse I've asked, "When and where did you lose yourself? If you lost yourself here, why go someplace else to find yourself?"

Someone has defined home as "the place where you're treated the best and act the worst." Too often that's true. Athletes "find themselves" by submitting to great coaches, and musicians to great teachers, and young people find themselves by submitting to the Lord.

Eventually the boy discovered that the "self" he "found" away from home wasn't exactly what he expected to find. We have a way of lying to ourselves, convincing ourselves that we need a change of scenery when we really need a change of heart.

I think it was Ralph Waldo Emerson who said that a change in geography never overcomes a flaw in character. He was right. If anything, being away from home only makes character worse because we know that our friends and neighbors aren't watching.

The boy made his worst decision in the best place—home—and made his best decision in the worst place—the pigpen. The heart of every problem is the problem in the heart. "Above all else, guard your heart, for everything you do flows from it" (Prov. 4:23).

*   *   *   *   *

The father had a tender heart and open eyes. He kept watching and praying for his son to return home, which leads to the third surprise. When he saw the boy, *the father ran to welcome him!*

Why is that a surprise? Because in that time and place, older men didn't run. It wasn't considered dignified. They left the running to the servants and the children. When the neighbors saw the father run out of the field and down the road toward the traveler, they were shocked.

Why did he run? Obviously, his compassionate heart drew him to his son, especially when he saw the condition he was in. Augustine wrote in his *Confessions*, "You loved him when he set out and you loved him still more when he came home without a penny."[1] But there was another reason for his haste. The boy had brought disgrace both to his family and his village, and according to the Mosaic Law, he deserved to be stoned to death.

> If someone has a stubborn and rebellious son who does not obey his father and mother and will not listen to them when they discipline him, his father and mother shall take hold of him and bring him to the elders at the gate of his town. They shall say to the elders, "This son of ours is stubborn and rebellious. He will not obey us. He is a profligate and a drunkard." Then all the men of his town are to stone him to death. You must purge the evil from among you. All Israel will hear of it and be afraid. (Deut. 21:18–21)

By running to the boy and throwing his arms around him, the father was saying to the neighbors, "Go ahead and throw stones at him! You will hit me!"

It's a vivid picture of Calvary.

See what Moses wrote immediately after the above commandment: "If anyone guilty of a capital offense is put to death and their body is exposed on a pole, you must not leave the body hanging on the pole overnight. Be sure to bury it that same day, because anyone who is hung on a pole is under God's curse" (21:22–23).

Jesus committed no offense, yet He "'bore our sins' in his body on the cross" (1 Pet. 2:24). "We all, like sheep, have gone astray, each of us has turned to our own way; and the Lord has laid on him the iniquity of us all" (Isa. 53:6). The body of Jesus hung on a cross, and He was treated like a guilty criminal. "Christ redeemed us from the curse of the law by becoming a curse for us, for it is written: 'Cursed is everyone who is hung on a pole'" (Gal. 3:13). "But God demonstrates his own love for us in this: While we were still sinners, Christ died for us" (Rom. 5:8).

By running to the boy and throwing his arms around him, the father was saying to the neighbors, "Go ahead and throw stones at him! You will hit me!" It's a vivid picture of Calvary.

At the cross, the Father ran to us, opened His arms to embrace us and said, "Go ahead and throw the stones! You will hit me!" Paul said it clearly: "God was reconciling the world to himself in Christ, not counting people's sins against them" (2 Cor. 5:19).

Reconciliation! That's what the boy needed more than anything. Because he had been out of fellowship with his father, he was out of sync with everything else in life.

But reconciliation isn't cheap; it's very costly. Only Jesus can pay the price. "But because of his great love for us, God, who is rich in mercy, made us alive with Christ even when we were dead in transgressions—it is by grace you have been saved" (Eph. 2:4–5).

We are saved *because of* God's love but not by God's love. God loves the world, and yet the world isn't saved. We are saved by *love that pays a price and demonstrates itself in grace and mercy.* God in His mercy doesn't give us what we *do* deserve—judgment; and God in His grace gives us what we *don't* deserve—a bath, shoes, a ring, a robe, a feast—a new chance at life.

What a Father—great in love, rich in mercy, abounding in grace! And all this is ours in Jesus Christ.

*   *   *   *   *

This leads us to the fourth surprise: *The father gave his son more than the boy had before!* Everything the young man was seeking in the far country he found back home, and it was free.

The father didn't put his son on probation. Instead, he accepted him just as he was and gave him more than he expected or deserved. The son had planned to work his way back into the family circle, but he got no further than saying, "Father, I have sinned against heaven and against you. I am no longer worthy to be called your son."

At that point the father interrupted, and the son never had a chance to apply for work. *The only way to receive grace and mercy is to shut our mouth and receive by faith what God offers us in Christ!* "So that every mouth may be silenced and the whole world held accountable to God" (Rom. 3:19).

Salvation begins with sinners closing their mouths in conviction and fear before God. No excuses, no blaming somebody else, no arguing with God's plan—just silence.

That was Job's experience: "I am unworthy—how can I reply to you? I put my hand over my mouth" (Job 40:4). It was also the experience of Joseph's brothers: "But his brothers were not able to answer him, because they were terrified at his presence" (Gen. 45:3). "I was silent," said David, "I would not open my mouth, for you are the one who has done this" (Ps. 39:9).

Has your mouth ever been shut before the Lord? If not, you may never have experienced His grace and mercy, for He welcomes and forgives only those who admit their guilt.

Every mouth must be silenced before God. We can't boast about our religious achievements or defend our foolish actions.

"The LORD is in his holy temple; let all the earth be silent before him" (Hab. 2:20). There are no exceptions. We must be silent in guilt before we can call upon the name of the Lord and be saved.

*   *   *   *   *

In his poem "The Death of the Hired Man," Robert Frost writes, "Home is the place where, when you have to go there, they have to take you in." The son came home just as he was—bankrupt, dirty, hungry, unworthy, helpless and hopeless—and the father took him in, not because he had to but because he wanted to. His heart told him to.

Never forget that the "much more" Jesus is speaking about in this parable is not just human sentiment or parental love. God's love goes far beyond that.

The boy was cleansed, he was clothed with the best robe—his father's own robe—and then given the ring of authority and the shoes of a son. When you come to the Father, you're made a child in the family. "Yet to all who did receive him [Jesus], to those who believed in his name, he gave the right to become children of God" (John 1:12).

Servants go barefoot, but sons and daughters have shoes on their feet. Servants are penniless, but sons and daughters wear rings. Servants are fed but children are feasted. "The old has gone, the new is here!" (2 Cor. 5:17).

The Christian life is an exciting experience of "much more." "How much more shall we be saved from God's wrath through him!" (Rom. 5:9). "How much more, having been reconciled, shall we be saved through his life!" (5:10). "How much more will those who receive God's abundant provision of grace and of the gift of righteousness reign in life through the one man, Jesus Christ!" (5:17). "But where sin increased, grace increased all the more" (5:20). Our God is the God of the much more!

But never forget that the "much more" Jesus is speaking about in this parable is not just human sentiment or parental love. God's love goes far beyond that. Jesus is speaking about grace and mercy—*love that has paid a price.* Here is what P.T. Forsyth said in his book *The Sense of the Holy*:

> To understand all is not to forgive all. That is mere literary ethics, not the moralist's, certainly not the Christian theologian's. There was more fatherhood in the cross (where holiness met guilt) than in the prodigal's father (where love met shame). . . . It is not a father's sensitive love only that we have wounded, but His holy law. Man is not a mere runaway, but a rebel; not a pitiful coward, but a bold and bitter mutineer.[2]

Now listen to the apostle Paul.

> God presented Christ as a sacrifice of atonement, through the shedding of his blood—to be received by faith. He did this to demonstrate his justice, because in his forbearance he had left the sins committed beforehand unpunished—he did it to demonstrate his justice at the present time, so as to be just and the one who justifies those who have faith in Jesus. (Rom. 3:25–26)

In one sentence: There can be no forgiveness from the Father in heaven apart from Jesus Christ and His cross. Jesus Himself said, "I am the way and the truth and the life. No one comes to the Father except through me" (John 14:6).

The young man was lost (Luke 15:24, 32), and Jesus is the way to the Father. The young man was ignorant (15:17), and Jesus is the truth about the Father. The young man was dead (15:24, 32), and Jesus is the life from the Father.

Jesus was all he needed, and if you want to come to the Father, Jesus is all you need.

Five

The Hopeful Mother

I n his beautiful painting *The Return of the Prodigal,* Rembrandt has placed a woman in the background in a shadowy doorway, and some art critics think he meant her to be the boy's mother. In His parable, though, Jesus said nothing about the mother. Some people in our gender-sensitive world think this is a serious omission.

Jewish society in that day did honor and care for women, although it was a strongly masculine society. If you question our Lord's concern for the needs of the women, read Luke's entire Gospel and note how often He speaks of them and ministers to them. In His example, His teaching and most of all His sacrifice, Jesus has elevated women in society and enabled them to bring blessing to the whole world. Where would the church be without dedicated women?

God is spirit (John 4:24) and therefore has no body. This means He's without gender and is neither male nor female, even though the Bible speaks of Him in the image of a Father. In His incarnation, God the Son became a man be-

cause He is the "last Adam" who came to undo the consequences of the first Adam's sin (Rom. 5:12–21; 1 Cor. 15:22–
28). God the Holy Spirit is also without gender and indwells
all believers, male and female.

The prodigal's mother surely grieved when her baby boy
left home. Daily she wept over him in solitude, prayed for him
and watched anxiously for his return. Love "always protects,
always trusts, always hopes, always perseveres" (1 Cor. 13:7).

The prodigal's mother had lived in hope all the
time her son was away from home, and that
hope was not disappointed.

She rejoiced greatly to see her son again and agreed with
everything her husband said to him and did for him—but
like every modest Jewish wife, she stayed in the background.
She had lived in hope all the time her son was away from
home, and that hope was not disappointed. As she supervised the preparation of food for the feast, she praised God
that the family was now together and that her "little boy"
had come home a wiser man.

Scripture speaks eloquently about the "motherhood of
God."

*   *   *   *   *

Like a mother, *God is unchanging in His love.*

But Zion said, "The LORD has forsaken me,
the LORD has forgotten me."

"Can a mother forget the baby at her breast
and have no compassion on the child she has borne?
Though she may forget,
I will not forget you!"

(Isa. 49:14–15)

Yes, the father loved the son. But the mother had cradled the baby under her heart for nine months and nourished him over her heart until he was weaned. Even before his birth she had lovingly spoken to him, sung to him and prayed for him, and after his birth she had tenderly cared for him and dreamed great dreams for him.

When the boy left home, some of her gossiping neighbors may have said to her, "Be thankful he's gone! Forget him! That boy will never amount to anything!"

She didn't agree with them, but said nothing, for in her heart she knew he would come home and make a new start. "Love lives on hope, and dies when hope is dead," says a Spanish proverb, and Shakespeare wrote,

Love is not love
Which alters when it alteration finds.

Her son had changed, he had disappointed her; but she never gave up hope. He would come back.

"You deserted the Rock, who bore you; you forgot the God who gave you birth," Moses wrote in Deuteronomy 32:18. The statement is charged with images. God is unchanging like a Rock, but He is a *living* Rock, a Rock that gives birth to children. Those children abandoned Him, *but God didn't abandon them!*

The names of the twelve tribes of Israel were engraved on jewels and carried on the shoulders and over the heart of the high priest (Exod. 28:9 30). "I have loved you with an everlasting love," God told His people (Jer. 31:3), and we know Paul's words in First Corinthians 13:8—"Love never fails."

The *expression* of God's love for us is unconditional, but our experience of that love is conditional. How much parental love did the younger son experience in the far country? Did he feel their embraces or kisses? Did he hear their loving words? Were there any robes or rings or shoes to put on? Were there any joyful feasts to attend?

The mother and father still loved the boy, but his rebellion and distance from them robbed him of receiving it. It wasn't until he repented and returned home that he experienced their love and found healing.

*   *   *   *   *

Like a mother, God is *unfailing in His comfort.* "As a mother comforts her child, so will I comfort you; and you will be comforted over Jerusalem" (Isa. 66:13).

When frightened or distressed, children usually flee for comfort to their mother, or at times their grandmother. Fathers can say and do the same things as mothers, but for some reason their efforts don't generate the same results. It's a mother's love that children want.

When children have been rebellious and say they're sorry, they need comfort through our forgiveness (see Isa. 40:2). In the same way, Israel's disobedience had brought ruin to their nation, especially to Jerusalem and the temple, but God spoke with comfort and compassion to them.

"Comfort, comfort my people, says your God" (Isa. 40:1). "The Lord will surely comfort Zion and will look with compassion on all her ruins; he will make her deserts like Eden, her wastelands like the garden of the Lord. Joy and gladness will be found in her, thanksgiving and the sound of singing" (51:3). It reads like a description of the prodigal's welcome home party!

Children also need comfort when they are afraid. A neighbor's granddaughter was frightened during an especially severe thunderstorm, and her grandmother said, "The thunder is only God's voice, so don't be afraid." Her reply was, "God's voice is too loud!"

But the Lord speaks comfort to His people, because He is "the God of all comfort" (2 Cor. 1:3). "I, even I, am he who comforts you" (Isa. 51:12).

Substitution and distraction never dry tears or heal broken hearts. What the sorrowing really need is transformation, and only God can transform sorrow into joy.

I have visited children in hospitals and have seen the difference it makes when their mother is in the room. A mother's presence even affects adults! I recall a mature man who mumbled as he came out of the anesthesia, "Mommy! I want my mommy!" We never outgrow that need.

God comforts us when we mourn. He gives us "the oil of joy instead of mourning, and a garment of praise instead of a spirit of despair" (Isa. 61:3). Often we try to comfort children by giving them toys or candy, but substitution and distraction never dry tears or heal broken hearts. What the sorrowing really need is *transformation*, and only God can transform sorrow into joy.

The English word "comfort" comes from two Latin words that together mean "with strength." To comfort people doesn't mean to pamper them or entertain them. It means to help God put strength into them so they can accept the pain and use it for God's glory.

God "comforts us in all our troubles, so that we can comfort those in any trouble with the comfort we ourselves receive from God" (2 Cor. 1:4). "The truest help we can render an afflicted man is not to take his burden from him," said Phillips Brooks, "but to call out his best strength that he may be able to bear it."

*   *   *   *   *

Like a mother, the Lord is *unsparing in His joy*. "The LORD your God is with you, the Mighty Warrior who saves. He will take great delight in you; in his love he will no longer rebuke you, but will rejoice over you with singing" (Zeph. 3:17).

Our God is a God who sings! Here God the Father sings to His people to reassure them, as a mother does when she takes a child on her lap and sings it to sleep. God the Son sang at the last Passover before He went out to be arrested, tried and crucified (Mark 14:26). The Holy Spirit sings when Spirit-filled Christians assemble and worship God as He commands them (see Eph. 5:18–20). In fact, if our singing is not in the Spirit, He is grieved.

As God's children, we should seek to bring joy to His heart through our obedience to Him. When we rebel, He rebukes us and sometimes disciplines us; but when we confess our sins, He forgives us and replaces our tears with songs of joy. David expressed this joy after he was forgiven of his sin: "Open my lips, Lord, and my mouth will declare your praise" (Ps. 51:15).

How often have you seen a mother take a fretful child into her arms and comfort it with a song? Like a mother, God is unsparing in His joy; and love, joy and peace go together (see Gal. 5:22).

*   *   *   *   *

God is like a loving mother in that He is *unyielding in His purpose*. His goal for each of His children is *maturity*. David emphasized this in Psalm 131:

> My heart is not proud, LORD,
> my eyes are not haughty;
> I do not concern myself with great matters
> or things too wonderful for me.
>
> But I have calmed myself
> and quieted my ambitions.
> I am like a weaned child with its mother;
> like a weaned child I am content.
>
> Israel, put your hope in the LORD
> both now and forevermore.

A mother can't nurse her children all their lives; there comes a time when they must be weaned. But children don't like that idea. They want mother all to themselves—her love, her closeness, her protection.

Although weaning can appear unloving, even cruel, it's for the good of the child that the mother begins the process of separation and introduces new nourishment and new habits. The Hebrew word for "wean" means "to complete, to ripen, to treat kindly." It's a humbling experience, but very necessary for the producing of maturity.

Life is a series of "weanings," because letting go is one of the first steps toward maturity. "When I became a man, I put the ways of childhood behind me" (1 Cor. 13:11). There comes a time when we set aside the toys and pick up the tools. Life is a series of new beginnings, and it's the maturing people who put the most into life and therefore get the most out of life.

The key to successful maturing is submission. God takes away the good and replaces it with the better, and then He removes the better and gives the best.

The key to successful maturing is *submission*. God takes away the good and replaces it with the better, and then He removes the better and gives the best. Fretting over a less than ideal past only makes matters worse. God wants us to grow up and be "conformed to the image of his Son" (Rom. 8:29; see also Eph. 4:14–15), and that demands sacrifice and suffering.

A proud heart and a desire to meddle in "great matters" may inflate our ego, but it won't mature our character. People like Joseph and David endured years of "weaning" before

God entrusted them with their thrones. We must learn to quiet ourselves, feed on the Word and allow God to make us what He wants us to be.

*   *   *   *   *

God is *unwilling in His punishment.* Jesus was weeping when He spoke these words:

> Jerusalem, Jerusalem, you who kill the prophets and stone those sent to you, how often I have longed to gather your children together, as a hen gathers her chicks under her wings, and you were not willing. Look, your house is left to you desolate. (Matt. 23:37–38)

It's not until we become parents ourselves that we fully understood how our own parents felt when they would say, "This hurts me more than it hurts you." The hen sees trouble coming and calls her chicks to herself, sheltering them under her wings. But if one chick refuses to obey, it's in danger of losing its life. When a loving mother detects evidence of rebellion in a child's character, she knows it signals trouble ahead, so she disciplines the child to teach it obedience. Her loving heart hurts as she deals out correction, but it must be done. "The Lord disciplines those he loves" (Heb. 12:6).

"Do I take any pleasure in the death of the wicked?" God asks in Ezekiel 18:23, and He answers the question in verse 32, "For I take no pleasure in the death of anyone. . . . Repent and live!"

To make sure we don't miss the message, He repeats it in Ezekiel 33:11. Paul wrote that God "wants all people to be saved and to come to a knowledge of the truth" (1 Tim. 2:4), and Peter writes that the Lord doesn't want "anyone to perish, but everyone to come to repentance" (2 Pet. 3:9).

Whether it's the punishing of the unrepentant lost or the disciplining of His disobedient children, the Lord doesn't enjoy the experience. But this is part of the "motherhood" of God.

Six

The Spiteful Brother

(Luke 15:25–32)

M any preachers and evangelists make the mistake of stopping with the prodigal's return home, completely ignoring the elder brother. But the elder brother is as much a part of the parable as the prodigal son. He represents the self-righteous scribes and Pharisees who avoided "sinners" and who criticized Jesus for welcoming them.

If the younger son had not repented and returned home, Bible readers today would probably praise the older son as a model boy who always obeyed his father, worked hard and didn't barter his future for a mess of pleasure. But the return of the prodigal and the joyful generosity of the father focused a laser beam on the elder son's heart, revealing some ugly sins hidden there—sins like covetousness, anger, pride, malice, envy and an unforgiving spirit, to name but a few. It's possible to stay home, proud that you're obeying your father, and still be a sinner.

* * * * *

An act of gracious giving can powerfully expose people for what they really are. The expensive gift Mary of Bethany gave Jesus revealed the sinful attitude of Judas (John 12:1–8). The generous gift of Barnabas exposed the deception of Ananias and Sapphira (Acts 4:36–5:11). And now the father's gifts to his repentant son triggered shocking responses from the older one.

The younger boy sinned in the far country, and he admitted his wrongdoing. But his brother was guilty of sinning right at home—and successfully covering it up. If the prodigal was guilty of sins of the body, his brother was guilty of sins of the spirit (see 2 Cor. 7:1).

The longer the prodigal remained in the far country, the better the older brother looked as he diligently worked at home. But when the younger boy came home, his big brother openly revealed the truth about himself.

I fear that the attitudes of the older son are "sins in good standing" today, quietly tolerated even among professed Christians. People might be rejected from church fellowship because of drunkenness or adultery but rarely because of temper tantrums or displays of malice and envy. (Malice means we're happy when our enemies fail; envy means we're sad when they succeed. The elder brother was guilty of both.)

The longer the prodigal remained in the far country, the better the older brother looked as he diligently worked at home. But when the younger boy came home, his big brother openly revealed the truth about himself.

The father's loving welcome and generous gifts were too much for the older boy, for he had long craved a party of his own. Even more, he simply didn't understand the father's forgiveness and grace, just as the scribes and Pharisees didn't grasp the meaning of the grace of Christ toward tax collectors and outcasts.

We may try to pass off our sinful anger as "righteous indignation" (Eph. 4:26), but God sees our hearts, and He knows the difference.

When he first returned, the prodigal had a hard time accepting his father's forgiveness. The elder son, however, didn't feel his brother should have any forgiveness at all. He refused to agree with his father or speak to his brother. The attitudes of the self-righteous Pharisees and scribes were no different. Instead of rejoicing that wayward sinners wanted to make new beginnings, they rejected them and, like the elder brother, kept their distance.

*   *   *   *   *

When the older son came home after another day's work in the field, he was surprised to hear music and dancing. Had he really wanted his brother to return, he might have guessed that his parents' prayers had been answered. But his brother's homecoming was the last thing he wanted.

He asked one of the servant boys for an explanation, and what he heard made him very angry. His wayward brother *had* come home, and his father had killed the fattened calf and called the household and the village together for a celebration. The original Greek text informs us that the elder brother *repeatedly* questioned the servant. He wanted to know all the details. And the more he learned, the angrier he became.

Here are four questions to ask yourself if you want to make a quick test of your character:

- What makes me laugh?
- What makes me cry?
- What makes me angry?
- What makes me sacrifice?

The test isn't infallible, but if we answer the questions honestly, it's amazing how much we can learn about ourselves. You would think that the elder brother would have rejoiced to hear that his brother was home safe and sound, if only because it brought great joy to their parents. If he'd really had his parents' interests at heart, he would have rejoiced with them (see Rom. 12:15).

It's a basic principle that if we don't get along with the Lord, we won't get along with other people. So our first responsibility is to be right with God.

Instead, he exploded with anger and refused to join the party. The younger son had caused his parents embarrassment when he was far away, but now the older son was causing his parents grief and embarrassment right at home—in front of their friends and neighbors.

The feast was much more than a family celebration. The prodigal had brought disgrace to the village as well as to his family, so his father invited the neighbors to dinner as a gesture of reconciliation. In the east, to eat together is an act of brotherhood. No matter how much they may have disagreed in the past, once people have broken bread together, they forget their differences.

But if the older son wasn't ready to forgive his brother, why should the neighbors? By standing outside the house and burning with anger, the elder son was sending a conflicting message to the guests, one that embarrassed his mother, his father and his brother.

It's a basic principle that if we don't get along with the Lord, we won't get along with other people. So our first responsibility is to be right with God.

The prodigal hadn't gotten along with his father, so he abandoned the whole family and left home. Then later the elder brother despised the younger, disagreed with his father and defended himself angrily—and this put him outside the fellowship.

Speaking about the church members of his day, Jonathan Swift said, "We have just enough religion to make us hate, but not enough to make us love one another." It's a sad fact that many professed Christians not only hate the sins they see in others, but they hate the sinners as well, even after the people have repented and made new beginnings.

When D.L. Moody was preaching in Great Britain, one pastor said he didn't believe Mr. Moody was sent by God "because many of the people who are converted under him never went to a place of worship before. It is only the riff-raff that are brought in."

Charles Spurgeon's reply was, "Instead of ever sniffing at sinners as if we were better than they, let us welcome them with all our heart and praise the heavenly Father that he so lovingly takes them in."

Jesus never saw unconverted people as "riffraff." He saw them as sick patients who needed a physician (Luke 5:27–32) and as lost sheep, lost coins and lost sons that needed to be found.

The older son boycotted the feast because he was angry at his father for being "unfair." The father had never given him as much as a goat so he could feast with his friends—but for his wayward son he had killed the fattened calf. Not fair! But the elder brother had no understanding of the grace of God. If God did what was fair, all of us would be condemned forever. What we need is not justice but mercy!

We've already seen some of the surprising actions of the father, but there's one more: He humbled himself before his guests, going out to plead with his angry son to come inside and enjoy the feast. The verb means "he kept on beseeching him."

The father's food was getting cold, his guests were missing him from the table, and his younger son especially wanted him there; but the father continued to plead. The basic problem was that the father lived by grace, and his older son lived by law—*but the son never applied that law to himself.*

*   *   *   *   *

Contrast the elder brother with the father and you will get a better understanding of the relationship between law and grace.

Law accuses and condemns—"this son of yours who has squandered your property with prostitutes" (Luke 15:30). But grace forgives: "Above all, love each other deeply, because love covers over a multitude of sins" (1 Pet. 4:8).

Love doesn't cleanse us of our sins, for only God's grace through the cross can do that. But love covers sins so that we don't go around exposing the mistakes of others. Love "keeps no record of wrongs" (1 Cor. 13:5).

Law separates the obedient and the disobedient, but grace unites the humble and the repentant. Law can generate anger—at God, at others, and at ourselves—while grace provides a joy that we can share. Law boasts: "All these years . . . I've never disobeyed your orders." But grace helps us say, "I have sinned . . . make me like one of your hired servants" (Luke 15:18–19). Law puts us into bondage: "All these years I've been slaving for you" (15:29). But grace lifts us to liberty and life.

In one sense, the elder brother yielded to the same temptation our first parents did at the beginning of human history. "God is holding out on you," said the serpent to Eve. "Obey me and you will be as God" (see Gen. 3:1–5).

The elder brother wanted to enjoy a feast with his friends, but he felt his father was holding out on him. (Did the man even know his son wanted a feast?) But now the father *was* hosting a great feast, *and the elder brother refused to enjoy it!* He found it difficult to share because he wanted his own feast with his own friends. After all, wasn't he the elder son and the heir?

Paul wrote to the churches in Galatia to explain that God's people must not mix law and grace. Law encourages us to depend on ourselves, but this brings out the worst in us, "the acts of the sinful nature" (Gal. 5:13–21; Rom. 7:7–14). Grace, however, encourages us to depend on the Lord—and this brings out the best in us, "the fruit of the Spirit" (Gal. 5:22–25). Law is based on obeying rules, while grace is based on loving relationship and on doing the Father's will. Because of his sinful attitude, the elder brother was outside the fellowship. He was relationally deprived.

Yes, there's an important place for law in the Christian life. The law reveals the holiness of God and, like a mirror, shows us our sins (James 1:22–25). But you don't wash your face in the mirror. In His holy life, Jesus fulfilled the demands of the law, and in His death He bore its curse, so that our faith in Him releases us from its bondage (Rom. 6:14–15).

The elder brother wasn't a free person. To be sure, he worked hard, but it was not because he was a loving son; he worked rather as a dutiful slave.

What the law requires is "fully met in us, who do not live according to the sinful nature but according to the Spirit" (Rom. 8:4).

*   *   *   *   *

The elder brother wasn't a free person. To be sure, he worked hard, but it was not because he was a loving son; he worked rather as a dutiful slave. It wasn't a son's labor of love for his father but a servant's grinding toil. He wasn't seeking to please his father; he only hoped one day to have a feast with his friends. His alienation from his father robbed the elder son of the riches of his grace.

He was outside the feast because he wouldn't yield by faith to the grace of God. His father was more generous than the elder brother had realized. The critical scribes and Pharisees were outside "salvation's feast" for the same reason. *Grace puts everybody on the same level,* and proud legalists don't like that. They want to be a special elite.

Grace gives the glory to God, but proud legalists want to be honored for their accomplishments. Law says, "Do not come any closer. . . . Take off your sandals" (Exod. 3:5), while grace runs to the sinner with open arms and cries, "Put . . . sandals on his feet" (Luke 15:20–24).

The elder brother was a legalist. And legalism is still a problem for many today. It's usually the sin of good, even religious, people, and not of grossly evil ones. Good people strive to become better, but they often forget the grace of God.

If we depend on the Holy Spirit, growing in godly character can be a great adventure; but if we compete with others and make ourselves the standard, then we fail miserably. "When they measure themselves by themselves and compare themselves with themselves, they are not wise" (2 Cor. 10:12).

When the father addressed his elder son, he called him "child" (Luke 15:31, YLT), for the son was really an adult acting like a child. When we live only by rules so we can boast of our achievements, we reveal our immaturity, because mature people are motivated by love and for the glory of God.

"For whoever loves others has fulfilled the law. . . . Therefore love is the fulfillment of the law" (Rom. 13:8, 10). There are laws in every city that require parents to care for their children, but very few parents ever think about them. Fathers and mothers work and care for their home and family *because of their love for one another.* So it must be between us and our Father.

*   *   *   *   *

During more than fifty years of ministry, I've met many "outsiders," people who were angry at God, a family member or a friend, and who nurtured their grudges in painful loneliness. Usually they were hardworking people and upstanding citizens, but they were outside the joy of the fellowship.

I've pleaded with them to forget the past and make new beginnings in life, but they were in such bondage to disappointment, bitterness and resentment that they couldn't begin a new lifestyle. Without their bitterness, they would lose their identity. They were secure in their high opinion of themselves and their low opinion of others, and they didn't want to step out by faith and trust the grace of God. It takes courage to walk by faith and to live by God's grace.

People who imitate the elder brother pay a high price for the privilege of loneliness. For one thing, they are out of fellowship with the Lord. They see Him as a demanding employer instead of a loving Father. They serve Him, not out of spontaneous love ("doing the will of God from your heart"—Eph. 6:6) but out of sullen, rigid obedience.

God wants to be a Father to us (2 Cor. 6:14–7:1), but we can't enjoy that rich relationship if we ignore His grace and mercy. When we give Him our heart and ask Him to cleanse us of our sins, He draws us to Himself and gives us a new beginning. "My son, give me your heart and let your eyes delight in my ways" (Prov. 23:26).

But the older son was also out of fellowship with his family and friends. They were inside the house eating good food, while he was outside nursing his grudges. The elder brother could speak to one of his father's servants but not to his own brother! In fact, he wouldn't even use the word "brother"; he called him "this son of yours" (Luke 15:30).

But if the father had received the prodigal and forgiven him, the older brother should have done the same. "Get rid of all bitterness, rage and anger," wrote Paul. "Be kind and compassionate to one another, forgiving each other, just as in Christ God forgave you" (Eph. 4:32).

The older son was an adult acting like a child, a son acting like a slave, a brother acting like an enemy and an heir acting like a beggar. What a miserable way to live!

Then what is the remedy for this behavior? It's very simple: Listen to your Father, accept what He says and obey Him *no matter how you feel.* Join the family and friends at the feast. Apologize for being late. Speak graciously to your brother and update him on neighborhood news and the state of the farm. Be thankful that you have parents with loving, generous hearts, because you've sinned as well as your brother, and they've forgiven you.

Your Father is giving you another chance at life, so make the most of it.

*   *   *   *   *

There are two passages in the Bible dealing with angry men, and neither of them has an ending. We, the readers, must supply the ending, *and the ending we supply helps reveal the condition of our own hearts.*

One of these is the passage we've been reviewing, and the other is Jonah chapter four. Jonah was angry with the Lord because He spared the wicked people of Nineveh, the hated enemies of the Jews. The prophet was sitting outside Nineveh, waiting to see if the Lord would destroy the city, and the sun was beating on his head.

In His grace, God caused a gourd plant to grow and shade him, but there's no record that Jonah thanked Him. Then God sent a worm to chew the plant so that it withered and died, and Jonah became angry.

> But God said to Jonah, "Is it right for you to be angry about the gourd?" "It is," he said. "And I'm so angry I wish I were dead."
>
> But the LORD said, "You have been concerned about this gourd, though you did not tend it or make it grow. It sprang up overnight and died overnight. And should I not have concern for the great city Nineveh, in which there are more than a hundred and twenty thousand people who cannot tell their right hand from their left—and also many animals?" (Jon. 4:9–11)

If I sent a manuscript to an editor with that kind of cliffhanger ending, he would send it back and ask, "What happened next?" Yet the Lord did it in Scripture!

Did Jonah confess his hardness of heart and repent? Did he gladly accept the grace of God, get over his anger and return home a better man? Did he learn to love his enemies and want God's best for them? We don't know, and we never will until we get to heaven. How we answer depends on the state of our own hearts. How would *we* have responded to Jonah's behavior?

Did the elder brother confess his anger and renew his fellowship with God, his family and his neighbors? For his sake, we hope so, but we don't know. Again, how we answer depends on the condition of our own hearts.

If we haven't forgiven those who have sinned against us, we'll probably agree with the older brother and stay outside. But if we've experienced the pain of being sinned against and if we've paid the high cost of forgiveness, we'll want the elder brother to get rid of his bitterness and hardness of heart, forgive everybody and enjoy the banquet. No matter how much we may try to hide, the parable is a mirror in which we see ourselves.

"God's love for poor sinners is very wonderful," wrote Henry Drummond, "but God's patience with ill-natured saints is a deeper mystery."

The Christian life is not a funeral; it's a feast. "For Christ, our Passover lamb, has been sacrificed. Therefore let us keep the Festival, not with the old bread leavened with malice and wickedness, but with the unleavened bread of sincerity and truth" (1 Cor. 5:7–8). We don't have to murder somebody to become guilty sinners. All we have to do is nurture an unforgiving spirit and a hardening heart, and we have closed the door.

"If a brother or sister sins against you, rebuke them; and if they repent, forgive them," said Jesus. "Even if they sin against you seven times in a day and seven times come back to you saying 'I repent,' you must forgive them" (Luke 17:3–4). That's why Jesus the Savior died, and that's why Jesus the Advocate lives and ministers in heaven today. He wants us to be forgiven *and forgiving*, and to experience another chance at life.

"God's love for poor sinners is very wonderful," wrote Henry Drummond, "but God's patience with ill-natured saints is a deeper mystery."

"Instead he is patient with you, not wanting anyone to perish, but everyone to come to repentance" (2 Pet. 3:9).

Seven

The Joyful Neighbors

(Luke 15:5–7, 9–10, 23, 32)

We want very much to believe that the elder brother came to his senses, repented of his sins and joined in the celebration. But even if he continued to stubbornly pout outside the door, there was still joy inside the house where the family and guests were celebrating—and there was also joy in heaven.

Our homes are never more like heaven than when our family is rejoicing in the blessings of the Lord, particularly over the salvation of a lost person. The Christian life is supposed to be a celebration of the grace of God, and anything that hinders this joy comes from outside the will of God.

As the above references show, one of the major themes of Luke 15 is the joy people experience when the lost are found and restored to their rightful places. The shepherd, the housewife and the father were so happy when their treasures were found that they invited the neighbors to share their joy with them.

Jesus said that "there is rejoicing is the presence of the angels of God whenever the lost are found" (15:10). Nobody rephrased it better than C.S. Lewis in his *Letters to Malcolm,* "Joy is the serious business of heaven."

*   *   *   *   *

That phrase "serious business" reminds us that Christian joy isn't a cheap commodity you pick up at a flea market. Christian joy is very expensive because it involves sacrifice—and not just any sacrifice, but the death of Jesus Christ on the cross. "I am the good shepherd," said Jesus. "The good shepherd lays down his life for the sheep" (John 10:11).

> But none of the ransomed ever knew
> How deep were the waters crossed;
> Nor how dark was the night that the Lord passed through
> E'er he found His sheep that was lost.
> Out in the desert He heard its cry—
> Sick and helpless, and ready to die.
>
> "Lord, whence are those blood drops all the way
> That mark out the mountain's track?"
> "They were shed for one who had gone astray
> E'er the Shepherd could bring him back."
> "Lord, whence are Thy hands so rent and torn?"
> "They are pierced tonight by many a thorn."[1]

Jesus was "a man of sorrows and acquainted with grief" (Isa. 53:3, NASB), and yet He was also filled with joy. Luke 10:21 describes Jesus as being "full of joy through the Holy Spirit." He wanted His disciples to experience this too, and He prayed for the Father to grant it to them (John 15:11; 17:13). Believers today are included in that prayer, and the

Holy Spirit can produce this joy in us as we walk with Him, obeying God's will (Gal. 5:16, 22–23).

One of the key verses concerning Christ's joy is Hebrews 12:2—"For the joy set before him he endured the cross, scorning its shame, and sat down at the right hand of the throne of God." Like a runner in a race, Jesus kept His eyes on the goal, "the joy set before him."

Jesus wanted His disciples to experience joy, and He prayed for the Father to grant it to them. The Holy Spirit can produce this joy in us as we walk with Him.

What was that joy? I believe the answer is found in Jude 24—"To him who is able to keep you from stumbling and to present you before his glorious presence without fault and with great joy . . ."

The joy that enabled Jesus to endure the suffering of the cross was the expectation of presenting His glorious church in heaven to Himself and to the Father. "Christ loved the church and gave himself up for her to make her holy . . . and to present her to himself as a radiant church, without stain or wrinkle or any other blemish, but holy and blameless" (Eph. 5:25–27).

I think we can safely say that Jesus rejoices in heaven when the lost on earth are found and restored. After all, He loved them and gave Himself for them.

*   *   *   *   *

But the angels in heaven also rejoice. "In the same way, I tell you, there is rejoicing in the presence of the angels of

God over one sinner who repents" (Luke 15:10). "Heaven keeps holiday when some poor waif comes shrinking back to the Father," wrote Alexander MacLaren.

Peter tells us that the angels have a keen interest in God's plan of salvation. "Even angels long to look into these things" (1 Pet. 1:10–12). In the Holy of Holies in the Jewish tabernacle, the cherubim at either end of the mercy seat looked down at the ark where the blood was sprinkled and the holy Law was housed. When Jesus was born in Bethlehem, God sent an angel to the shepherds to announce "good news of great joy" (Luke 2:10). When the angels witnessed the first creation, "the morning stars sang together and all the angels shouted for joy" (Job 38:7). Now they rejoice over the new creation as they behold sinners become the children of God through faith in Jesus (2 Cor. 5:17).

If lost people could see themselves and this world through the eyes of the angels, they would immediately cry out to the Lord for salvation. The angels know why humans were created and how much people are missing by rejecting Christ. They see this present age as it really is and what judgments lie before those who refuse to acknowledge Jesus as Lord. The angels beheld the destruction of Sodom and Gomorrah (Gen. 19:1–29) and know how foolish it is for people to delay their decision to trust Christ. Angels know that the Lord has no pleasure in the death of the wicked (Ezek. 18:23), and they wonder why sinners don't turn to Him now for salvation.

When the prodigal son was a rebel in the far country, "he began to be in need" (Luke 15:14). When he came home repentant, his father hosted a feast and "they began to celebrate" (15:24). *Believers on earth and angels in heaven are still celebrating and will celebrate for eternity!* Will you be left out?

*   *   *   *   *

Those who have witnessed to the lost, prayed for them and sought to win them will rejoice with them when they meet in heaven. "For what is our hope, our joy, or the crown in which we will glory in the presence of our Lord Jesus when he comes? Is it not you? Indeed, you are our glory and joy" (1 Thess. 2:19–20). One of the special joys of heaven will be seeing people there who eventually trusted Christ because of our prayers and witness *when we didn't even know it.*

In one of the churches I pastored, we had a retired schoolteacher who taught for many years in the primary department of the Sunday school. She loved her pupils, prayed for them and sought to win them to the Lord, and even after they got older and left her department, she kept praying for them by name.

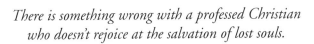

There is something wrong with a professed Christian who doesn't rejoice at the salvation of lost souls.

On more than one occasion when I gave a gospel invitation at the close of a message and an older child or a teenager would respond, she would go forward and stand by them with tears in her eyes and joy on her face. Here was somebody she had prayed for, and now the Lord had answered! Even after she got old and had to give up her class, her prayers for her pupils never ceased. She's in heaven now, and when she arrived, I'm sure she met people who had come to Christ because of her witness, and she hadn't known it.

"Those who are wise will shine like the brightness of the

heavens, and those who lead many to righteousness, like the stars for ever and ever" (Dan. 12:3). There is something wrong with a professed Christian who doesn't rejoice at the salvation of lost souls. Can you imagine one of the neighbors in the parable not rejoicing when the sheep or the coin was found, and especially when the wayward son came home?

For the elder brother not to join in the feast was evidence of a hard heart. Let's beware lest we follow his bad example.

*   *   *   *   *

Have you met yourself in this parable?

Are you a prodigal, wasting your life and in need of returning to the Father? He will run to meet you, so don't delay.

Are you an elder brother, missing out on the feast because of an unforgiving spirit and a hardening heart? Then confess your sins to the Father and discover the joy of reconciliation.

Jesus welcomes sinners and eats with them. The Father welcomes critics and gives them new hearts so they can enjoy the feast and the fellowship.

Today—right now—Jesus offers you a new chance at life. Don't waste it.

"You make known to me the path of life; you will fill me with joy in your presence, with eternal pleasures at your right hand" (Ps. 16:11).

Eight

The Forgotten Son

There are actually three sons involved in this parable: the elder son, the younger son—and the eternal Son, Jesus Christ, who told the parable. We must not forget Him! If you compare Jesus with the younger son, you will find the lessons of the parable reinforced in your heart in a new way.

Both were beloved of their father.

It was the father's love for his younger son that moved him to give the boy his inheritance and allow him to leave. No doubt the neighbors thought the man was foolish, but the father knew what he was doing, and he was willing to pay the price. The boy would have to learn the lessons of life the hard way, and only the father's patience and love could make that possible.

We often emphasize the Father's love for a lost world and the Son's sacrifice to save that world, and the emphasis is good. But we are prone to forget the Father's love for Jesus and the Son's love for His Father. "The Father loves the Son and has placed everything in his hands" (John 3:35). "For the Father loves the Son and shows him all he does" (5:20).

The prodigal received only part of his father's wealth and never asked for guidance. He was motivated by selfishness and pleasure, and he didn't think about consequences until he was bankrupt.

The Father in heaven gave Jesus everything He had and lovingly told Him how to use it, and the Son obeyed. Jesus said, "I love the Father and do exactly what my Father has commanded me" (John 14:31).

It's remarkable that the Father loves believers today as much as He loved His own Son from eternity!

It's a remarkable fact that the Father loves believers today as much as He loved His own Son from eternity! Jesus said to his disciples, "As the Father has loved me, so have I loved you" (John 15:9). And to His Father, "Then the world will know that you sent me and have loved them even as you have loved me" (17:23, 26). How much the younger brother missed by not remaining at home and rejoicing in his father's love!

Both left home.

The prodigal left home because he wanted to "enjoy his freedom." Had he consulted his father, he would have learned that freedom without discipline only leads to bondage. The very pleasures he sought to enjoy would gradually enslave him and then lose their power to please him. The result would be emptiness and slavery.

But Jesus left heaven and came to earth as a servant who obeyed His Father's will, even though it meant "death on a cross" (Phil. 2:8). "I seek not to please myself," He said, "but him who sent me" (John 5:30).

Both were lavish in their spending.

The word "prodigal" means "wasteful, extravagant" and describes how the younger son spent the inheritance his father gave him.

Jesus wasn't wasteful in that sense, because all He did was in obedience to the Father's will. Paul says it best: "For you know the grace of our Lord Jesus Christ, that though he was rich, yet for your sake he became poor, so that you through his poverty might become rich" (2 Cor. 8:9).

At His birth, Jesus was placed in a feeding trough; during His life He had no place to lay His head; at His death He was stripped of everything and treated like a criminal—and He did it all for undeserving sinners like us!

Jesus was lavish in His ministry as He taught the crowds, healed the sick and injured, fed the hungry and raised the dead. As the great Physician, He even made house calls and never once sent a bill for His services. His ultimate gift was His own life laid down on the cross, and all this was motivated by a love greater than that displayed by any person in human history.

Yes, people have laid down their lives for their friends, but Jesus laid down His life for His enemies (Rom. 5:10).

Both became poor.

The prodigal became poor because he was foolish and wasted his wealth on sin instead of investing it in service. "After he had spent everything, there was a severe famine in that whole country, and he began to be in need" (Luke 15:14).

The word translated "be in need" is used by Paul in Romans 3:23, "for all have sinned and *fall short of* the glory of

God." There comes a time when the sinner must confess his poverty and the inability of others to help. Then all he can do is throw himself on the mercy of God.

Jesus became poor so He could make us rich (2 Cor. 8:9), and those who trust Him are rich indeed! Through Jesus Christ, God the Father has lavished on His people the riches of His grace (Eph. 1:7–8) and gifted us with every spiritual blessing we can ever need (1:3). "And my God will meet all your needs according to the riches of his glory in Christ Jesus" (Phil. 4:19).

Both became servants.

The prodigal son became a servant very unwillingly, but Jesus willingly submitted Himself to the Father. During His three years of public ministry, Jesus made Himself available to all kinds of people at all hours of the day and night. Some people even interrupted His sermons and asked for help. Like a common slave, Jesus even washed His disciples' feet.

Each of us must decide whether we will be "slaves to sin, which leads to death, or to obedience, which leads to righteousness." It's only in our submission to Christ that we can find true freedom.

Jesus "made himself nothing by taking the very nature of a servant" (Phil. 2:7). When the disciples disputed over which of them was the greatest, Jesus calmly reminded them, "I am among you as one who serves" (Luke 22:27).

Each of us must decide whether we will be "slaves to sin, which leads to death, or to obedience, which leads to righteousness" (Rom. 6:16). The younger son was a slave to the sins of the flesh. It's only in our submission to Christ that we can find true freedom.

Both were forsaken.

The father never once forsook his younger son; he watched daily for his return. The boy was certainly forsaken, however, by his so-called friends in the far country. Once his money ran out, they abandoned him, not caring whether he lived or died. The Gentile farmer who hired him gave him the worst job on the farm, hoping he would refuse it and leave, but he had no place to go. Nobody fed him or even checked to see if he was alive.

Jesus, too, was forsaken. The religious leaders of His own nation asked that He be crucified. Judas turned on Jesus and betrayed Him; and when Jesus was arrested, the other disciples "deserted him and fled" (Mark 14:50).

Even the heavenly Father forsook His Son when Jesus cried out from the cross, "My God, my God, why have you forsaken me?" (Mark 15:33–34; Ps. 22:1). Jesus had made Himself an offering for sin—your sin and mine—and the Father's eyes "are too pure to look on evil" (Hab. 1:13). But the Father accepted His sacrifice and raised Him from the dead. Now none of God's children can ever be forsaken (Heb. 13:5; Deut. 31:6).

Both were welcomed home again.

It took weeks for hunger, loneliness and shame to teach the prodigal that everything he really needed and wanted would be found back home, but finally he got up and went to his father.

He was willing to earn his way as a menial laborer, but the father would have nothing to do with such plans. With hugs and kisses he welcomed his son, cleaned him up, dressed him up and then filled him up with the finest food, including specially dressed veal. What a welcome!

Forty days after His resurrection, Jesus ascended to heaven and was welcomed by the Father, the angels and "the spirits of the righteous made perfect" (Heb. 12:22–23). In His glorified body He ascended "through the heavens" (4:14, NASB) and was enthroned at the right hand of the Father.

In answer to Jesus' prayer, He was given back the glory He had laid aside when He came to earth (John 17:5). "Lift up your heads, you gates; lift them up, you ancient doors, that the King of glory may come in. Who is he, this King of glory? The LORD Almighty—he is the King of glory" (Ps. 24:9–10).

One day all who have trusted Christ will see and share His glory in the Father's house forever (John 17:22, 24). Jesus is now ministering to His people as high priest and advocate (Heb. 4:14–16; 1 John 2:1–2) and is equipping us to serve Him (Heb. 13:20–21).

What a wonderful Savior is Jesus our Lord!

No matter how far you may have drifted, Jesus still welcomes you home when you come to Him by faith.

He offers you another chance at life, a new beginning that has no end.

"So they began to celebrate" (Luke 15:24).

Will you join the celebration?

Endnotes

Chapter 1

1. *para*—"alongside" and *ballo*—"to cast, to throw," Merriam-Webster Dictionary, 11th edition (Springfield, MA: Merriam-Webster, 2004).
2. William Golding, *A Moving Target* (New York: Farrar, Straus & Giroux, 1984).
3. Erik H. Erickson, *Identity: Youth and Crisis* (New York: W.W. Norton & Company, 1968), p. 25.
4. Barbara Tuchman, *Practicing History* (New York: Alfred A. Knopf, 1981), p. 254.

Chapter 2

1. Dean William R. Inge, *Outspoken Essays, Second Series* (New York: Longmans, Green & Co., 1922), p. 185.
2. The *diaspora* here refers to "the dispersion of the Jews" or "the places where they settled." Webster's New World Dictionary (New York: Collins-World Publishing, 1978). Published by Houghton Mifflin Company. All rights reserved.
3. P.T. Forsythe, *Positive Preaching and the Modern Mind* (London: Independent Press Ltd., 1922), p. 28.

Chapter 3

1. A.W. Tozer, *The Knowledge of the Holy* (New York: Harper & Brothers, 1961), p. 11.

Chapter 4

1. Augustine, *Confessions*, Book 1, Section 18.
2. P.T. Forsyth, *The Sense of the Holy* (Eugene, OR: Wipf and Stock, 1996), p. 24.

Chapter 7

1. Elizabeth C. Clephane, "The Ninety and Nine" (hymn), 1868.

This book was produced by CLC Publications. We hope it has been life-changing and has given you a fresh experience of God through the work of the Holy Spirit. CLC Publications is an outreach of CLC Ministries International, a global literature mission with work in over 50 countries. If you would like to know more about us or are interested in opportunities to serve with a faith mission, we invite you to contact us at:

CLC Ministries International
P.O. Box 1449
Fort Washington, PA 19034

Phone: (215) 542-1242
E-mail: orders@clcpublications.com
Website: www.clcpublications.com

DO YOU LOVE GOOD CHRISTIAN BOOKS?
Do you have a heart for worldwide missions?

You can receive a FREE subscription to *HeartBeat*, CLC's newsletter on global literature missions.

Order by e-mail at:

clcheartbeat@clcusa.org

Or fill in the coupon below and mail to:

P.O. Box 1449
Fort Washington, PA 19034

FREE *HeartBeat* SUBSCRIPTION!

Name: _____

Address: _____

_____

Phone: _____ E-mail: _____

READ THE REMARKABLE STORY OF

the founding of

CLC International

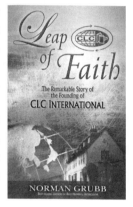

Expert Lifemanship
Mastering the Art of Living

Warren Wiersbe & Ken Jenkins

What do we do with life?

When life's predicaments—or even its predictability—threaten to overwhelm us, it is easy to crumble. But God intends us to overcome—to be experts at living. With His help we can face life's hard realities and come out victorious on the other side.

This grand theme is explored in the heartening words of Warren Wiersbe, punctuated by the stunning nature photography and commentary of Ken Jenkins. What is created is an appealing invitation to reexamine your level of expertise at life—and maybe make a fresh beginning. Full color photos and text included.

Coffee Table Book • 120 pages • 978-0-87508-988-1

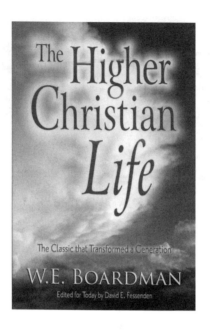

The Higher Christian Life

W.E. Boardman

Read this book and let Christ's power bring you higher!

The Classic that Transformed a Generation

When first published in 1858, this book sparked a revival in England, and was a foundation for the birth of the Keswick movement. When brought across the ocean, it stirred revival in North America as well. Among the many people it influenced was A.B. Simpson, who went on to start the Christian and Missionary Alliance.

Now edited for today's reader and published in a new edition, *The Higher Christian Life* assures us that the Christian life need not be a continuing cycle of trying and failing, but that Christ's power is available for those who take Him by faith as their *sanctification* as well as their salvation.

Trade Paper • 164 pages • 978-0-87508-894-5

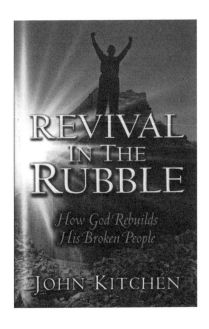

Revival in the Rubble

How God Rebuilds His Broken People

John Kitchen

Can spiritual life and renewal ever be found in the midst of rubble and devastation? "Yes!" says John Kitchen. "When God wants to do a fresh, reviving work in His people, He finds a person and breaks his heart."

Do you read of revivals in the past and find yourself asking God, "Why not here? Why not now? Why not me?"

If so, pick up this book now.

Trade Paper • 261 pages • 978-0-87508-873-2

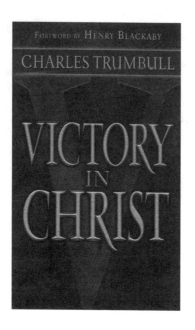

Victory In Christ
Charles Trumbull

Do you long for a righteous life,
yet struggle constantly with secret sins?

In this down-to-earth, practical book, Trumbull reveals insights
into the full reality of our victory in Christ, who has achieved by His
work on the cross the freedom that every believer desires.

Break free of the struggle between faith and works.
Experience true victory—*in Christ!*

Mass Market • **128 pages** • 978-0-87508-533-3

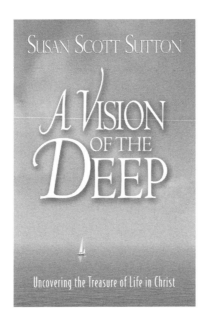

A Vision of the Deep
Uncovering the Treasure of Life in Christ

Susan Scott Sutton

Has your walk with Christ become
a duty rather than a passion?

Susan Sutton takes us beyond a sense of obligation and responsibility in the Christian life to give us a "vision of the deep." If you are dissatisfied with "surface living," join Susan in this life-altering venture to lose yourself in the fathomless depths of Jesus Christ.

Trade Paper • 189 pages • 978-0-87508-786-3

In the hot summer of 1939 war was
National Socialists were on the move and few doubted that
only twenty-one years since the final shells were fired in the
war-to-end-all-wars, another major conflict seemed inevitable.
Only the timing remained in doubt but the signs were clear. On
March 7th 1936, in a blatant contravention of the Versailles
Treaty, Hitler marched his army into the demilitarised
Rhineland. There were lots of hot words from European leaders
but neither Great Britain nor France had the stomach for a
fight. 'Appease rather than oppose' appeared to be their default
strategy and unsurprisingly it emboldened the German dictator.
Two years of rapid re-armament later, on March 12th 1938,
Hitler launched his Anschluss and annexed Austria, again
unopposed by the governments of Germany's neighbours. In
September of that same year, following the Munich conference
on the 30th, Germany annexed the Sudetenland with the supine
approval of Great Britain and France. Chamberlain returned to
the UK waving a piece of paper and proclaimed that it was
'Peace for our time.' Hitler said it was the end of his
expansionist ambitions for Germany but everyone knew it was
just the beginning. Yet despite the storm clouds, British tourists
were taking advantage of favourable exchange rates and
flocking in hoards to the capitals of Europe. Even in Berlin, at
the centre of the storm, there were tourists everywhere.

One such tourist was Duncan Buchanan, a Scottish student
who was reading German at Glasgow University. He had
finished his second year and intent on improving his
conversational German going into his final year, he was

spending most of the summer vacation travelling on his own across Germany. He chose to travel alone rather that with a companion because it forced him to engage with the locals who for the most part were more than happy to talk to him. He had a natural flair for the language and after speaking only German for weeks on end his pronunciation and accent improved dramatically, to the point where towards the end of his trip he was frequently mistaken for a native. On discovering he was British it was only a matter time before the standard question was posed to him. *'What do you think of Adolf Hitler?'* It was a tricky question because to a large extent his answer depended on what the questioner thought of Adolf Hitler and that was not usually obvious. People were generally guarded when expressing anything other than wholehearted support for Hitler and the National Socialists. So he learned to duck the question and pose it back to the questioner. If the response was unqualified and enthusiastic support, then his answer was usually along the lines of. *'Well, he has certainly raised the self-esteem among the German people and the economy seems to be strong.'* The danger came when he detected antipathy towards Hitler. Such feelings were never expressed openly but at times it was clear that the person he was talking to was too scared to speak out. When this happened he would immediately change the subject and comment on how beautiful the weather was in Berlin that summer and how much he had been enjoying practising his German and how friendly everyone had been.

It was now late July and his boat back to the England from Amsterdam was leaving in a week's time, so it was time to head north. There was a direct train from Berlin to Amsterdam which took nine hours but there was no point in arriving in

Amsterdam more than a couple of days early. His train ticket allowed him to stop off somewhere along the way so eventually he decided to take a break in Hannover which was about half way to the Dutch border. There was nothing in Hannover that he particularly wanted to see, but he knew in a large industrial city he would have lots of opportunity to meet people and put the finishing touches to his German. When he arrived at Berlin Hauptbahnhof he realised how much he was looking forward to getting back home. The tension in the German air was palpable and there were rumours of troop movements towards the Polish border. In the back of his mind he began to worry that if war broke out before he could get across the border into Holland then life could become very tricky indeed. However, unless something delayed him unexpectedly in Hannover he'd be in Holland the following day.

The train station was mobbed with travellers all urgently going about their business and circulating among them were many uniformed police with peaked caps and red Swastika armbands checking identity documents. He was also sure that the notorious Gestapo would be present, also on the lookout for anything suspicious. Tourists were few and far between and it was obvious that for one reason or another many of the travellers were in the process of trying to get out of Germany. Families anxiously struggled with heavy suitcases as they picked their way across the busy concourse to the platforms. Suddenly realising he stood out as a foreign tourist, he hurried to the ticket office.

'A single ticket to Amsterdam, please - third class.' He said in German, lowering his head to speak through the mouse hole at the bottom of the glass panel. As he spoke he realised it

might have been better to have spoken in English, or at least in broken German but it was too late. As he collected his ticket he felt a tap on his shoulder. *'Please let me see your identity papers.'* Said a smartly dressed man wearing a homburg hat and looking for all the world like an important businessman but for the fact he wasn't carrying any baggage - not even a briefcase. As Duncan took off his rucksack and fumbled in the top pocket for his passport, he smiled to himself, this man was unmistakably a member of the secret police. Despite his plain-clothes he stood out from the crowd like a sore thumb. Finding his passport he handed it over and watched as the man carefully examined every page. After an agonising period he said, *'please come with me.'*

'But I have a train to catch.' He protested quietly.

'Routine check. It won't take long. Come with me.' He said, gripping Duncan's arm tightly and steering him towards a door into a room which was part of the ticket office. Inside was a simple desk and two chairs. The man gestured to him to sit down and then took the seat opposite. Saying nothing he produced a watchmaker's eyeglass from his pocket and proceeded to study the passport carefully. Duncan glanced nervously at his watch, noting that the departure time of this train was fast approaching. He was tempted to point this out but something told him it would make no difference whatsoever, in fact it might encourage the secret policeman to take longer than was necessary. After what seemed an age the secret policeman removed the eyeglass and said. *'Everything seems to be in order. I see you are now returning to England after spending the summer here with us in Germany. Have you enjoyed yourself?'* It was the opening he needed and he quickly

explained that the purpose of his visit was to improve his German. *'Then your visit has been a success. You could quite easily be mistaken for a German citizen.'* He said as he rose to his feet. *'Mr Buchanan you may go. I hope you have a safe journey home.'* The curt nod and the instinctive click of his heels plainly betraying his identity as a member of the German State Secret Police, the Geheime Staatspolizei, otherwise know as the Gestapo.

As he raced to the platform and climbed aboard the train it became clear to him that many people, especially Jews, must be trying to get out of Germany before the storm burst and anyone like him who was purchasing a single ticket out of the country would arouse suspicion. The ticket officer must have pressed a button to summon the secret agent when, as an apparent German citizen, he'd asked for the one-way ticket to Amsterdam. The incident unsettled him and as the train got underway he began to think it might be better not to stop off in Hannover and get out of Germany as quickly as possible. As they pulled away from the station and headed westwards out of the city he made his way along the train to the restaurant car and bought a beer to settle his nerves. By the time he'd finished it he had decided to stick with his original plan and break the journey in Hannover. It was already late afternoon and when the train arrived at Hannover station so his first priority was to find somewhere to spend the night. The next morning he could catch the first train to Amsterdam and then spend his final couple of days in Europe sightseeing while he waited for the ferry. Several times during the three and a half hour journey uniformed officers moved up and down the carriages randomly checking tickets and identity papers. However, apart from a railway employee who routinely checked his train ticket, his journey to Hannover was uninterrupted.

The train sped through the rural countryside of Lower Saxony, passing the new town of Wolfburg on the way. This industrial town was constructed only a year previously to house the workers who built the latest modern automobile in Germany, the Volkswagen 'Beetle' as it had quickly become known. The vast, sprawling factory employed tens of thousands of assemblers, testers, engineers and office workers, all housed in dull blocks of identical concrete apartments which surrounded what he'd heard was one of the largest car assembly plants in the world outside of The United States. He was wondering what other vehicles were being manufactured there when the train passed an enormous field crammed to the edges with military vehicles. Germany really was gearing up for war.

His guide book waxed lyrical about the ancient city of Hannover. Founded in the thirteenth century there would be plenty for him to see had he had more time. But now his priority was to find somewhere to spend the night, preferably near the station. He would catch the midday train to Amsterdam the following day and spend his last few hours in Germany sightseeing near the station. Alighting from the train he made his way out of the station into the bustling city. During his time in Germany he had mostly stayed in Youth Hostels but occasionally he'd had no choice but to look for bed and breakfast accommodation. This he usually did by asking a barman who invariably knew which locals were prepared to put up a student overnight for a modest fee. Sometimes he'd found a room over the bar but that wasn't his preferred option as it was usually very noisy.

It was a sultry evening and an old inn on the square outside the station beckoned. He sat up at the bar and in English ordered a half-litre of lager. The barman looked friendly enough but after his brush with the secret police in Berlin he had no wish to attract their attention again.

'Are you just passing through on your way back to England?' Enquired the barman.

'Yes' he replied switching to German, 'I've spend the past six weeks in Germany brushing up on my German. I'm a student - Glasgow University - it's my final year coming up next term. I'm heading to Amsterdam tomorrow at midday and then back to England on the ferry a couple of days later.'

'Have you enjoyed yourself?' He enquired and not waiting for an answer he continued, 'we live in troubled times but still the tourists come and go as if everything was normal.'

Ignoring the invitation to discuss the current political situation in Europe, he replied. 'It has been a great trip for me. Travelling alone has forced me to speak German almost all the time and it has undoubtedly improved my conversational German. Of course that doesn't help much in my exams which concentrate on German grammar and I've not done much of that while I've been here.' He said, acknowledging the smile from the barman with a brief nod. He sipped his beer and then said, 'I was wondering if you knew any locals who could put me up for the night?'

'You could try Frau Schneider. She has a room to let and she lives only a half a kilometre from the station. I'll give you her address and please tell her it was me who recommended *her. My name is Hans.'* He was already writing the address on a napkin as he spoke.

'I'm Duncan. Pleased to meet you.' He said, reaching across the bar with his outstretched hand.

They shook hands and he downed the rest of his beer. *'Thank you for your help, I hope our paths cross again sometime.'*

'And good luck to you, Duncan. Safe home.' He said.

As he left the inn the barman called after him *'By the way, you speak German like a native!'*

'Thanks.' Replied Duncan who was reflecting on the 'safe home' comment and wondering if there was any darker dimension to this tradition farewell to a traveller. Maybe he was getting neurotic but the barman did seem to emphasise the word 'safe' a little more than usual. There was an inescapable yet unspoken feeling that war was imminent. It was in the air. At a personal level, however distasteful he felt the German regime was, he felt no malice to the barman or to any of the normal Germans he'd met during his holiday, but there was a dreadful tide of anti-Semitism spreading across the country like an influenza epidemic. Early on he'd learnt not to engage in any conversation either about the Jews or National Socialism. Often, at some point in most conversations an apparently innocent question would be floated but he quickly became an expert at spotting it and taking evasive action. The skill wasn't entirely unknown to him. In Scotland the first question posed in a conversation with a stranger was more often than not. *'What school did you go to?'* If the answer was Saint something or other, then it was assumed you were a Catholic, which had been the point of the apparently innocent question.

Enjoying the early evening sunshine he strolled down Bahnhofstrasse and took a right turn past the church to a row of five-storey apartments which in his native Glasgow would have been called tenements. The address he'd been given was on the third floor overlooking the church. He climbed the stairs and knocked on the door of apartment number sixty-two.

Expecting Frau Schneider to open the door, he was taken aback when a girl of similar age to himself opened the door. She was stunningly beautiful and groping for words amidst the fog he finally managed to speak. *'I'm sorry, I was looking for Frau Schneider - to see if she could put me up for the night - the barman in the station bar, Hans, gave me this address - am I in the right place - this is her apartment - no?'*

She smiled and her brown eyes twinkled in silent acknowledgement of his embarrassment before responding. *'This is Frau Schneider's apartment. She is my mother. Hold on and I'll get her.'*

What had happened to him? Yes, she was a very pretty girl and yes, she had not been who he'd been expecting to answer the door but before he could fully regain his composure Frau Schneider appeared in the doorway with her daughter behind her. *'Hello,'* she said *'my daughter says that our friend the barman sent you?'*

He nodded and replied. *'Yes, I'm a British student and on my way back home after spending nearly six weeks in Germany brushing up on my German. The ferry leaves from Amsterdam in a couple of days time so I was hoping to spend one night or maybe two in Hannover before catching the train to Amsterdam. Can you put me up?'*

'We do have a spare room and you are welcome. If you wish I can also serve you dinner and breakfast?' She said, beckoning him to follow her into the apartment. *'We will be eating shortly as my daughter is going to the ballet in the Congress Centrum this evening. If you want join us for dinner, please do.'*

The room was clean and tidy with a single bed, a small table and chair and a view from the window onto the Church plaza. He dropped his rucksack beside the table and flopped down on the bed, his head still spinning from his first encounter with Frau Schneider's daughter. It was some minutes before he felt back in control and after changing his shirt he made his way to the dining room where an extra place had already been laid and enticing smells were emanating from the kitchen where Frau Schneider was in the final stages of preparing dinner. Her daughter emerged from the adjacent room, smiled at him and said. *'I'm Ruth.'*

In his best German he replied. *'A pleasure to meet you. My name is Duncan - Duncan Buchanan - I'm from Scotland.'* Realising he was beginning to run off at the mouth again he abruptly stopped speaking. What had happened to him? Every time he spoke to this girl he seemed to ramble incoherently.

'I've always wanted to visit Scotland,' she said wistfully, *'but I can't see that happening anytime soon.'*

It was yet another oblique reference to the fragile political situation so he evaded the inferred question and responded. *'You never know what's around the corner, Ruth. Life is full of surprises. You would like Scotland, I'm sure. I would happily show you around.'* Once again he had to hold himself in check. Here he was, having just met the girl and already offering to show her around Scotland. He smiled awkwardly at her, realising he was probably making a fool of himself when thankfully Frau Schneider emerged from the kitchen carrying a tray which was laden with food.

'Please take a seat Duncan. I hope you like goulash.' She said.

'I certainly do and it smells delicious.' He replied, quickly moving around the table to hold Ruth's chair for her. Nothing was said but the polite gesture didn't go unnoticed and he felt he was beginning to regain some composure. Over dinner the discussion ranged across the usual topics but always steering clear of politics. It was obvious that people were afraid and Frau Schneider and her daughter were no exception. But openly sharing views was perhaps only confined to close friends and definitely not up for discussion between casual acquaintances. Over coffee Ruth glanced at her watch and said. *'It's a thirty-five minute walk to the concert hall and I'll need to be off soon if I'm to get to there in time. It's my favourite ballet - Prokofiev's Romeo and Juliet.'*

'It's also my favourite.' He replied.

There was a noticeable pause before Ruth spoke again after a quick glance across to her mother. *'I'm not sure if you could get a ticket but if you want to take the chance, you're welcome to come with me?'*

His heart leapt 'I'd like that very much,' he said, before adding. *'If that's OK with you Frau Schneider?*

'I'd be very happy to know that Ruth wasn't walking there and back on her own. These are worrying times.' She said, shaking her head from side to side. It was as signal that she wanted to talk so instead of avoiding the subject he said. *'They*

certainly are. I was stopped by the secret police in Berlin, they checked my passport and once they discovered I was British they let me go but it was an uncomfortable experience.'

Out of the corner of his eye he could see Ruth glancing again at her watch. *'I'm sorry Frau Schneider, it seems we have to be off now but we'll have more time to chat tomorrow I'm sure. Thank you for dinner, you are an excellent chef!'* He said enthusiastically.

As they walked down the stairs he wondered briefly what he would do if he couldn't get a ticket to the concert but the answer was obvious. He would hang around outside the concert hall until it ended and then accompany Ruth back to the apartment. They exited the apartment block into the fresh evening air and headed off eastwards, the sun casting long shadows ahead of them. As they walked together he noticed with pleasure that she made it easy for him to walk on the outside of the pavement. He wanted to take her hand, especially when they crossed the road but he held back for fear of stepping over a hidden line. All the time his heart was racing. He had never felt like this before - not even close - and yet he'd only known her for a couple of hours. What was she thinking? No matter how controlled he tried to be she must have sensed his discomfort. Meanwhile, All the time she seemed to be so composed while he, despite his most earnest efforts, was ill-at-ease and struggling to behave normally. For a while they didn't speak but it was a special silence and in it he could feel their friendship grow.

'If I can't get a ticket, I'll wait for you,' He said as they joined the throng of people streaming towards the concert hall.

She looked directly at him and smiled. *'There's really no need. The performance lasts more than three hours so you might prefer to head back to the apartment? I can make my own way home.'*

'I'll wait,' he said, *'really I don't mind. I can find a local bar or coffee shop and practice my German - the time will fly by. I'll meet you in the foyer after the show.'*

When they got to the ticket office he could barely believe his good fortune that thanks to a last minute cancellation, the seat next to Ruth's was available. He barely noticed the cost of the ticket which was at least one day's allowance but he didn't care, he was in heaven. He bought an over-priced programme and they took their seats just as the orchestra began playing the overture. He glanced across at Ruth and touched her hand. *'Thank you for allowing me to accompany you tonight. Even though the ballet hasn't started, I will never forget this evening.'*

She flashed a smile at him before turning to watch the curtain rise. He continued to look at her in wonder. She was the most beautiful girl he had ever seen and here he was, sitting beside her at the ballet, watching Prokofiev's Romeo and Juliet. It was a moment of supreme happiness. In the interval he bought her a glass of white wine and in the crowded bar they chatted easily about the ballet. Every now and then when she was making a point she reached across and touched his arm, as though to make sure he could hear her, so when the bell rang he boldly took her hand and led her out of the crowded bar and back to their seats. She was in tears at the end and how he wished he'd had a clean white handkerchief to give her to wipe her eyes.

'I always cry at Romeo and Juliet - it is so very sad.' She said, *'at the same time it is the most beautiful yet the most tragic love-affair imaginable.'*

He took her hand in the darkness as they walked back to the apartment. On the way they made small talk about the ballet, the weather and everything except what was happening between them. He knew that to open up to her about his feelings would be to risk all, it might break the magic, so he continued the small talk until they were at the apartment door by which time he felt his heart was on the verge of exploding. He could contain his feelings no longer. *'Ruth,'* he said in a voice trembling with emotion. *'I don't quite know what is happening to me but even though we've just met, it's crazy but I think I'm falling in love with you.'* He'd barely finished the sentence when the door opened sharply and Frau Schneider welcomed them inside saying. *'How was it? Did you get a seat?'* She produced a bottle of schnapps and poured out three small liqueur glasses. They drank a toast to family and friends before Ruth said. *'I've got to be up early for work tomorrow so I'd better be off to bed. If I miss you in the morning, I hope you have a safe trip back to Scotland.'*

Fearing he might never see her again he blurted out. *'I'm an early riser. I could see you at breakfast and walk you to work - that is, if you'd like...?'*

'That would be nice Duncan. Breakfast at six-thirty then?' She said cheerfully, flashing another of her beautiful smiles at him before giving her mother a kiss and disappearing into her bedroom.

He lay awake all night in torment. On the other side of their thin adjoining wall was the girl that he loved more than life itself, yet in all other respects she was infinitely beyond his reach. He had fallen into a vortex from which there was no escape, his emotions oscillating between extreme happiness and extreme sadness. It was supremely ironic that they should have just watched Romeo and Juliet at the ballet. Should he stay in Hannover for another night or should he perhaps stay in Hannover for ever? He could speak fluent German and getting a job should be relatively easy. Should he ask her to come with him back to the Britain? What if she wouldn't leave he mother? Should he ask them both to come to Britain? Even if they both agreed to uproot their lives for him, they would need to apply for an exit visa and German citizens were no longer allowed to travel freely abroad. That could take weeks or even months and in the meantime what if war erupted across Europe? Through the long night these questions swirled inconclusively around in his head until finally, towards dawn, he eventually fell asleep.

A knock on his door awakened him and within seconds he was back in the cauldron of indecision which had kept him awake all night. He washed, dressed quickly and automatically stuffed his gear into the rucksack. Still red-eyed and bleary he entered the kitchen to the smell of coffee and bacon. Ruth and her mother were already sitting at the table.

'Please sit down Duncan,' said Frau Schneider, beckoning him towards the empty seat, *'I hope you slept well?'*

It must have been plain to them that he'd had a sleepless night so he opted for honesty. *'To be truthful, it took me a long time to get to sleep. Different bed, lots to think about etcetera....and then when I eventually dropped off it was into the depths - that's why I look so bleary - apologies. A cup of coffee and I'll be fine!'*

'The weather is still good so we will have a pleasant walk to my work. The office is on the way to the station so rather than returning here, you could go straight to the station and catch an early train to Amsterdam?' Ruth had phrased it as a question but there was something in her tone and in the way she looked at him told him otherwise. His mind raced. It seemed that Ruth had decided she wanted him to leave. Swallowing his discomfort and forcing a smile, he replied. 'That would make sense. I've already packed my rucksack - it's a habit one develops when always on the go.' As he spoke he looked across at Frau Schneider and saw the warmth and sadness in her eyes. She knew how he felt, of that there was no doubt. He settled up with Frau Schneider, bade her farewell and followed Ruth downstairs and into the sunshine of another beautiful late summer's day. He wanted to hold her hand but she was carrying her briefcase between them and if she had wanted to hold hands, he assumed she would have switched the briefcase to her other hand. Although they walked in silence he sensed an emotional warmth between them. Eventually she spoke. 'Duncan, last night at the ballet was very special for me. I won't ever forget it. We barely know each other yet during the entire evening, anyone who saw us would have been forgiven for thinking we were a couple who had been together for years. If you lived here maybe we would be a couple but we are ships passing in the night. You are travelling back to Britain tomorrow and I am staying here in Hannover with my mother.' She paused, as if to let the message sink before continuing, 'my father died when I was ten. He fought in the trenches during the first World War and was poisoned by mustard gas. As I child growing up I watched him suffer... When he died mother *looked after me and then when I grew up I looked after her. I will always look after her. We are a good team, my mother and I.'*

There was silence between them for a while. He didn't know what to say. Everything he'd wanted to say had been summed up in those few words of love he'd spoken at the door of the apartment the previous night. Then she stopped and spoke again. *'You are a fine man Duncan, a gentleman and you will make a good husband for some fortunate Scottish girl. This is my office...'* She turned to face him and before he could say anything she kissed him lightly on his cheek and whispered something in his ear. Then she handed him a small envelope and turning abruptly away she opened the office door and disappeared inside.

Stunned and speechless, he stood motionless on the pavement while he struggled to come to terms with what had just happened. Then as he turned to slowly walk away he felt a dull ache in his heart, an ache which felt as if it would last for an eternity. He had arrived at the station before he realised he was still carrying the envelope she had given him. Stopping in the middle of the concourse he gently opened it to find it contained a photograph of her. On the back was her address and a sequence of marks he didn't recognise. He looked at her photo again and amidst the bustling commuters he broke down. Passers-by stared at him but he saw nothing other than Ruth. It was several minutes before he regained control. He replaced the photo in the brown envelope and put it carefully in his breast pocket next to his aching heart but it didn't ease the pain. A short while later he boarded the early train to Amsterdam and as it pulled out of the station he drifted off into a dreamless sleep.

Meanwhile in the office where Ruth worked, her friend on the adjacent desk said. *'How was the ballet?'*

'It was very special.' She replied as the hot tears welled up in her eyes. *'I think I've got something in my eye...I'll be back in a minute.'* She rose from her chair and walked quickly to the Ladies where she locked herself into a cubicle and sobbed silently. Afterwards she tried to console herself by remembering what a special evening it had been but the tears kept coming. It was impossible not to think of what might have been. That evening when she returned to the apartment she could see that her mother knew.

'He was a very special boy - wasn't he?' she said as they hugged.

'Yes Mutter, very special and I will find it hard to forget him.'

'Maybe he will come back one day - you never know. Unless I am very mistaken, he will find it hard to live without you.'

Duncan awoke sharply as the train shuddered to a halt at Minden and it took a few minutes for his head to clear as he came round from his coma-like sleep. The dull ache in his heart was still there and it reminded him of when he'd first left home to go up to university. For a while he'd thought he was ill but after a couple of days he realised it was simply homesickness. Now he was love-sick and no medication existed to cure his condition. Somehow he had to see her again, but how and when? At least he had her address so he could write to her and maybe he could ask her to come and visit him in Scotland but the future was so uncertain. All the signs were that Europe was on the brink of war and if hostilities erupted it would change everything.

As the train pulled out of the station a family of four joined him in his compartment. They were laden with baggage and after helping them stow their suitcases they exchanged pleasantries, being careful to avoid commenting, even obliquely, on the political situation. The man and his wife were holding hands and exchanging what seemed to be nervous glances while their two girls sat quietly reading. After a while their conversation dried up and he resorted to staring out of the window as they sped through the Lower Saxony countryside, stopping at Bad Oeynhausen, then at Osnabruck and finally at Rheine. At each station more and more people piled onto the train and by the time they pulled out of Rheine even the aisles were full. It was obvious that most if not all of the passengers were heading to Amsterdam with one purpose in mind - to get out of Germany before the storm burst. Apart from picking up on the language he had no way of knowing the nationalities of the passengers. There were a lot of people speaking Dutch and he assumed that like him they were keen to get out of Germany but the majority, as best he could tell, were Germans. At first he found this puzzling but on reflection he realised there was one category of German citizens who would be desperate to get out of the country - the Jews. He suddenly realised that his nearby travelling companions, the couple with their two well-behaved children, were almost certainly Jewish. It was nothing to do with their appearance but if they were Jewish it would explain their obvious anxiety. He wondered what the family had left behind? All they now had was in the four suitcases he had helped them store in the overhead rack. Feeling fortunate to be British he felt strangely detached from any of the mounting tension that surrounded him. It was as if his British Passport would guarantee him a trouble-free passage across the border. After all, his paperwork had already been thoroughly checked by the secret police in Berlin but the closer the train got to the border the more electricity there was in the air. The final stop before crossing into Holland was at Bad Bentheim, only a few miles from the border. When the train pulled into the station the platform was strangely empty, however, at regular intervals along it stood three or four people - one person in plain clothes with two or three uniformed officers in attendance. This must be the border police he thought, once the train leaves Bad Bentheim, presumably it would not stop again until it was is inside Holland. Some shuffling at the end of the carriage and a dramatic lull in the conversation indicated they were in for a thorough identity check and at the rate at which they were progressing it was apparent that the train would be stopped for at least an hour. He no longer felt as detached as before and despite the knowledge that his papers had been cleared in Berlin he couldn't help worrying. Meanwhile, across from him he could see the couple exchanging increasingly nervous glances as the officers slowly worked their way down the carriage. There was now total silence, no one spoke apart from the plain clothes border policeman demanding identity papers and questioning the passengers. When it came to his turn, he handed over his British passport which was returned to him with no more than perfunctory glance.

The border policeman then addressed the father of the family sitting opposite him. *'Papers please.'* He ordered bluntly, his hand outstretched. The father was visibly shaking as he placed the documents in his hand and his trembling hand didn't go unnoticed. With mounting alarm Duncan realised that a drama was unfolding in front of him. The papers were scrutinised carefully and then handed to one of the uniformed guards. *'Your exit visas are not in order.'* He said curtly. *'We need to do further checks. You will all leave the train now with one of my officers.'* Fighting to suppress the terror which was clearly visible in his eyes, the father of the family quietly protested only to be interrupted rudely. *'You will leave the train now - with your baggage. You will not be going to Holland on this train.'* He gestured to one of his attendants who hauled the father to his feet in front of his now sobbing wife and terrified children. Duncan leapt up to help get the bags down from the luggage rack before resuming his seat and watched powerlessly as the sad family was ushered off the train. *'Juden.' S*aid the border policeman to nobody in particular before carrying on with his checking. As far Duncan could tell there were no more 'incidents' in his carriage but he could see from his window seat that several other passengers had been disembarked and were being taken across the platform to the station offices. After an eternity of waiting the border check was completed and the policemen dismounted from the train. Then the whistle blew and at last the train pulled away from the station. A collective sigh of relief filled the carriage and the deathly silence that had been present during the check was slowly filled again with subdued talk. A short while later the train finally crossed the border into Holland to a ripple of applause from the relieved passengers. Duncan did not join in. He remained shocked at what had happened to his travelling companions and it required a considerable mental effort not dwell on their possible fate.

The atmosphere in the carriage quickly became warm and relaxed. People smiled at each other and talked quietly about how glad they were to be safely across the border and how frightened they'd been. Nobody mentioned the poor passengers who had been removed from the train. It was as if they had never existed. Later that afternoon the train finally arrived at Amsterdam. His ferry to England was in two days time on August 30th and before today he had been looking forward to some sightseeing in the city. Now all he wanted to do was to get back to Britain. He found accommodation in a Youth Hostel near the centre and ordered a quiet meal and a beer in a nearby restaurant. He was glad to be alone as he reflected on his summer in Germany. Although his German had improved to the point where he was frequently mistaken for a native and it had been a successful trip in almost every respect, staring at Ruth's picture while he ate brought tears to his eyes and the ache in his heart returned.

During the next two days he spend his time drifting aimlessly along the banks of the canals, stopping for the occasional coffee or beer and always thinking about Ruth. The newspapers were full of reports of an incident on Germany's border with Poland and there were rumours of German troop movements and a buildup of armaments in response. Everywhere there was talk of war yet he had mixed feelings as he boarded the ferry. He wanted to get back home and finish his degree but at the same time he desperately wanted to return to Hannover and find Ruth. From the moment he'd met her his life had changed for ever.

That night in London he stayed with friends before catching the sleeper to Edinburgh the following evening. In normal times his visit would have been a cause for celebration but these were far from normal times. *'What's the matter with you Duncan?'* His friends had said. *'You seem very subdued, yet you should be happy to be safely back in Blighty after your summer in Germany.'* He wanted to talk about Ruth but he wasn't ready yet to open up to anyone, his feelings were too raw and too intimate to share. The news of Germany's invasion of Poland broke while he was waiting on the busy concourse at Kings Cross Station. Word spread like wildfire through the waiting throng and the word on everyone's lips was that it would only be a matter of days before Britain and France would have to honour their pledge to defend Poland's sovereignty and declare war on Germany. For the foreseeable future all hopes of seeing Ruth again or even communicating with her were dashed. Would he ever see her again? He boarded the train and after leaving his rucksack on the upper berth of his compartment he made his way to the restaurant car for some dinner where he found himself assigned to a table immediately opposite a young lady who looked up from the menu and smiled.

'The train seems to be busy, I'm sorry to disturb you.' He said as he took his seat. He'd have preferred to be alone but perhaps the company might distract him.

'My name's Duncan.' He said, reaching across the table to shake hands.

'I'm Rachael.' She replied as she took his hand.

The train pulled out of the station and quickly gathered speed as it travelled north. When the steward came to take their dinner order, on an impulse Duncan ordered a bottle of red wine. It would be a long evening and apart from the occasional beer he'd barely touched alcohol, rationalising that the wine would also help him sleep. Over dinner they struck up a conversation and as he consumed the red wine his tongue loosened and before he knew what was happening he started pouring his heart out to his anonymous travelling companion who listened carefully, interjecting sympathetically when he paused from time to time. Sharing his story with a complete stranger was somehow easier than sharing it with a friend. *'Thank you for listening to me Rachael. You must think I'm a sad case. Please help me finish this wine before I completely break down.'* She nodded and he filled her glass. There was quiet between them for a while as the train chuffed its way northwards. Without thinking he reached into the inside pocket of his jacket and brought out Ruth's picture. *'This is her.'* He said wistfully as he passed it across the table. She looked at the photograph for a while before responding. *'She is very beautiful.'*

'Apart from my memories of our evening at the ballet, this is all I have. She wrote her address on the back but what use is that? If we declare war on Germany I won't even be able to write to her.'

She casually turned over the photograph. *'I see she lives in Hannover. I'm told it is a lovely old city.'*

'It is.' He replied, noticing that Rachael was still looking at the back of the photograph. Her brow furrowed slightly and she looked up and directly into his eyes.

'Is something wrong?' He said, reaching across to take the photograph.

'No, nothing is wrong but do you know what this means?' She said, pointing at the curious markings beneath the address on the back of the photograph.

He shook his head and she smiled softly. *'Duncan, this is Hebrew and it says - I love you.'*

Tears welled up in his eyes as he wrestled with his swirling emotions. Her message of love also told him that she was Jewish and suddenly the anti-Semitism he had seen during his travels in Germany took on a a more ominous significance, they became personal yet he was utterly powerless to help in any way. For a few moments he was unable to speak and then he remembered something else. When they had parted she had kissed his cheek and whispered something in his ear. *'Rachael, can you please tell me what 'I love you' sounds like in Hebrew?'* He asked, knowing the answer before she spoke.

'Ani ohevet otkha.' She whispered softly.

Unable to speak he nodded and reaching across the table he squeezed both her hands tightly as his tears flowed down his cheeks. It was the most bittersweet moment of his life. In his mind's eye he watched again as she disappeared beyond the office door and he heard again the rude clunk as it sprang closed behind her.

When he awakened the next morning the train was stationery at the platform in Edinburgh's Waverley Station. Although his fare included breakfast he chose to leave the train immediately. He needed to clear his head and much as he had greatly appreciated his encounter with Rachael, he felt it would be awkward and embarrassing for both of them if they had breakfast together. It was early morning and well before the rush hour so the air was fresh, birds sang and he breathed deeply as he headed up the hill out of the station towards his parents' house in Stockbridge. They were mightily relieved to see him, with war looming they had been terribly worried he would get stranded in Europe. That evening they had a celebratory meal in one of the city's best restaurants and he regaled them with tales from his travels but he did not mention Ruth. That was too personal and too emotional to share with his parents whose advice would only be to try and forget her. He could almost hear his father saying. *'Move on son. You need to concentrate on your studies. You'll meet other girls but the time to get serious is after you've got your degree.'* His mother would feel his pain and sympathise but there seemed no point in burdening her with his emotional problems.

Two days later Britain and France declared war on Germany, dashing the slender hopes he had that one day in the not too distant future he might see Ruth again. However, he knew he could never forget her so he placed his memories of her in a special room in his head where they would be safe. When he needed to he could unlock the door and spend time reliving their all-too-brief time together. He decided that the only person who would know about her would be Rachael, the girl he'd met on the train and it seemed highly unlikely that their paths would ever cross again. The days passed slowly until the start of his term and he took to doing long runs to lonely places where he could look at Ruth's photograph and talk to her without anyone else seeing or hearing their conversation and all the time the reports from Germany of increased violence against the Jews scared him.

When the university term started he knew his heart wasn't in it. Some of his friends has enlisted within days of the outbreak of war and were already in training. It seemed wrong that he should continue his studies while others were prepared to risk their lives for King and Country, so one day he walked into the RAF recruitment office in Glasgow and signed up. His parents were shocked but by then it was too late so when he left home to start initial training as a pilot they told him how proud they were and they wished him well. He was posted to a training camp in the south of England where, assuming he passed all his exams and flying tests, he would gain his wings in nine months time - at the end of May 1940. Becoming a pilot was a much more exciting proposition than finishing his degree. In any event the university told him they would welcome him back after his service duty ended. Boarding the London sleeper train at Waverley Station brought back memories of his chance encounter with Rachael, the Jewish girl who had translated the Hebrew writing on the back of Ruth's photo and who also told him how a girl would say *'I love you'* in Hebrew. As the train drew away from the platform he patted the left breast pocket of his smart new RAF uniform where Ruth's picture would always be kept, next to his heart.

In Germany, apart from those involved directly in the invasion of Poland, nothing much had changed during the first few weeks of the war. There was a sense of foreboding but most Germans had confidence in their country's military strength and many hoped that before long a lasting peace agreement would be secured. For the majority the current aggression was aimed at correcting the punitive Treaty of Versailles which had ended the First World War by humiliating Germany and crippling the country's economy. All the time the persecution of the Jews increased. Hundreds of thousands of Jews escaped to other European countries and further afield before war broke out. With few exceptions they left everything they had behind them. All Jewish assets were seized by the Nazis and used to fuel the fascist regime. In Hannover, Ruth and her mother believed no-one in the apartment block knew they were Jews. They had never actively practised their Jewish faith since Frau Schneider had married a Gentile. Shortly after their marriage they moved to Hannover from the country so that Herr Schneider could be closer to better medical facilities and to the best of their knowledge nobody in the apartment block could possibly know that Frau Schneider and her daughter were Jews. Confidence in their anonymity grew when they escaped the horrors of the pogrom and the Kristallnacht, however Frau Schneider's birth and marriage certificates showed that her maiden name was Grünberg and she knew that sooner or later the SS would knock on her door. At work Ruth worried about her Jewish name but she was good at her job and in those early days following the outbreak of war her employers had bigger problems to worry about. In the evenings Ruth and her mother spent many hours discussing what to do. Essentially they only had two alternatives, the riskier of which was to try and leave Germany by crossing the border into one of the neighbouring countries. Holland was the obvious choice being the closest but that border was now fully militarised and virtually sealed. The other alternative was to sit tight and hope the SS would not track them down before the war ended. Like most Jews who were still trapped in Germany in those days they opted to sit tight and hope for the best but as time passed their anxiety grew. The months slipped by and Ruth deliberately avoided anything other than the most casual of relationships. She had many admirers but none were able to get close to her and most stopped bothering her after a while, assuming she had a steady boyfriend. Eventually even the most persistent admirer gave up and in one acrimonious exchange she was accused of being a lesbian. It was hard for her to maintain her distance without running the risk of raising the suspicion that she had something other than a secret boyfriend to hide. Anxiety about Frau Schneider's maiden name grew and they discussed visiting the towns in which her birth and marriage were registered and somehow destroying them. But the idea was impractical and unlikely to be successful. She had been born in Bavaria and married in Hamburg and all the travelling and enquiring would in itself have aroused suspicion. They decided it was better to let sleeping dogs lie rather than to try and erase the records but every day there were incidents of anti-Semitism in Hannover and like everyone else they looked the other way.

Back in Britain in the barracks at the training airfield Duncan also drew suspicion that he had a secret girlfriend and for all he knew he might also have been suspected of being homosexual. Every Saturday night a group of trainees would head to a pub in the village called The Swan which had by no means the best beer in town but by some distance it did have the best looking barmaid. Vera was the owner's daughter and had it not been so, she would have undoubtedly been poached one of the other pubs in the area. Vera brought in the business with a smile and by flirting with the men, both officers and trainees but never letting anyone get close. It was only a question of time before every new recruit made a pass at her. The old hands watched with amusement, making bets at how and when he would get the brush-off. Regularly during the evening she would come from behind the bar to collect glasses and when she did every male head in the bar watched her. Dressed in a tight jumper and an even tighter skirt she would sashay amongst the tables confidently batting away the good natured banter which followed her. Only when she returned behind the bar did the conversations revert to discussions about the training, the war and always - girls. Duncan alone had never made a pass at Vera and this didn't go unnoticed. Then on one occasion when it was his round, Vera fluttered her eyelids and asked him directly. *'Do you have a steady girlfriend, Duncan?'* which was coded way of asking the real question. *'Why do you never try to chat me up?'* Under the influence of several pints and for the first time since he'd shared dinner with Rachael on the train to Edinburgh he dropped his guard. *'I suppose I do.'* He responded wistfully. As she looked down at the pint she was pulling she continued to probe. *'Tell me about her'* adding a - *'please'* - as she put the brimming pint on the counter in front of him. She spoke kindly and with no hint of her customary flirtation so he felt confident that any secrets shared with her would remain their secret. *'Not now.'* He said with a nod and a smile to acknowledge her sincerity. *'It's too noisy here - maybe somewhere quieter.'*

'Well, Duncan, I see you finally made a pass at Vera.' Said one of his group as Duncan carefully lowered the beers onto the table. Everyone looked at him with eyebrows raised as they awaited his response. He answered with a wry smile but said nothing. Eventually their pestering died down and the

conversation reverted to the usual topics, their flying course and the war. His group was approaching the end of the eight-week Initial Training and there was excitement at the prospect of starting into the next phase, the ten-week Elementary Flying Training School. Only one person in his group didn't pass out from Initial Training and Duncan was complimented on his performance by the CO. *'Good job Duncan, keep this up and you'll make a fine pilot.'*

The trainees were given two days leave before entering the next stage and all of his group chose to visit their homes. For Duncan that was out of the question so in the morning he went for a run around the airfield and then drifted into the village for lunch. The pub was quiet with only a few regulars at the bar, each on his customary stool and each with his own pint mug which was stored behind the bar. Combined with the usual smells of smoke and stale beer was the unmistakable whiff of strong cleaning fluid, however a fire was burning warmly in the wood-burning stove so after his initial reluctance, he ordered some soup and bread which Vera brought over to him.

'Hi Duncan, I guess Edinburgh was too far to go?' She queried.

'You're right but I'm enjoying the break anyway. My dorm is empty so for the first time since I got here I won't be kept awake by a chorus of loud snorers!'

She sat down in the chair opposite him and warmed her hands at the stove. *'So it's also too far to go to visit your - I suppose - girlfriend?*

'I suppose,' he replied with a brief smile followed by a long silence while he stared thoughtfully at the wood-burning stove. *'I wonder if she is OK, you see - she's German - a German*

Jew.' He glanced up at her with sad eyes and she silently stretched out her hand to touch him gently on the arm.

'It's my night off. If you like, we could go to the cinema tonight - they're showing The Rains Came?' She said softly.

He looked across at her and realised what he had suspected since the 'I suppose' moment. This was her true self and the flirting barmaid was only an act, perhaps an act of self-defence? *'I'd like that.'* He said, lifted by the sincerity of her invitation. *'Shall I see you here or would your prefer it if I met you at the cinema?*

'Perhaps we should meet at the cinema. If we're seen leaving here together the rumours will start flying. The show starts at six-thirty. See you then.' And with that she rose from her seat and gracefully as ever she returned behind the bar. He finished his lunch and walked slowly back to the camp where he lay down on his bunk with his hands behind his head and for a long time stared at the ceiling. Eventually he dropped off to sleep and as usual he was thinking about Ruth but in the background a new thought was emerging, was there something happening between him and Vera?

As they'd agreed he met Vera at the entrance to the cinema where he purchased two tickets in the stalls. In the near darkness they were reasonably assured of their anonymity, not that he worried overly about that. If they were seen - so what? They were simply friends who went to the cinema together but he knew that if word got out in the camp it would cause quite a stir. He led her to a row near the middle of the stalls, pointedly walking past the two of rows at the rear which like most cinemas had double seats. They sat through the show in silence, only broken when he asked her if she would like an ice cream in the interval. She declined but took advantage of the break in the silence to enquire. *'Are you enjoying the show?'*

'It is good but maybe a little on the sad side for me. Some people like a good weepy movie, but not me - at least not at present - I'm weepy enough at the moment.' He said, looking across at her. She understood the coded signal that he would be happy to talk about Ruth.

'We can talk later - after the show - when you walk me home?' She said with a quick squeeze of his arm while leaning a little closer towards him.

When the show ended and the strains of the National Anthem had died away, he led her from the cinema and out into the night. It was cold but dry and the forecast was for a light overnight frost. Not sure what to do with his hands he thrust them deep into his overcoat pockets. She walked beside him for a while before he felt her arm slip inside his. They looked for all the world like a couple. As they walked back to the pub he opened up his heart to her, much as he had done to Rachael on the train to Edinburgh the day after he returned from Europe. He felt a lot more comfortable talking about matters of the heart with a woman than with a man. Women were better listeners and Vera barely said a word until they reached the pub door where he awkwardly pecked her on the cheek and said. *'Thank you for a lovely evening and thank you for listening to me. You must think I'm crazy to have fallen hopelessly in love with a girl I spent so little time with.'*

She smiled at him and then turned to leave, stopping half-way to say. *'To be so much in love must be a very special feeling and although it obviously hurts, you're fortunate to have experienced it. I'm sure most people go through their entire life without ever having such strong emotions.'* She paused and looking straight into his eyes she said. *'It must be really hard for you Duncan, I wish I could help you, but thank you for taking me to the cinema. We should do it again perhaps?'*

As the door of the pub swung closed behind her he felt a pang of guilt. Was he being fair? He had talked selfishly of his love for a beautiful German girl in the presence of an equally beautiful English girl. How did she feel? He suddenly realised how self-centred he had been. He hadn't asked her a single question about her life, loves and ambitions. For all he knew, she was also pining for someone, perhaps a soldier who was posted abroad? On an impulse he followed her into the bar where the sound of the door behind her caught her attention. She turned to see him standing in front of her. *'Please can we go out again soon?'* He said. *'And I promise I won't talk about myself and my problems all the time.'*

She grinned broadly and said. *'That would be lovely.'*

On the long walk back to the camp he had plenty of time to reflect on the evening. The last thing he wanted to do was to lead her on. He viewed their relationship as purely friendship but how did she view it? By the time he was climbing into his bunk he had made up his mind, he would make his position quite clear the next time they went out together.

The trainees returned from their leave and faced new challenges in their training and after a tedious eight weeks of theory and classroom work, the next ten weeks would finally get them into the air. At last they would learn to fly. Their first outing in the sky was as a passenger in a de Havilland Tiger Moth, the biplane in which he would hopefully gain his Wings.

From the moment he climbed into the forward cockpit he was hooked, his first flight lasted only thirty minutes but it changed his life for ever. He was consumed with a passion for flying and for the first time in months he had something else other than Ruth to concentrate on. Not that his love for her was in any way diminished or was to any extent replaced by his love of flying. Quite the opposite. In his mind, learning to fly seemed to shorten the distance between them. When he was in the air he was theoretically only a few hours away from Hannover. He made startling progress and rapidly emerged as the leading trainee in his group and all the time he could never get enough time in the air. His leisure time was spent working alongside the ground crew helping to keep the planes airworthy and their magnificent Merlin engines running perfectly and it was some weeks before he returned to the pub where Vera worked. His group was well known to the locals who noticed the new swagger about them since they had started 'proper' flying training but it proved to be no help in the perpetual quest to date Vera.

'It must be your round, Duncan. I can't remember when you last stood us a drink - you're such a swot!' Said one of the trainees, in a voice loud enough for most of the other occupants of the pub to hear. Vera looked up and smiled broadly as he approached the bar *'Well stranger, nice to see you again. You wouldn't have been avoiding me, would you?'* She said in her best flirting voice which drew no special attention from his pals - it was what she would have said to any of them. However, to him it had a special meaning, he knew it and she knew it.

'*Been working.*' He replied and then leaning forward he quietly added. '*When is your next night off? We could go to the cinema again...*'

She smiled and nodded but said nothing as she handed across the last of the five pints he'd ordered. He returned to the table with the tray of drinks worrying that he had hurt her by not being in touch since their evening out together.

'*What's the matter Duncan, you look miles away? It can only mean one thing - you've fallen under Vera's spell at last.*' Said the most vocal of the trainees to a chorus of laughter from the table. Duncan now felt distinctly uncomfortable. It was inevitable that at some point his visit to the cinema would become common knowledge but he couldn't really talk about it without speaking to Vera first. He could just imagine the howls of derision if he played the '*We're just good friends*' line, so rather unconvincingly he smiled weakly and said '*I suppose so.*' immediately changing the subject to talking about flying. However, his discomfort did not go unnoticed by Vera who was also wrestling with her own feelings. Although she was now attracted to Duncan she held her feelings carefully in check. She had no desire to allow herself to fall in love but at the same time she wanted to continue their friendship, mostly for herself but there was something very vulnerable about Duncan and she felt she could help.

Later, as he passed the bar on a visit to the Gents, Duncan had a quick word with Vera which went unnoticed by his friends who were busily arguing about the relative merits of the Spitfire versus the Hurricane. '*Can I call you on the telephone sometime - I need to arrange our next outing to the cinema?*' He said surreptitiously.

'Call me on the pub's number at nine o'clock tomorrow night. I take a break then and I'll stand by the phone.' She whispered back to him, flashing one of her trademark smiles.

He felt a tingle of excitement which was immediately replaced by an upwelling of guilt. In the Gents he quickly got out Ruth's picture and briefly touched it to his lips. 'I'm sure you understand.' He said, without really understanding himself. The following day he called her as arranged. She must have been standing next to the phone because it had barely started to ring when she answered. 'Hi Duncan, Vera here.'

'Vera, although I said I'd like to go to the cinema again I'd really much prefer to have dinner with you on your night off - so we could talk. I could buy you a meal in the hotel at the other end of town - The Spread Eagle?' his voice was awkward and hesitant, he wanted to explain that he felt uncomfortable with their clandestine relationship on a number of accounts but he needed to do that face-to-face. The last thing he wanted was to hurt her and that would be far too easy over the phone. He knew that communication depended not just on the spoken word. In a conversation a lot more than dialogue mattered and he needed to gauge her reaction to his words in real-time in order to avoid a misunderstanding, so he kept the telephone call as brief as possible, simply arranging the time of their assignation.

Snow fell that day and it was on a still evening that Duncan crunched his way to the hotel at the end of the village. Deterred by the snow his group of trainee pals had opted for an all night poker session rather than having the usual few drinks in the pub. Duncan wasn't a poker player so his decision to head into the village didn't attract any unwanted attention. He arrived a few minutes early and was sitting at the table when Vera arrived at the door of the restaurant. He leapt to his feet, greeted her with a peck on the cheek and led her to their table where he helped her off with her coat and hung it over the back of her chair. The restaurant was less than half full so he'd been able to choose a table which was both discreet and still close enough to the log fire to feel its glowing warmth and hear its soft crackling. They ordered drinks as they looked at the dinner menu. *'Not much on offer,'* He said, *'I guess it will be like this until the war is over.'* When their drinks came they drank a toast to friends and family. *'Looks like we might have snow for Christmas,'* she said *'Ah, Christmas,'* he replied *'I suppose that's the busiest time of the year for you. Will you have any time off during Christmas and New Year? I was wondering if you'd like to go to our New Year's Eve Ball?'* Vera looked surprised, even startled at the invitation while he wondered where that had come from - it was way off script. He wanted to have a quiet evening together to talk over what their relationship meant and then, out of the blue, he'd invited her to the RAF New Year's Eve Ball. Before she could reply he hastily added, *'maybe I'm getting a bit ahead of myself?'*

'Perhaps you are.' She replied, *'it would definitely start tongues wagging if I showed up at the Ball with you! I presume none of your mates know we were at the cinema last week?'*

'That's right but I'm not trying to hide anything, I just wanted to make sure that we've discussed and agreed whatever we tell anyone, or even if we tell anyone.' He added, feeling awkward again.

'You're making this sound like a business meeting Duncan. I understand your position and I appreciate you're trying to do

the right thing but please don't worry. Let's just enjoy our meal and see where the conversation takes us. I'm sure that if we try too hard to understand each other we'll end up in a muddle.' There was a hint of exasperation in her tone which he countered with a fleeting touch of her hand across the table. *'You're right Vera.'* He said with a broad smile. *'How about you tell me a bit more about yourself - I realise that up to now I've done most of the talking.'*

Their food came and while they ate she spoke softly about herself. *'Most people have a stereotype image of a barmaid in their head and I probably fit that image. I can handle the typical banter I get from you boys in the RAF - give as good as I get, I'd say. I'm a good listener, a shoulder to cry on and a friendly welcome to any stranger who comes through the door of the pub. That's the job and I reckon I'm quite good at it.'* At this he nodded in agreement. *'You certainly are.'* He said as she continued. *'But I also have dreams, dreams that at times seem so far beyond the horizon that I sometimes wonder if they're worth hanging onto, dreams that have had to be put on hold because of the war. My parents assume that my goal in life is to meet a nice boy, get married, settle down and have a family. Not that there's anything wrong with that it's just that there are places I'd like to see and things I'd like to do before I do all that, because obviously, once I settle down - that's it isn't it?* At this she looked directly at him and raised her eyebrows as if inviting a comment. Understanding that the question was rhetorical his only response was another brief nod of the head. Between mouthfuls she continued to speak of her desire to go to university, to travel in Europe and America, to climb mountains, sail seas and live a full life. At some point she hoped to meet Mr Right but rather than settle down, she dreamt of continuing a life of adventure with him and then, when they had children, encouraging them to have dreams and cling to them, while still doing something creative and intellectually stimulating beyond running the home. She wound up her story by saying. '*Sorry about the rant but I'm probably not much different from a lot of barmaids and why shouldn't a woman have ambitions? And shouldn't there be more to life than - settling down.*'

As she finished he realised how conditioned he was by the stereotype image of a barmaid and how wrong it had been. The same probably went for policemen, doctors, priests, builders, teachers, lawyers, estate agents, prostitutes etc, he had a stereotype image for everyone. It amused him to recognise that almost without exception the opening line in a conversation with a stranger was '*What do you do?*' Which immediately led to a stereotype image popping into his head and conditioning his behaviour towards that person.

'*Stereotypes are dangerous.*' He mused and she nodded in agreement. '*It is too easy to misjudge a person simply because of the job that they do. I know I'm guilty of doing that - perhaps we all are? We need a reference point from which to open up a conversation and I suppose it's better to start with the question - What do you do? - rather than to ask whether you're a Catholic or a Protestant?*' He said, choosing a lighthearted way to make a serious point. '*So already you have made me realise something Vera - I shouldn't prejudge what a person is like because of the job that they do.*' Their conversation carried on in that vein over coffee and a final round of whisky until, glancing at her watch. '*My goodness, is it that time already?*

I'll need to be getting back home or my Dad will come looking for me!' She joked as he held her coat for her. He settled up and they left the hotel into a clear and frosty night. The stars glittered and twinkled in the blackout darkness as they walked arm in arm though the glistening snow back to the bar. *'Thank you for a lovely evening and thank you for listening to me,'* She said, squeezing his arm more tightly. *'And I'd love to come with you to the New Year's Eve Ball - if the offer is still open?'*

'Of course!' He replied as she gave him a goodnight kiss on his cheek and disappeared into the near-empty pub. For a while he just stood there looking at the door, casting his mind back over the evening they'd had together and wondering if he was doing the right thing. Almost without thinking he slipped his right hand beneath his RAF greatcoat and touched his breast pocket where Ruth's picture was kept. He felt a familiar pang of guilt as he thought about the danger she was in. Anti-Semitism was spreading like a flu epidemic which wasn't solely confined to Germany and even in England Oswald Mosley was propagating hatred of the Jews. If only he had some way of communicating with Ruth. His fervent hope was that Ruth and her mother would be able to keep the fact that they were Jews a secret. Extensive rationing in Germany was just being introduced around the time he was returning to England and special ordinances imposed a strict curfew on Jewish individuals, prohibiting them from entering designated areas in many German cities. Then when food rationing was introduced, Jews received reduced rations and further decrees limited the time periods in which Jews could purchase food and other supplies. Furthermore, access to certain stores was restricted with the result that Jewish households often faced

shortages of the most basic essentials and there were rumours of deportations and concentration camps. The uncertainty coupled with his feeling of utter helplessness was eating him up.

Duncan spent Christmas with his parents in Edinburgh where he also met up with some of his old friends from University. Not many were around, as like him most had joined the armed forces and moved away. It was a quiet, relaxed time and although he felt close to his parents and they quizzed him on his social life he chose not to mention either Ruth or Vera. He was glad to get back to the camp the day after Boxing Day. Meanwhile the phoney war continued. Following the German invasion of Poland in September, there had been only one Allied military action in the Saar Offensive where, in the week following their declaration of war, eleven French divisions advanced along a twenty mile line near Saarbrucken. Despite weak German opposition the French attack was half-hearted and it did not result in the diversion of any German troops. After taking the heavily mined Warndt Forest the assault stalled and it appeared as if France with support from the British Expeditionary Force had decided to fight a defensive war from behind the Maginot Line. In the RAF camp there was more talk about when the war would start than when it would end.

Preparations for the RAF New Year's Eve Ball were completed in an atmosphere that was more subdued than usual due to the blackout and noise restrictions but with rationing of bacon, butter and sugar just around the corner it felt like it might be the last proper celebration for a while, so no expense had been spared and the planned buffet would be something to remember in the dark days which almost certainly lay ahead. In a clandestine meeting Duncan and Vera agreed to make public their plan to attend the Ball together and although they decided to continue their relationship on a 'just good friends' basis, they knew that to announce it as such would attract universal disbelief. So they decided to tell people nothing other than that they'd agreed to go to the Ball together.

At their table in the RAF mess hall the following lunchtime, Duncan casually dropped the bomb. *'By the way, Vera is coming to the Ball with me.'*

The reaction was a few seconds of stunned silence followed by a clamour of comment which took some time to die down. Throughout it all Duncan tried to maintain a dignified silence but he couldn't help grinning broadly at the way his news had been greeted. Then his best mate summed up on behalf of the group. *'My, aren't you the wily one! Anyway well done - round one to you, but if you think for one minute we'll give up on trying to lure her away from you, you're very much mistaken!'* Duncan limited his response to a slightly embarrassed grin and was very glad that he and Vera had decided not to pursue the *'We're just good friends'* line.

It was a strange time in Britain. Apart from Germany's invasion of Poland the war had not really started. Taking the maximum advantage of the hiatus in the war Britain had dramatically ramped up the manufacture of arms and planes, ships, tanks and guns were rolling off the production lines in ever increasing volumes. Reports leaking from Poland made awful reading with alarming stories of dreadful persecution of the huge Polish Jewish population. Duncan worried constantly about Ruth and her mother but buried his concern in his training. It was rumoured that the German Luftwaffe was getting ready for a massive assault sometime early in 1940 and Britain desperately needed to be ready. It only took a couple of weeks to make an aeroplane but many months to train a pilot. This showed through on Duncan's course when instructors went out of their way to help students who for one reason or another were struggling. This didn't apply to Duncan who had moved head and shoulders above his fellow trainees and was already attracting attention from his superiors. Flying had become his passion and as he accumulated hours in the training aircraft, all he could think about was getting into a Spitfire or a Hurricane and taking on the German fighters. There was constant debate in the mess as to which was the better fighter. Most chose the Spitfire simply because it was more modern and faster but all concluded they would be more than happy with either. During those days all they could think of was fighters and none of them wanted to be a bomber pilot but they knew that at least half of them would end up in bombers. The glamour was in the fighters and that's where their preferences lay but for now all that mattered was getting their wings. Only when they had completed their training and were assigned to an active squadron would they know what they would be flying.

Preparations for the New Year's Eve Ball ramped up as the big day approached and everyone on the camp lent a hand. No expense was spared. The mess hall was festooned with decorations and a net filled with balloons was strung to the ceiling. The stage at the end of the hall was set up as a bandstand and a full sound system was rented for the occasion. The dance floor took up the half of the hall in front of the bandstand and the area behind that was set out with tables, each with six places . At the opposite end of hall was the buffet and a bar which sold beer, wine and soft drinks but no spirits. A bus had been arranged to bring the ladies from the village at 7pm and take them back again at 1am. The men were lectured on the need for good behaviour and a stern warning was issued that no young ladies were allowed in any of the dormitory huts. Sanctions for offenders ranged from a period confined to barracks to loss of leave and a lengthy spell on latrine duty. Despite this, most of the trainees privately agreed that if the opportunity arose they'd be prepared to take the risk. When the preparations in the hall were complete it was time for the men to get themselves ready for the party. Singing rang out from the communal showers, chins were carefully shaved, moustaches were trimmed and lots of time was spent combing hair. Shirts and uniforms were ironed, and buttons, belt buckles and shoes were polished until they gleamed. Only for the passing out parade would so much care be taken to look their best.

Eventually the coach from the village arrived and the band struck up a Glen Miller number as the guests filed into the mess hall. Coats were taken, drinks were bought, tables started filling up and before long the dance floor was full. Duncan led Vera to the dance floor where in the privacy of the crowded dance floor he whispered in her ear. *'Vera, you look absolutely stunning tonight - I really hope you have a good time.'* Realising how corny this sounded he quickly added. *'I'm not much of a dancer, my mother taught me a few years ago while I was still living at home and to be honest I've not had much practice since but I can see you've trod the boards before!'* She smiled broadly at him and then holding him more tightly she spun him around in a turn. *'There you are - not so bad after all! I think we'll be fine.'* When the dance set finished he sat her at a table and as he went up to the bar for some drinks he joked. *'Don't go away and please don't talk to any strange men.'* As he stood in the drinks queue he glanced back at her, she flashed a smile at him and raised her hand in a tiny wave, he couldn't remember the last time he'd felt this happy.

As the evening progressed several of his group asked Vera for a dance but as far as he could see, none of them 'tried it on' with her. There was plenty of good-natured banter around their table and the mood was universally happy. The evening wore on and when the time came the band led everyone in the final countdown to midnight when the balloons were released in a brightly coloured shower. They held each other in the midst of the crowded dance floor. *'Happy New Year Vera.'* He said *'this has been a wonderful evening.'*

'It was lovely,' She replied and they kissed, not a peck this time but a long, passionate kiss and he felt her body pressed against him, all the way down to his knees. Their embrace took them both by surprise and as they looked into each other's eyes their happiness was underpinned by uncertainty. Neither of them knew what was happening. For the first time since he'd met Vera, Ruth was not there in the background, either for him or for her. Before that kiss everything between them had taken place in her presence. She lived in that private room in his head, a room where the door was usually left open but on this occasion the door was shut. It wasn't that he'd deliberately closed Ruth out of his mind, it had just happened and for the first time as Vera looked into his eyes, she couldn't see Ruth. They held each other for a long time and kissed again, only to be interrupted. *'Come on Duncan, give someone else a chance!'* Said one of his friends, whisking her off for a dance. It broke

the spell and for the next few minutes there was mayhem in the hall as the balloons were burst, the band played a boisterous Glen Miller number and everyone kissed everyone else wishing them Happy New Year. Although the atmosphere in the hall was upbeat and happy in the background lurked dark fears about the year which lay ahead. During the so-called 'phoney war', apart from the blackout, some noise restrictions and the impending rationing of some food basics, there had been little or no impact on everyday life in Britain. But as the country drew breath and readied itself for the conflict, Germany had established a brutal occupation of Poland and it was clear Hitler would not stop there. There was constant speculation on when and where Germany would strike next. In the air that night was the thought that this might be the last New Year's Eve party for a long time.

At 1am sharp the bus arrived at the RAF mess hall to take the girls back to the village. Goodbyes were said with hugs, kisses and whispered promises as the band played them out with 'We'll meet again.' Duncan and Vera gently embraced in the chilly darkness outside the hall. Each felt somehow restrained after the passion of their midnight kiss.

'Just good friends?' she whispered softly in his ear.

Back in the Swan pub in the village the following day Vera's life returned to the usual round of pulling pints, tidying up and chatting to the locals.

'How was the Ball?' Her father had asked her on New Year's Day. *'It was wonderful, Dad, really great.'* She'd replied.

'And how about that man of yours - Duncan isn't it?' He'd asked.

'Like I said Dad, it was a wonderful evening.' She'd said with a smile which her father correctly interpreted - the subject was closed. It was too early to start talking about relationships but there was now a tiny flame in her heart which had been kindled by a single passionate kiss on New Year's Eve.

Meanwhile, in Hannover, Ruth and her mother were also wondering what 1940 would bring. Their New Year's Eve celebrations were muted and confined to a special dinner for the two of them. Ruth had declined an invitation to attend her office New Year's Eve party on the grounds that she had to look after her mother. Far from being disappointed she was happy to have a good excuse, her previous experiences of the office New Year's Eve party had not been good. She was one of only a few young ladies working in the office, all of which had to endure the advances of tipsy managers, balancing their desire to slap the occasional face with the knowledge that to do so would almost guarantee dismissal. Ruth also had another problem. Recently her mother had become noticeably forgetful, to the point where Ruth worried that it might be an early sign of dementia. They prepared a special meal together and then sat across the small dining room table and chatted the evening away over a bottle of wine. Eventually her mother asked. *'Do you ever think about Duncan?'*

Loathe to tell her the truth she replied wistfully. *'From time to time I wonder where life will take him - but I will probably never know. This war has changed many lives already and before it ends for sure it will change a lot more.'* She looked at her mother who had seen the sadness in her daughter's eyes.

'I wish you didn't have to stay in with me Ruth. It doesn't seem fair, a beautiful young woman like you should be out having fun dancing the night away, making the most of life, meeting your future husband.' Said her mother with great tenderness.

Smiling bravely Ruth replied. *'I'd rather be with you Mutter, now tell me the best New Year's Eve celebration you ever had.'*

Soon her mother was lost in happy memories of the days before she'd married Ruth's father and as the candles on the table flickered low they wished each other a happy New Year, tidied up the dishes, hugged and went to bed. But for Ruth sleep didn't come. All night she tossed and turned with her head swimming with worries about the future, everything seemed to be closing in on her but uppermost in her mind was the growing aggression towards the Jews. At the moment nobody appeared to suspect that she and her mother were Jewish but it seemed inevitable that sooner or later someone from the SS would go through the church records and discover the truth. Then would come the knock on the door at 3am and after that? Also, it had only been four months since she'd said goodbye to Duncan and instead of that memory fading, if anything it had grown stronger. Futile though it was, she hung onto the hopeless dream that one day soon he would reappear magically at their door and take her and her mother away to somewhere safe where they could live happily ever after. *'I wonder if he ever thinks of me?'* She pondered before eventually dropping off into a troubled sleep.

He was thinking of her, which was hardly surprising because he almost always thought about her as he drifted off to sleep.

He could see her smiling face and feel again the brush of her lips on his cheek and hear her whisper *'I love you'* in Hebrew into his ear and then, as usual he felt guilty about Vera. Had he crossed the line between being just good friends and having a proper relationship? Was his brief but incredibly intense relationship with Ruth more important than the developing friendship-cum-relationship he had with Vera? Was he being fair to Vera? Would he carry the spectre of his first love, Ruth, to the grave and would it spoil his chances of falling in love again? Was a relationship with Ruth a hopeless dream which he should ditch before it ruined the rest of his life? There were no easy answers so he took refuge in the need to concentrate on his training.

The pace of flight training stepped up noticeably in January and Duncan added to his studies with a course in engine maintenance. The magnificent Merlin engine in the Spitfire was as much a part of its success as the beautiful airframe for which it was better known. To truly understand his aeroplane, he needed to understand the engine and so while his days were filled with flying, his nights were filled with study. One or two of the other trainees shared the course with him but most concentrated only on their flying skills. During this time he developed a passion for the engine and he began to dream of life after the RAF when the war was over and opening an engineering workshop which maintained and tuned engines. Getting the most out of an engine both in terms of its reliability and its performance became a passion for him and he spent every spare hour working with the engine maintenance staff on the one-thousand-eight-hundred horse-power, twenty-seven litre V12 monster which powered the Spitfire. Unlike most of his colleagues, he did not see his long term future as a pilot, however glamorous it might seem. Despite the accelerated manufacture of fighters and bombers in readiness for the oncoming fight with the Luftwaffe, it was obvious that the training of new pilots was on the critical path so becoming a fighter pilot was his priority and nobody worked harder than Duncan. His group were scheduled to complete their training and be assigned to a fighting squadron by mid-May 1940 but that changed and a few days into the new year they were called together for an announcement.

Coming straight to the point the CO stood on the stage in the mess hall and said *'Gentlemen, the good news is that we've changed the training schedule and those of you who pass will now get your wings a month earlier than previously planned.'* He paused as a ripple of enthusiasm swept through the ranks. *'However, this does not mean we're not taking any shortcuts in your training - you will still have to do the same amount of work but do it in less time. From next Monday you will have to work longer days and six days a week instead of five.'* At this there was a collective groan from the trainees *'In my opinion the increased intensity of your training will make you better pilots so although this will mean less leisure time for you all, I'm sure you're as pleased as I am about this revision to the schedule and the opportunity to be operational as an RAF pilot by mid-April.'*

The meeting was dismissed without any opportunity to ask questions and the men headed back to their classroom in silence. There was no dissension, to a man they wanted to get into the air as soon as possible. Although some of his colleagues regretted losing much of their spare time, Duncan was in no doubt this was what he wanted. Over the previous weeks he'd become increasingly impatient with the course which seemed to him to be overly pedantic and cautious. The phoney war couldn't continue indefinitely and he wanted to be ready to fight when the conflict began.

Towards the end of January, after a hard morning in the classroom he was having a coffee when out of the blue one of his pals asked *'How are things between you and Vera?'* For some time Duncan had wanted to have someone in whom he could confide, even just someone who would listen but he didn't want advice. However, he knew it would help if he tried to articulate his dilemma to someone who wouldn't judge him. It wasn't that he felt defensive, but how could anyone who wasn't in precisely the same shoes as him offer any advice of value? He needed a sounding board, someone he could trust to keep his confidences between the two of them.

'It's complicated.' Duncan responded.

'I'd figured that out!' Said his pal with a smile. *'I'm happy to listen if you're happy to tell me.'*

Over the next half hour Duncan bared his soul and when he'd finished he said. *'Thanks for listening. I needed a shoulder to cry on. You don't have to say anything if you don't want to - I'm not asking for advice but just explaining the situation I'm in has helped clarify it in my own mind. I'm no nearer knowing what to do other than just take one day at a time in the hope that something will pop up and suddenly it'll all become clear....'*

'All I would say,' came the reply *'is that Vera won't wait for you for ever. I doubt she likes playing second fiddle to someone who in truth, you barely know - even though you fell*

head-over-heels in love with her. As someone who has yet to fall in love for the first time, I'm actually jealous of your problem. You've already fallen in love once and if you'd only admit it, you're probably in the process of falling in love for a second time. In your position I've no idea what I'd do - probably take it one day at a time as you are but beware, the stakes are high for you. You must surely realise that the chances of ever seeing Ruth again are next to zero and while you're taking things day-by-day Vera might announce one day that she's met someone else. She may want you to make your mind up but she won't necessarily push you on it because she wouldn't want to put you under pressure - pressure she might regret later. Your one-day-at-a-time approach might leave you with neither.'

Duncan sighed deeply and then said. *'So you think I'm falling in love with Vera?'*

His friend took a deep breath before replying. *'Bearing in mind I have absolutely no experience in these matters, I'd say that had it not been for your memories of Ruth you'd not only have fallen in love with Vera by now but you'd also probably have proposed to her. She's a wonderful girl and for reasons none of us can understand she seems to be nuts about you.'*

'No matter what I do I feel as if I'd be betraying one or the other.' Duncan said sadly before continuing. *'I'll say it before you do - a bird in the hand is worth two in the bush. Come on, we need to be going or we'll be late for our next lesson.'*

That night before dropping off to sleep Duncan knew he had to decide about Vera before the weekend when he'd arranged another evening meal with her. The advice he'd received had definitely focused his mind. There was no doubt that even before the midnight kiss he'd felt himself resisting the forces which were in play between him and Vera. That resistance would almost inevitably be interpreted by Vera as an unwillingness to commit to a deeper relationship as long as there was even a glimmer of hope that he might see Ruth again. Finally he had to accept one important thing, if he'd never met Ruth he probably would have already fallen in love with Vera by now. Feeling he was closing in on an 'answer' which was still agonisingly just beyond his reach he finally drifted off into an uneasy sleep.

Over the next few days Duncan went round and round his situation. There were times when he even wondered if his encounter with Ruth had really happened. Maybe it was all just a dream? After hours or wrestling with his conscience he decided that he'd try not to go into the 'Ruth room' in his head until after his evening out with Vera and just see how things developed. S, when Saturday came around, for the very first time, he left Ruth's photograph in his bedside locker. As he pushed the drawer closed he felt the familiar stab of guilt, it was as if he'd begun the process of abandoning her.

Less than three hundred and fifty miles away as the crow flies Ruth and her mother were keeping a low profile. The ever-present fear of being exposed as Jewish wrapped them up in a cold cloak of perpetual anxiety. Each knock on the door caused their pulses to race and there was always palpable relief when it proved to be entirely innocent. Every sideways look from a passerby was a possible indication that they were suspected of being Jews. The only place they could properly relax was in the apartment but even there the thought that at any minute the

Gestapo might knock on the door kept them on edge. Ruth's life consisted only of work, shopping and looking after her mother who for some months now had never left the apartment on her own. If the weather was nice at the weekends they occasionally would take a walk by the river, always being careful to avoid contact. From time to time they encountered other residents of their apartment block in the stairwell but apart from exchanging the usual pleasantries they never engaged in conversation. How she wished they had left Germany along with almost three hundred thousand other Jews before the Nuremberg Race Laws were passed in 1935. Since then life as a Jew had been getting harder by the day so she knew their best and maybe their only hope was for their secret to remain hidden. Despite her failing memory Ruth's mother worried about her daughter, thinking that a beautiful girl like her should have lots of friends and lead an active social life. Even though there was a war on life in Hannover continued more or less as normal for most Germans, other than the Jews. *'Wouldn't you like to go out in the evenings some time - to the ballet or the cinema? You don't have to stay in with me every night.'* Ruth's mother pleaded.

'It's best we keep ourselves to ourselves as much as possible Mutter. Let's hope the war ends soon and maybe then we can leave Germany and go to America. They don't persecute Jews in America.' Ruth replied, effectively closing down the conversation. That night she dreamt that Duncan was trying to find her but although she could sense he was nearby, despite desperately reaching out to find him he remained out of sight. It was a dark, troublesome dream that she found difficult to dismiss and fruitless though it was she kept looking for some

deeper meaning in it. Duncan was the only light in her life, everything else had become fear and darkness and she clung to her memories of that magical night when he'd told her he'd fallen in love with her. How she wished that she had a photograph of him. Memories fade in time, how long would it be before she forgot what he looked like? Recently, one of her work colleagues had teased her that she must have a secret lover because she didn't participate in any of the festivities over the Christmas and New Year. Ruth had used her mother as an excuse, explaining that she now required almost constant care and could no longer be left on her own, especially in the evenings. She hoped that when this information was gradually disseminated around the office it might deter the continuing stream of advances she received from male members of staff who had not been conscripted into the armed forces. These were mostly single men over the age of forty-five or the fortunate ones who had secured exemptions, some for physical reasons and some because they knew the right people in high places. Since war was declared, there were few if any men in the office that she would even consider dating so it wasn't difficult for her to turn down the occasional invitation to dinner, the theatre or sometimes the ballet. Thankfully, her refusals didn't appear to raise any awkward questions and the story about her mother engendered sympathy rather than suspicion.

It had been a while since Duncan had been out with Vera and he was looking forward to seeing her again but he was also nervous about how it would go. The symbolism of leaving Ruth's picture in his bedside cabinet really mattered. After his heart-to-heart with his trainee pal he'd made up his mind to see Vera without carrying the picture of Ruth in his breast pocket and it was the first time he'd gone anywhere without her. Perhaps this would make it easier to see Vera more clearly and help him decide what to do? Also, not having Ruth's picture with him would perhaps allow Vera to see him more clearly? In some ways it would be like a first date. The rain was coming down in sheets when he got to the hotel so rather than hanging around outside he sat down in one of the comfortable chairs by the fire in the foyer and watched the door for Vera's arrival. It was an anxious wait as he turned over in his head how best to open up a discussion about their future together. He'd reached no conclusion on this when she walked through the door, shaking her umbrella and beginning to take off her wet overcoat. Duncan leapt to his feet and helped her off with her coat, hanging it alongside his on the stand by the door.

'Thank you Duncan. What an awful night it is out there.' She said as he steered her over towards the seats by the fire.

'Why don't we sit here by the fire and dry out a bit before we go in for dinner?' Duncan replied already feeling his heart quickening at the prospect of the evening ahead.

For a minute or two they both leant towards the fire, warming their hands and enjoying the comforting glow of the burning coals. They had the foyer to themselves and without saying so, both were enjoying the privacy. For a while their conversation was the verbal equivalent of the pavement dance that approaching walkers frequently do when each is trying to avoid bumping into the other but end up hopping from side to side in concert. Both knew that what they really wanted to discuss was their future together but neither knew how to embark on it and neither wanted to go first. It was a deeply emotional subject and each knew that matters of the heart weren't easy to discuss rationally. Finally Duncan said. *'Let's have a drink here by the fire and then go through to the dining room when we've finished. We can order our food here - I'll go and get the menu.'*

As he walked off to the dining room to find a menu Vera ran her fingers through her hair and whispered to herself. *'After all the rain I must look a mess but one way or another I don't want to leave here tonight without settling things between us.'*

They made their choices and placed the order with the waiter who told them he'd come and fetch them when their starter was ready to be served. *'Thank you,'* They both said in concert and then their eyes met with a 'moment of truth' look. There was a tiny pause before both of them started to speak at the same time. *'You go first '* They both said and then a smile warmer than the fire bridged the awkwardness and the mood became relaxed and reflective as they sipped their gin and tonics.

'Ok then, I'll go first,' said Duncan with a broad grin. *'You look absolutely beautiful Vera - as always - but it's not just your film star looks that I find attractive...'*

'Now you're being silly, Duncan,' She scolded.

'No really Vera, you are beautiful, you've got a sparkling personality, you're a great conversationalist, you're an incredible listener and you have the warmest of hearts. Honestly, there isn't anyone in the world I'd rather be with at this moment than you.' The words slipped spontaneously, almost accidentally from his mouth and in the timeless moment it took for them to float in slow motion across the space between them, he realised the significance of what he'd said. It

was a watershed moment in his life. His heart had spoken, not just to Vera but to himself and for the very first time he realised how much she meant to him.

For a while Vera said nothing, as if giving him time to either correct or qualify what he'd just said. When he remained silent, she reached her hand across the small gap between them and touched his knee. '*Me too.*' Was all she could manage before the waiter broke the spell to tell them their table was ready. He took her hand and squeezed it tightly as they rose from their seats and walked through to the restaurant. She looked up at him and drew closer as they exchanged smiles which for the first time were completely uninhibited and honest. Those smiles heralded the beginning of a wonderful new relationship and with them came a huge feeling of relief for Duncan who now knew the path he had to follow.

Later, while walking back to the camp in the darkness he was unable to recall much about the meal or their conversation that night, all he could remember was their parting kiss and the thrill of falling in love again. Once again he felt the tingling excitement of crossing an emotional frontier and arriving into a state of pure bliss. Nothing on earth could dampen his spirits. The weather front had cleared through and after many dull days of rain and wind it was now cold and still. Above him the sky was lit by a million stars, tiny pinpricks of brilliant light which had travelled through space for countless millennia to shine on him that night. As he dropped off to sleep he thought about the room where his memories of Ruth were kept but for the first night since their brief encounter in Hannover he chose not to go in.

Back in her room above the pub Vera snuggled down into her bed, wishing Duncan was beside her but feeling his presence all around her. Although she'd never felt like this before she knew what the feeling was - she was falling in love with Duncan and as she tumbled though space she neither knew nor cared where she would land but wherever that place was, it would be in a different world from the one she had just left. It had all started with the New Year's Eve kiss but it was their second kiss which had tipped her over the edge. She'd kissed lots of boys before but not like this. Should she have told him how she felt, or did he already know? Were words really necessary or were they even adequate? Surely what she was feeling couldn't ever be summed up in three simple words? And did he feel the same? She smiled to herself as she drifted off to sleep. *'We're more than just good friends now - we're lovers.'* She murmured to herself contentedly.

As Winter gradually gave way to Spring the mood across Europe continued to darken and tensions rose. The phoney war gave Britain the opportunity to re-arm but to what degree that was being offset by the massive German build up was impossible to determine. Finally in April the dam burst and Germany simultaneously launched attacks on both Denmark and Norway. Denmark succumbed in six hours however, aided by the British the Norwegians put up a stubborn resistance but the campaign was beset with problems and towards the end of the month the trainees heard the news that the British were pulling out of Norway. The Chamberlain-led government in the UK inspired little confidence and it became clear that sooner rather than later he would have to go. The talk in the mess was all about who would take over as Prime Minister and among the men Winston Churchill was by far the most popular choice. Meanwhile alongside the French army the British Expeditionary Force was digging in along the French/Belgian border in the expectation that Germany would launch a blitzkrieg assault within weeks.

The trainees all received their wings in a passing out parade attended by their families and friends. Duncan's parents travelled down from Edinburgh and proudly watched their son as he formally became a pilot in the Royal Air Force. Vera also attended the ceremony and at the reception which followed the parade Duncan awkwardly introduced her to his parents. For some reason he'd not mentioned her in the weekly letter he'd been writing home, so this came as a surprise.

'Mum, Dad, this is Vera.' He said, taking her hand in a clear signal that they were in a relationship.

'Very pleased to meet you.' Replied his mother, wondering why Duncan had never talked about her in his letters but tactfully deciding to leave that question until they had time alone with him.

'You must be very proud of Duncan.' said Vera to his parents before turning to look up at him and continuing. *'I certainly am - he looks so handsome in his uniform, don't you think?'* She said, squeezing his hand tightly.

They made small talk over their tea and cakes before Vera excused herself to 'powder her nose' and disappeared off to the Ladies.

'It's obvious you're more than just good friends Duncan. She's a beautiful girl and you make a lovely couple but why didn't you ever tell us in your letters?' Said Duncan's mother, her sad smile and the tone of her voice making it clear to him

that she was hurt. Before Duncan could respond and seeing his discomfort his father tried to come to his rescue but succeeded only in adding to the awkwardness of the situation. *'I'd try to hang onto that one Duncan, she seems to be really nice and just the sort of girl we'd love to have in the family.'* He said lightheartedly but with obvious enthusiasm.

His comment received a glare from his wife and a smile from Duncan. *'She is a marvellous girl Dad, we are more than just good friends and Mum I'm sorry I didn't let you know beforehand, it was thoughtless of me, I know it sounds lame but I just never got around to it. Anyway, if it's ok with you, I'd like Vera to join us at the hotel for dinner this evening?'*

'Of course Duncan, we'd very much like to get to know her better.' She said with a smile which signalled to Duncan that he was being forgiven. Vera returned and to her satisfaction the conversation began to flow a little more freely, as if the previous awkwardness had been cleared away by a light breeze. Her visit to the loo had been well-timed she thought, smiling inwardly. After they'd seen his parents to the taxi Vera gave him a quick kiss and said teasingly. *'You're parents are lovely but it seemed as if I was a complete shock to them. Have you been keeping me a secret, Duncan?'*

Slightly flustered he replied. *'It wasn't deliberate, it just sort of happened. I know it was selfish but I wanted to have you all to myself for a while. Somehow it made our relationship more special.'*

'Nice answer,' She replied with a raised eyebrow and giving him another kiss.

He continued. *'Vera, can you join us for dinner at the hotel tonight? My parents would like to get to know you better and I'd like them to see that we're…'*

'…more than just good friends?' She queried.

'Yes, that's exactly what I was going to say - more than just good friends.' He replied hugging her tightly. The mess hall was full of people but for a few moments they were lovers, all alone in their own private world.

'And maybe it's time you met my parents?' She said, flashing another of her special smiles.

The dinner at the hotel that evening went much better than Duncan expected. He had foreseen a rather formal, stilted atmosphere but right from the start Vera put Duncan's parents at their ease with her natural charm but also with her years of experience chatting to the locals and the airmen across the bar. She knew when to talk and when to listen, she was good company and an expert at heading off awkward silences with a swift change of subject or a brief anecdote. Duncan watched in awe as his parents fell under her spell - just as he had done. When they'd finished Duncan's mother said. *'This has been a beautiful evening and it has been lovely to meet you. We have to catch the early train tomorrow and it's a long journey back up to Edinburgh but you really must come and visit us soon Vera. We would love to show some Scottish hospitality and give you a tour of the city.'*

Vera glanced across at Duncan before replying. *'I've never been to Scotland, in fact I've never been north of Manchester but thank you for your invitation - I would love to come up to see you again and it has been lovely to meet you.'*

'*Goodnight Mum, goodnight Dad,*' said Duncan happily, '*have a safe trip home and I promise to write to you once a week from now on.*'

Duncan put his arm around Vera's shoulder as they watched his parents leave the dining room and head upstairs to their room. Then he leant across and whispered in her ear. '*I wish we had a room here for the night.*'

'*Me too,*' She said, '*but it wouldn't be right - not here and not now but maybe sometime soon.*'

A late frost glistened on the pavement as they walked back across the village to the pub. They said little but their love deepened in the quiet. He kissed her goodnight at the door and said. '*Thank you Vera for being marvellous with my parents, they loved you.*' Then adding, '*tomorrow I'll hear which squadron I've been posted to and as soon as I get the news I'll telephone you. I should have a couple of days Leave before the move and I want to spend them with you. Could we go away together - to the seaside perhaps - for a couple of nights? It might be a while before we can see each other again?*'

'*Yes let's do that.*' She replied. '*I'll do some thinking. I've got a friend who lives in Brighton and she's always saying I should visit her.*'

They kissed again and then she turned away and was gone. As heavy pub door closed noisily he realised that more than anything else in the world he wanted to marry Vera. It was a defining moment and although he'd previously been aware of the vague thought that one day they might get married, that thought had now crystallised into a flawless gemstone of priceless value. In that moment everything had become clear, he would propose to her when they were at the seaside and tomorrow he would buy the ring! He walked back to the camp through the blackout darkness with his heart racing and it was a long time before he managed to get to sleep that night. The following day he received formal notification that he had been assigned to a fighter squadron based at RAF Bodney in Norfolk, an airfield over fifty miles away. Without much hope he asked the Commanding Officer if he had any choice in the matter. *'Afraid not Duncan. You've been one of our star trainees and the squadron you've been assigned to is top notch. You'll be flying a Spitfire and when the war finally comes to us you will be in the thick of it.'*

He broke the news to Vera in a telephone call. *'Vera, I've been assigned to Bodney in Norfolk. It means we'll be apart. The day after tomorrow I start on five days Leave so how about contacting your friend in Brighton and seeing if she can put us up?'* He asked anxiously.

'I'll telephone her straightaway. Will I see you in the pub tonight?' She replied.

'The lads are planning to have a few celebratory pints this evening so we can snatch some time together when you're on your break.' There was a pause and then he added. *'Vera, if she can't put us up we'll go anyway, right?'*

'Definitely,' She replied, her voice full of enthusiasm and he felt himself squeeze the handset tightly.

'See you tonight then Vera.' He said, blowing a kiss into the mouthpiece. He heard the return kiss and then she hung up.

As he dressed to go out that evening his hand lingered briefly over the knob on the uppermost drawer of his bedside cabinet, the drawer in which he kept the picture of Ruth since he'd stopped carrying it in his breast pocket. He wanted to talk to her and explain but something told him it would be a bad idea and the moment passed. The picture stayed in the drawer but her image still occupied that secret room in his head and even though the door to the room was shut tight he could feel her presence. At some point in the near future he would have to unlock that door and explain to her what he was doing and ask for her forgiveness and understanding. He also knew that Vera would be wondering about Ruth so he would need explain clearly to her where he stood. That would not be easy as he really didn't know himself where he stood, should he try to forget Ruth completely? Would that even be possible?

That evening in the pub Vera excitedly told him that her friend had said they were welcome to stay with her and that she was looking forward to meeting Duncan. *'You'll like Grace, we've been friends since school days. She's got a steady boyfriend but I don't know if they are living together or not. Anyway, we're all set - isn't it exciting?'* She said *'I hope you don't mind but I told my parents we were going to spend your Leave together. They were fine with it but it would be good to introduce you to them tomorrow morning before we set off. I told Grace we'd be arriving in Brighton during the afternoon sometime so there'd be time for you to have a quick cup of coffee with my parents before we go....is that OK?'*

'No problem. I'd like to meet them properly - see you about ten? Now what about those pints you were supposed to be pulling? I'm going to be in trouble if I don't get them back to the table soon.' Although Duncan was smiling when he spoke, his head was already swirling with what he would say to Vera's parents the next day. Most of the trainees were spending their Leave at home with their parents but rather than reveal his

plans, even to his best mate, Duncan chose a white lie. *'I'm going to visit friends in Brighton.'* He said before quickly changing the subject back to the war, their postings and aeroplanes. When he arrived at the pub to collect Vera the following morning Duncan had already paid a quick visit to the village jeweller to buy an engagement ring. Understanding that her client was in a hurry, the jeweller said with a smile. *'Don't worry, if she wants to exchange it for some reason you can always bring it back - provided it's not damaged in any way of course.'* As he counted out his money he noted that she hadn't said he could have his money back if she refused his proposal. The ring he chose was a pale blue sapphire surrounded by tiny diamonds, he thought the sapphire matched Vera's bright blue eyes. The friendly lady carefully placed it in a red velvet nest before snapping the tiny, square jewellery box shut. *'Good luck.'* She said, smiling at him with eyes alive with kindness.

Vera's father answered the door. *'Morning sir,'* said Duncan as they shook hands. *'Morning Duncan, come through,'* he replied. *'I thought we could have a quick word?'* It wasn't really a question and Duncan was pretty sure what was coming. He followed Vera's father through to a small room behind the bar where he seated himself in a high-backed chair and indicated to Duncan to take a seat facing him.

'Duncan, I'll come straight to the point. Vera's mother and I have no objection to you taking Ruth off to Brighton for a few days but we would both like reassurance that your intentions are honourable.' He said with his steady gaze fixed on Duncan whose mind was racing. He was kicking himself for not having prepared an answer because this question from Vera's father was hardly unexpected. Fighting to control his discomfort at

being put on the spot he searched his mind for an answer which would not only satisfy Vera's father but would also fairly describe how he felt about her. For a very awkward five or ten seconds he said nothing and then it hit him. He was planning to propose to Vera so what better than to use this occasion to ask her father for his permission? Why hadn't he thought of this before? Duncan felt a surge of confidence as he fumbled in his coat pocket for the tiny jewellery box. *'Well Sir, I wanted to talk to you before we went away because I need your permission to ask your daughter to marry me. I've got the ring here and if you agree then all I need is to wait for the right moment when we're in Brighton.'* Breathing an internal sigh of relief Duncan stretched out his hand and showed him the ring box. *'I'll show you the ring if you want?'* He said, noticing that the awkwardness he had been feeling had transferred to Vera's father.

'No, no!' He replied immediately. *'That would be wrong. Vera should be the first to see the ring.'* Then there was a long pause before he continued. *'Well Duncan, I'm happy to say yes but it seems to me that once this phoney war ends and Germany attacks Britain as surely he must, then you will have just about the most dangerous job there is. Vera will be worried sick. Why couldn't you have been a bank clerk or an accountant instead of a fighter pilot?'* He paused again and then getting to his feet he stretched out his hand and smiled as he said. *'But they probably wouldn't be Vera's type so I wish you well.'*

'Thank you sir.' Said Duncan gratefully shaking his hand.

Later in the taxi on the way to the train Vera looked over at Duncan and enquired. *'How did you get on with Dad? At first I thought of not telling my parents that you were going with me to Brighton but that didn't feel right so I told them the truth - that we were in love. I hope you don't mind?'*

'I'm glad you told them and your father was OK with us going to Brighton together.' Replied Duncan as he put his arm around her, meanwhile his other hand was deep inside his overcoat pocket squeezing the ring box and felt his heart beat faster. It was the 9th of May 1939 and that morning on the BBC News he'd heard the announcement that the conscription age had been raised to thirty-six. It was yet another worrying reminder that the phoney war could not continue indefinitely but just then he couldn't have been happier, his mind was a long way from the war and the role he would play in it.

Across the Channel in Hannover everyone was aware that a major assault on the west was being planned. Long trains heavily laden with tanks and armoured vehicles laboured slowly westwards towards the Dutch/Belgian border and convoys of troop-carriers rumbled through the city. It seemed that no effort was being made to disguise their intentions and residents waved and cheered as formations of Wehrmacht soldiers marched smartly past. For a while following the invasion of Poland Ruth had hoped that a peace agreement would be reached and things might perhaps return to normal but it was only the faintest of hopes and Hitler's belligerent speeches gave little comfort to the peacemakers. It seemed inevitable that the Nazis were set on further conquests and even the most optimistic German citizen felt they were now in for a long and bloody war which sooner rather than later would touch everyone. Ruth's employer was a specialist manufacturing company which supplied parts to the massive

VW Plant at Wolfsburg, 90km east of Hannover, so the war had brought an increase in orders for the company and unlike many of her friends who worked in jobs which were not directly associated with the war effort it meant better job security for the staff. However, conscription had taken its toll on the workforce and women were now being recruited to do jobs which hitherto had been exclusively done by men. With fewer men around at work Ruth had proportionally fewer advances to fend off but if that aspect of her life had become easier, it was more than offset by her mother's slow descent into dementia. It was hard to watch as her mother became unable to do even the simplest things herself and Ruth worried about having to leave her alone in the apartment through the day while she was at work. Although she told her mother never to leave the apartment on her own, it became necessary for her to lock the apartment door when she left for work each morning just in case her mother felt the urge to go out. There was some respite at the weekends and if the weather was good Ruth would take her mother out for a walk along the river bank. Sometimes they stopped at a small café where they had a coffee and shared a slice of gateau. It was Spring and with all the trees coming into bloom it was hard to reconcile this surge of natural beauty with the ugliness of the man-made war that was raging. The German propaganda machine convinced the majority that the war was forced upon them but although Ruth could see through the lies she never dared to voice this opinion. With the success of the blitzkrieg in Poland had come a terrifying arrogance among the Nazi elite that Aryan Germans were the master race, destined to rule the world and as this myth grew so the persecution of the Jews relentlessly increased and along with the other restrictions, Jewish rations were significantly reduced to well below what the non-Jewish community received. There were relatively few Jews in Hannover but worrying rumours circulated about the treatment of the Jews in Poland where they were ten percent of the population. On each occasion when Ruth collected her ration book at the town hall, fear gripped her heart and she had to work hard to suppress it to avoid arousing suspicion in the official behind the desk. Every day at work she tried to behave as normally as possible, even on occasions mocking the Jews in the hope that it might deflect any doubts her colleagues might have held. Ruth's life was stressful and without any prospect of an imminent improvement she felt trapped in a terrible downward spiral. Back in 1933 the Nazis had introduced enforced sterilisation laws, ostensibly to purify the German race by eliminating people with handicaps or abnormalities of all descriptions. It was clear to Ruth that at some point her mother would be considered mentally incapable and what would happen to her then? When she could no longer look after her mother it was obvious that the State wasn't going to help - quite the opposite. At night Ruth bemoaned what had happened to her country. How had basically decent, good Germans been brainwashed into believing that the Jews had caused all Germany's problems? Where did the hatred come from? Deep in her heart she still clung to the hope that someday, somehow, Duncan would return to take her away to a new life where they could raise a family and live in peace. It was only the faintest hope but it was enough and that tiny flickering light kept her going. Every morning she'd briefly try to convince herself that maybe today was the day that Duncan would magically reappear.

The train shuddered to a halt in Brighton station as Duncan and Vera collected their luggage and climbed out of their compartment to join the tide of travellers heading towards the exit. Even in the station the smell of the sea was unmistakable. They were halfway to the exit when they heard a cry and out of the throng with arms outspread dashed Vera's longtime friend.

'Vera, how lovely to see you!' She exclaimed as they embraced.

'Grace, this is Duncan.' Said Vera, proudly.

'Very pleased to meet you Duncan,' she responded gleefully, *'I'm looking forward to getting to know you. Vera's told me a lot about you already and I have to warn you, you've got a lot to live up to. I hear you are a fighter pilot - how glamorous!'* She took Vera's other arm and then the three of them walked arm-in-arm across the busy platform to the station exit and the taxi rank. That evening they had dinner together in the apartment where the two girls got up to date after not seeing each other for more than a year. Grace had recently split up with her boyfriend and was enjoying playing the field. She was an attractive, lively girl who undoubtedly would never be short of suitors so she felt no urgency to 'settle down'. Every so often she would tactfully try to draw Duncan into the conversation but that evening wasn't about him and he enjoyed listening to the flow of conversation between the two long term friends while the engagement ring burned a hole in his pocket. Time passed quickly and before they knew it the clock struck 10pm.

'Right,' Said Grace, placing both hands on the table and standing up. *'I'm going to chase you two love-birds off to bed*

now while I do the tidying up. I'll probably be gone before you get up in the morning so just make yourself at home. When you go out there's a key on the hook by the hall mirror and please make sure you lock the door behind you. Usually I'm back here by 6pm so I'll see you then.'

The air crackled with electricity as they nervously got ready for bed and it was obvious to both of them that neither was exactly experienced in the bedroom department. *'I tell you what,'* said Duncan, *'I'm a bag of nerves, why don't we just snuggle up tonight and enjoy being together. I know if I rush things I'll almost certainly mess everything up. My love for you is so much more than just making love - sorry, that sounded really trite but you know what I mean don't you? We're here for another five nights so why don't we just take it slow and let things develop naturally, what do you say?'* He paused briefly and before she could respond he added. *'I hope I've not disappointed you?'*

Vera's smile said everything he needed to hear. She stood up in silence, walked around to his side of the bed, took both his hands in hers and drew him to his feet all the while looking directly into his eyes. Then she kissed him with her whole body pressed tightly to his. *'That's a great idea, Duncan. This is a very special time for us and we don't have to rush things so let's just snuggle up as you say and enjoy being together.'* It wasn't long before they fell sound asleep, two lovers wrapped in each other's arms without a care in the world. While in Europe a terrible storm was about to break.

The following morning after breakfast while Grace was at work, they walked down to the front and along to Brighton's famous pier which despite the war was in full swing. They strolled hand in hand to the end of the pier where they found a quiet table in the restaurant and ordered lunch. By the time it arrived Duncan could contain himself no longer. Ever since he'd bought the ring and asked Vera's father's permission, the urge to blurt out a proposal had been almost impossible to contain. Yet he wanted the circumstances to be just right, preferably romantic and accompanied by a well-rehearsed speech. However, he knew this was ridiculous because if Vera was going to say 'yes' it wouldn't be because of a silver-tongued proposal beneath a full moon in an idyllic spot that would forever be 'their special place'. If Vera was going to say yes it would be because she loved him and wanted to spend the rest of her life with him. No words could persuade her to feel that way about him so he fumbled for the ring box and said. *'Vera my darling, I'm going to explode if I don't do this now. I'm hopelessly in love with you and there's nothing more I want in this world than for you to be my wife - will you please marry me?'*

Tears welled up in Vera's eyes as she answered. *'Duncan Buchanan, I've longed to hear those words from you since our first proper kiss on New Year's Eve. Yes, yes, yes! I want to be your wife - let's get married as soon as possible so I can come with you to your posting. I don't think I could bear to be apart now even for a few days.'* She opened the ring box and wiping away a tear she said. *'It's beautiful Duncan, really beautiful.'* He took the ring carefully out of the box and slipped it on to the third finger of her outstretched left hand. *'It fits perfectly,'* she said, *'can I wear it now?'*

'Of course Vera, I want everyone to know that we are engaged.' He replied.

Their exchange had not gone unnoticed in the restaurant and a small ripple of applause spread around the room. The happy couple acknowledged the diners' good wishes with broad smiles and then the waitress surprised them with two slices of chocolate cake. *'On the house!'* She said as she put them down on the table. That same evening on the BBC they heard the fateful news. Hitler had launched a massive attack on Belgium and Winston Churchill had been called to form a Government of National Unity. The Phoney War was over.

During the remainder of the week they walked and talked, making plans for their marriage, the future and how many children they would like to have but in the background were the unknown concerns about the war and how it would affect them. At night they made love and dreamt of a family home in the countryside, filled with life, laughter and love. On his return Duncan would be posted directly to his new base and shortly thereafter could expect to see active duty in the air. It would be a dangerous life but not for an instant did either of them doubt that getting married was the correct thing to do. Vera phoned her parents with the news about their engagement and asked them to think about organising the marriage as soon as possible. There was some initial hesitation about 'there being no need to rush' but this was swept aside by Vera's determination to be with Duncan when he took up active duty as a fighter pilot. He would need all her support and she knew that if they were apart, it would only add to the operational stress he would have to endure once the fighting began in earnest.

Back at the training base he packed his gear and got ready for the move to the Spitfire squadron. While decanting the contents of his bedside cabinet into his suitcase he was forced to decide whether to pack Ruth's photograph away or to slip it into his breast pocket for safe keeping. Holding the envelope which contained her photograph he felt the old familiar stab of guilt as the memories of their brief encounter, now nine months old but still so fresh he could smell her perfume and feel the brush of her lips on his cheek. After a week of bliss with Vera in Brighton Ruth's hold on him had reasserted itself. Rather than face her he slipped the unopened envelope into his breast pocket and whispered to himself. *'Even if I tried, I know I could never forget you Ruth.'*

The following week Duncan got two days special leave to marry Vera. It was a very simple ceremony with one of Duncan's trainee friends as his best man and Grace, Vera's friend from Brighton as bridesmaid. Duncan's parents travelled down from Edinburgh to attend the ceremony along with Vera's parents and this small group had a meal together in the hotel where the happy couple had reserved a room for the wedding night. In the morning Duncan and Vera took the train to Duncan's new squadron and settled into a small flat in the nearby village of Watton. After all the excitement it was hard for Vera to adjust to being the wife of a fighter pilot who could be scrambled at any minute and might never return. Duncan worked shifts and lived in a Nissen Hut on the base during the five days he was continuously on call. He then had two days off with Vera before returning for another stint. Missing the social contact she had enjoyed when tending her father's bar, Vera started looking for work to help her pass the time when Duncan was on call at the camp. They both tried to make the weekends as special as possible but it wasn't easy for either of them. If boredom was a problem for Vera for most of the summer it was also a very real problem for Duncan. Like all the newly trained pilots he was desperate to see action but it would come soon enough. In Europe the war was going badly, Belgium and Holland fell in quick succession and the French and the British armies were in full retreat towards the coast at the English Channel in northern France. Towards the end of the month the action that Duncan so dearly craved finally arrived and his first sortie was to defend the three hundred thousand beleaguered troops who were trapped on the beaches at Dunkirk. He and his colleagues engaged the Lufwaffe fighters and Stuka dive bombers in bitter dogfights during which every nerve in his body was stretched to breaking point. More than anything he was deeply moved by the sight of the troops, huddled in defenceless groups on the beach waiting for a miracle to occur. Each sortie didn't last long but the strain and the intensity took their toll and by the time his five day shift was up he was absolutely drained. Back in the flat during those five days, Vera waited anxiously each night for his telephone call *'Vera, it's me. I'm OK.'* Was aways his opening line. Although there were restrictions on what he was permitted to say over the phone he had no desire to talk about his experiences. When they were together he just wanted their life to be as normal as possible, a happily married couple doing the sort of things that happily married couples did. But underlying the time they had together was the ever-present knowledge that when he returned to the base after the two-day break, it might be the last she'd ever see of him.

At the end of May the miracle happened and during a period of a few days over three hundred and forty thousand British,

French and Belgian troops were successfully evacuated from the beaches of Dunkirk by a huge flotilla of small boats, skippered by their owners and crewed by volunteers all of whom risked their lives to rescue the remnants of the British Expeditionary Force and over a hundred and twenty thousand of their brothers-in-arms from France and Belgium. Duncan was immensely proud to have played his part in this incredible exercise - a massive defeat but in a sense an astonishing success. The day after the last of the troops were taken from the beach Churchill made a speech to Parliament which was re-played on the BBC and broadcast over the camp loudspeakers. Across the country it left few unmoved. Duncan and his fellow pilots spontaneously rose to their feet as Churchill intoned, '...*we shall go on to the end. We shall fight in France, we shall fight on the seas and oceans, we shall fight with growing confidence and growing strength in the air, we shall defend our island, whatever the cost may be. We shall fight on the beaches, we shall fight on the landing grounds, we shall fight in the fields and in the streets, we shall fight in the hills; we shall never surrender...*' As Churchill finished, everyone in the camp burst into applause. The speech was pure inspiration, fuelling their spirits for the epic conflict which lay ahead.

In Germany there were mixed feelings about the way the war was progressing in the West. The victories in Belgium, Holland and finally in France filled most of the nation with pride. At last the humiliating terms of the Versailles Treaty had been avenged but Hitler's military ambitions alarmed many of the older generation in particular and they wished he would sue for peace with Britain. There were some who viewed the pause in the Panzer divisions' rampage as a sign that he might not want to pursue the war with Britain because during this inexplicable break three hundred and forty thousand men had been successfully evacuated from the beaches at Dunkirk. Yes they had left all their military equipment behind but arms and machinery could be replaced much more quickly than recruiting and training an entire army. For the most part however Germany was immensely proud and revelled in the pictures from Paris of the German Army marching down the Champs Elysee and of Hitler and his henchmen gazing at the Eiffel Tower. These were heady days for the Nazis but there were many unspoken worries about where this conflict would lead and ultimately how it would end. Most German citizens knew that Hitler's greatest fear was the growth of communism and people wondered if the treaty with Russia was going to last and if it didn't, what would follow?

Ruth and her mother lived from day to day, keeping themselves to themselves and only at weekends emerging into the town for their customary walk along the banks of the river Leine. Frau Schneider's dementia was progressing and Ruth needed to take her mother's arm to steady her. They walked slowly in step admiring the beauty of the tree-lined river as it sparkled in the summer sunshine. At times they thought that their fears of being exposed as Jews were unfounded but it only took a passing SS Officer to remind them that as long as Hitler was in power in Germany they were not safe. If peace was negotiated with Britain then Ruth had already decided they would sell up and try to move to England. Anti-Semitism was rife across Europe and although not unknown in Britain, by all accounts it was the least infected country in Europe. They would be safer in England and there was also the remote chance that she might meet again the one person in all the whole world apart from her mother that she loved.

Then one day while on their weekend walk by the river, Ruth and her mother were passed by a smartly dressed SS Officer who like them was enjoying the sunshine. He had just passed by with a friendly *'Guten tag.'* when Ruth's mother stumbled and fell. It wasn't a bad fall, more embarrassing than injuring but any fall at her age was a matter of concern. She cried out and Ruth immediately held her mother as tightly as she could but it was to no avail and they both tumbled onto the pathway in a heap. Ruth disentangled herself and was in the process of getting to her feet when she felt the supporting arm of the SS Officer grab her and gently help her up. *'That looked like a nasty fall,'* he said sensitively as he helped Ruth's mother to her feet *'We should sit over there on the seat for a minute and check to see no bones are broken.'*

Shocked and uncertain what to do Ruth instinctively protested that she was sure they were both fine. *'Thank you very much for your assistance.'* She said but before she could continue with their walk he stretched out his hand and introduced himself. *'My name is Johann Schmidt and I am happy to have been able to help. Are you really sure you're both OK? I think it would be better if perhaps we had some coffee over there?'* He said, gesturing towards a riverside café only a short distance away.

Ruth's mind raced. He seemed to be a perfect gentleman but being an officer in an SS uniform set off alarm bells. Not wishing to arouse suspicion or draw any unwanted attention she took the path of least resistance and acquiesced. *'Thank you Herr Schmidt, that would be a good idea.'* She said.

He led them to a table, held the chair for Ruth's mother and then did the same for Ruth before seating himself opposite the pair of them. After he'd ordered coffee for them he said. *'Maybe a brandy would have been more appropriate?'*

'No, really, we're fine now. It probably looked much worse than it actually was. We were lucky - I think we're both fine. Mutter, how are you feeling?' Replied Ruth, trying her best to behave normally.

'I'm embarrassed to have caused trouble. It was a simple slip and as far as I can tell I'm not hurt but thank you so much for your concern and your assistance.' Ruth's mother was obviously warming to the courteous officer. So was she but with no desire to encourage any further interest, after a few polite exchanges she downed the last of her coffee and said. *'Herr Schmidt you have been most kind and we really appreciate your help but we must be off now. Auf wiedersehen.'*

'May I escort you back to your home.' He enquired.

'No need,' She replied *'We've already caused you enough trouble and interrupted your walk.'* The last thing Ruth wanted to do was to arrive back at their apartment accompanied by an SS officer. It would start unwanted gossip from the neighbours and more worryingly, it might encourage the officer to come calling. She could see that he was attracted to her and without being rude she wanted to extinguish his interest in her before it took hold. Maybe she was doing him an injustice but being safe rather than sorry seemed like the best approach. *'OK I will be on my way then. Goodbye Ruth and Frau...?'* Realising that the officer didn't know their second name and preferring to keep it

that way, she pretended not to notice his question and interrupted hastily. *'Mutter, say goodbye to Herr Schmidt.'*

He nodded briefly and clicked his heels. *'It has been a pleasure to meet you. It would be nice if our paths crossed again sometime.'*

They went their separate ways and for a long time Ruth had to physically restrain herself from glancing back to see if he was following them. Casting her mind back over the incident she could think of no reason why he might in any way have been suspicious, in fact he seemed only to have been interested in helping and throughout their encounter had behaved like a perfect gentleman. But his obvious attraction to her had been obvious. To many of her female work colleagues an SS Officer would be considered quite a catch but to her as a closeted Jew, a relationship with Herr Schmidt could only end badly.

It was some weeks before Ruth and her mother again ventured out for their customary walk along the banks of the Leine. During the intervening period Ruth had exhaustively analysed the situation and finally concluded that even if they did encounter the SS Officer again they had nothing to fear. If they did meet him again she felt confident that she could handle his advances. If necessary she could tell him that she was already committed to someone and from what she'd seen of Herr Schmidt, he was a perfect gentleman who would not continue to pursue her under these circumstances. One lingering worry tugged at her from time to time, he knew her name was Ruth and although not exclusively a Hebrew name it was certainly commonly used by Jews.

They didn't meet the SS Officer again and soon the encounter was a distant memory which surfaced only when they saw other off-duty members of the SS. She concluded there must be an SS camp somewhere near Hannover. Following the fall of Belgium, Holland and France it was the job of the SS to ensure that the German occupation was secure so Ruth presumed Herr Schmidt had moved on. The news continued to proudly boast of victory and conquest and it was only the rationing and the blackout that reminded Ruth and her mother that Germany was still at war. There were rumours that the German armed forces were drawing breath in preparation for a September invasion of England and it was also darkly rumoured that the SS had begun to round up Jews and ship them east for resettlement. During these times Ruth's mind often turned to Duncan and she wondered how he was faring. If the propaganda was to be believed England would be overcome and occupied by Christmas and what would become of him then? She presumed he had been conscripted into the armed forces as had most young men in Germany, but beyond that she could only imagine how his life was unfolding. Most of all, she wondered if he ever thought of her.

'He was a nice young man.' Said Ruth's mother one day.

'Yes he was, Mutter, a very nice man.' She replied with a sigh.

'It would be good if you could meet up with him again one day.' Continued her mother. *'He seemed very fond of you.'*

'Indeed he was but the chances of our paths ever crossing again are almost zero. Duncan is British and we are at war with England so goodness knows what will happen but one thing is for sure, if we ever meet again it will be a miracle.' Ruth was gazing absent-mindedly out of the apartment window

as she spoke and she didn't see the confusion in her mother's face.

'Who is Duncan? I was talking about Herr Schmidt, Ruth, did you not like him?' Said her mother. As the months slid by Ruth had noticed that Frau Schneider's memory had begun to deteriorate quite rapidly, to the point where she no longer felt comfortable continually reminding her mother of her forgetfulness. It had been some months since she'd left the apartment on her own and she'd recently started to find it difficult performing even the simplest of tasks like starting the fire or cooking a straightforward meal. All Ruth could do was to try to keep her amused and as happy as possible but that was becoming increasingly difficult and the prospects were only that things would get worse. These days her mother most enjoyed reminiscing about the old times when Ruth was young and life was good. Thinking too much about what lay in store often brought Ruth to the brink of despair so she resolved to take life on a day-by-day basis but it wasn't easy. Her life had become a grinding routine of caring for her mother and work. Very occasionally she would allow herself to imagine what life might have been like without her mother and always it was the same dream. She and Duncan were happily married with two children and living in a beautiful house in rural America, far from the war, the anti-Semitism, the hatred and the suffering. Then she would feel the awful stab of guilt which would sweep away the dream and all hope of a happy life. Her hand of cards had been dealt and all she could do now was to play those cards as best she could.

'He was a nice gentleman Mutter, maybe much nicer than the average SS Officer but I don't think there's much chance

we'll ever see him again.' Responded Ruth, and in an attempt close down that topic of conversation asked. *'What would you like for dinner?'*

On the tenth of July the German Luftwaffe launched a massive onslaught on the shipping in the Channel and Duncan's squadron was scrambled to intercept the raiders. Alarmed at the number of German planes he followed his flight leader directly towards the heart of the formation. For a few moments chaos reigned until he realised that more by accident than design he was right on the tail of an enemy fighter. He pressed the firing button on his joystick and within seconds black smoke began to belch from the Messerschmitt's engine. It was doomed and as though mesmerised he watched in horror as it plunged vertically into the sea and vanished in an instant.

'Well done Duncan, now keep concentrating or that will happen to you.' His squadron leader's steady voice on the radio shook him back to reality and probably saved his life. Another few moments of distraction could well have spelt his end. When he safely returned to the airfield after the sortie the first person he sought out was his leader. *'Thank you Sir. Without your wake-up call I'd probably not have survived.'* He said, trying to keep the lid on his emotions.

'You did well Duncan. I saw your kill and together we downed fifteen Germans with only three lost on our side. John and Vic baled out and have been rescued from the Channel but Arthur didn't make it I'm afraid.' His voice was matter-of-fact but both men knew it was a thin veneer hiding the wretched feeling of loss which lay beneath. *'You need to get some rest now. This feels like the start of a major onslaught by the Luftwaffe. Hitler and his cronies know that as long as we*

control the skies above England he can never hope to successfully invade us so we're in the front line now Duncan and the country is depending on us.'

Feeling overwhelmingly tired he bolted down a sandwich and headed to his dorm via the mess telephone. *'Vera, it's me, I'm Ok. Must get some sleep now as we're almost certain to be out again before long. The feeling here is that the Germans have launched something big this time and we're probably in for a helluva fight. God I love you Vera, how I wish I could hold you in my arms just now, even for a minute.'* She could hear that his voice was beginning to break up so she interrupted. *'I hope you sleep well my love. I can't wait for your next break and in the meantime, you're always in my thoughts.'* By the time the call ended Vera was fighting tears. The war had only just begun for them and already the strain was starting to show.

Over the next few weeks the battle for the skies above SE England raged without a break. The grim statistics in the air led only to one conclusion and every pilot knew that the next sortie could well be his last. Brave faces were put on but each telephone call to a loved one before a sortie was an unspoken goodbye and each call on a successful return was filled with thankfulness just to be alive. The easiest part for the pilot was the actual dogfight where the action, adrenaline and excitement left no room for fear or caution. Each encounter with an enemy plane was a fight to the death and every pilot knew that without a break, sooner or later their number would be up. The stress of airborne combat was cumulative and if they hadn't been given time off after a fixed number of sorties the risk of a complete breakdown increased dramatically. Planes were readily replaceable but even in an accelerated programme a new pilot took at least four months to train. Compressing that process further would mean less experienced pilots taking to the air and a consequential increase in deaths. It was a ruthless equation but the formula was working and British pilots continued to down their German counterparts on a two-to-one basis. Also, and perhaps even more important, when a British plane was shot down three out of four pilots survived to fight again but the same was not true for the German pilots. When they were shot down a similar percentage survived the dogfight but for the German pilots the war was over and after a period of interrogation they were sent straight to POW camps. As time wore on the percentage of relatively inexperienced German pilots in any formation increased so there were easy kills to be had but once in a while a German ace would be engaged and then the odds changed dramatically. The primary goal of the British pilots was to bring down the German bombers who were concentrating their efforts on rendering the British airfields unusable but to get at the bombers, first their fighter escort had to be neutralised. In those weeks of continuous and at times unbearable tension, Duncan became one of the most successful Spitfire pilots in the squadron with a tally of ten kills, three of which were German bombers. Whilst his peers looked up to him, his success made no impact on him whatsoever. All he was trying to do was to stay alive in the never-ending airborne gladiatorial combat above the green fields of England. Day after day the Luftwaffe formations appeared and day after day they were engaged by the dogged RAF pilots in the squadrons based in the SE of England until one day in mid-September when the skies above Kent were strangely silent. By then one third of Duncan's colleagues had died in defence of their country and Duncan was on the brink of a mental breakdown. Despite the loving support of Vera who was also stretched to the limit, Duncan had closed in on himself to the point where even the dialogue with his maintenance crew, the men who kept his plane airworthy, was reduced to purely technical comments instead of the jovial banter which had characterised their earlier relationship. When Duncan phoned up on the evening of the first quiet day since July 5th he had difficulty believing himself when he said. *'Vera, we've not been scrambled today. Something has changed. The Germans may have given up on trying to beat us in the air. God I hope so. Can't wait to see you at the weekend. If the skies are still empty by the time I come home, we'll celebrate.'*

'I've got my fingers and toes crossed Duncan. Even though this war has only just started I've got a good feeling that for us - we might be through the worst.' She knew it was tempting providence but at times during what was being dubbed The Battle of Britain, their relationship had been strained. She had lain awake beside him in bed and heard him cry out in his sleep. On one occasion amidst the incoherence she was sure she'd heard the word 'Ruth' but to have raised that as an issue in the morning would only have added to the stress. So, as best she could Vera buried the nagging doubt that despite their loving and happy marriage, there was still place in Duncan's heart that belonged to Ruth, his first love. Putting this to the back of her mind she resolved to make Duncan's next homecoming extra special and with the help of her father, she managed to procure a bottle of Moet & Chandon champagne. No expense would be spared, her husband had been through

hell and so had she, this homecoming was special and she wanted it to be a watershed in their marriage, a punctuation mark which signified the start of a new life for them and more than anything she wanted them to start a family. She put on her best dress and met him at the door of the apartment with arms stretched wide in welcome. They embraced tightly with what they now called their 'New-Year-Kiss.'

'Close your eyes,' She said with an impish smile.

He dropped his kitbag and coat in the hall and taking Vera's hand followed her into the kitchen where soft music was playing on the gramophone. He noticed it was warmer than usual and even though his closed eyes he could tell that the light was dim.

'OK, you can open them now!' She said, her voice alive with excitement and emotion. He opened his eyes and gasped in amazement. The room was filled with candles on every horizontal surface and the table was set for two in the style of an upmarket Parisian bistro. On a red gingham tablecloth were two place settings between two tall silver candlesticks and at the side sat a gold champagne ice bucket with the chilling bottle of Moet & Chandon champagne leaning nonchalantly on the side of the bucket, its label clearly visible. Beside the champagne bucket stood two shining saucer champagne glasses which glimmered romantically in the flickering candlelight.

'Golly Vera, I'm stuck for words and how did you manage to get a bottle of Moet & Chandon?' Was all he could manage as he pulled her to him for a bear hug and lifting her off the ground he spun her around. *'What did I do to deserve this?'* He said.

'You came home.' She replied.

Neither of them wanted to openly acknowledge the fact that he was lucky to be alive after nearly two months of non-stop action during which so many of his friends and colleagues had lost their lives. All across Britain young wives like Vera were grieving the loss of their husbands, so while he and Vera were thinking how fortunate they were, thoughts of those who were not so fortunate were close to the surface. It was a beautifully slow candlelit dinner with long spells of comfortable silence and periods of gazing into each other's eyes. When they'd finished and extinguished the candles, he led her through to the bedroom. As they entered the room she turned him round and said. *'I think it's time we started a family Duncan, don't you?'*

"I do.' He said as he pulled the bedroom door shut behind them.

It was the seventh of September 1940 and the start of the London blitz. This signalled a dramatic shift in the German strategy and as summer passed into autumn the threat of an imminent invasion slowly passed. Despite the carnage in London and other major cities across Great Britain the entire country breathed a collective sigh of relief but there was no letup for Duncan whose squadron was deployed continually to attack the German bomber formations. Despite downing the enemy planes in large numbers, wave after wave of them came, night and day across the channel to pulverise the capital and other industrial concentrations in England. There seemed no end but after an interminable seven weeks of hell, it was clear that the worst of the blitz had passed leaving a quarter of London in ruins but the spirit of the Londoners undamped. Duncan flew sortie after sortie and before each, both he and Vera wondered fearfully if it would be his last and only after his safe return and his *'Vera, it's me, I'm Ok.'* call on landing could they relax for a few hours until the next scramble. Despite the relentless pressure, Duncan found a strange balance where his instinctive fear was counterbalanced by his determination to continue come what may. He convinced himself that every sortie was a standalone event and the fact that he'd come unscathed through many sorties did not alter the survival equation of the next sortie. He believed that the chances of dying did not increase with every sortie that he survived, in fact he deduced that his chances of surviving actually improved, simply because each sortie that he survived added to his experience and it was experience which kept him alive. Others argued that the more sorties he flew the greater his chance of encountering a German ace but he countered that by continuing to push his case that the riskiest time in the air was during the early sorties when the pilot had no experience. Duncan felt that this was the moment he'd been born for, he was doing something worthwhile and he was proud to be playing a key role in the defence of his country. He had been promoted to Flight Lieutenant and the extra responsibility, rather than increasing the stress on him actually helped him cope. He remembered clearly his first sortie as he'd watched the fatally wounded Messerschmitt nose-dive into the sea, when his leader had sharply reminded him over the radio to concentrate or die. That was his job now. It was up to him to steady the raw, inexperienced pilots which were arriving from training on a daily basis. Almost without exception new pilots were like he'd been, superficially gung-ho but beneath the surface quaking with fear. Duncan was at pains to point out to them that to not be afraid was first of all very unusual but more important, almost certainly fatal. Fear kept a pilot hyper-alert with all his senses keenly tuned to one end - shooting down the enemy before he was shot down. However, fear could become a ruthless master and if it gained control the fear became terror and that meant certain death. Nobody was immune to the accumulative effects of stress and he urged the pilots in his wing to open up when they felt they were on the point of breaking. But they never did. It was rarely the pilot himself who noticed the hairline transition point when the pressure turned into stress. Pressure improved productivity and performance but too much pressure for too long and that equation changed radically. The cumulative effects of stress drastically reduced productivity and performance and the only cure was space and time, neither of which were easy to come by in those days. He'd learned early on that it was a bad mistake to seek escape in alcohol and he kept a careful watch on the amount of beer his pilots were consuming. It was always difficult approaching a colleague and bringing up the subject because the response to the question. *'Are you feeling stressed?'* was invariably a flat-out denial. It was seen as unmanly to admit to any form of weakness and they all instinctively wanted to tough it out. He tried to use analogies to explain the issue, saying. *'The difference between pressure and stress is a bit like the difference between having a cold and having the flu. In the early stages they feel just the same, you can tough-out a cold but if you try that with the flu you'll end up in hospital and it will take weeks to recover - in some cases the flu can kill you.'* When he spotted a pilot that was near the edge he'd argue for a couple of days leave for him but that was usually refused, so it became an order. *'Take two days off, spend time with your sweetheart or your family, relax and try not to think about the war. Trust me, not only will it make you feel better but it might help to keep you alive.'* Sometimes and reluctantly he'd have to bluntly point out that the pilot in question was becoming a liability - a danger to the rest of them and needed to stay out of the air for a couple of days. This was always the last resort but after the initial shock it usually worked.

Then one evening the Squadron Leader called Duncan into his small office. *'Duncan,'* he said, *'we're looking for volunteers to escort a bombing raid on the Ruhr. There are some huge armaments factories which we'd like to put out of action. How would you feel about leading the escort wing?'* As usual the request was put to him in a manner which made him feel he really had a choice but he knew otherwise. He'd been selected for the job and only if he had an exceedingly good reason could he decline the request.

'Of course Sir I'd be honoured. I'd enjoy giving the Germans a taste of their own medicine.' He replied, with obvious enthusiasm. *'When is the raid?'*

'Thank you Duncan, well done. Briefing will be in two days time at 5pm and it will be a night raid. OK?' Continued the Squadron Leader, *'well Duncan that will be all for now.'*

Duncan saluted and left the office feeling positive. This raid indicated that Britain was beginning to take the fight to the Germans rather than being on the defensive all the time. That was the good part. What he found a bit more troublesome was the fact that if he was shot down over Germany he would most probably have to sit out the remainder of the war in a POW camp. Up until now if he had to bale out it was over home soil.

This mission would be a bit like being a tightrope walker and performing without a safety net for the first time. It didn't scare him but it added a distinct frisson to the mission. As usual he was unable to share any of this with Vera but that evening over dinner she had some much more important news for him.

'Duncan, it's early days but I missed a period a while back and the doctor reckons I'm pregnant. Imagine that, we're having a baby!' Said Vera, her smile broader and happier than ever. *'We'll keep it a secret until we're absolutely certain and then we'll have to either go back to visit my folks or invite them to come up here. I can't wait to see my parents' faces when we tell them!'*

Beneath Duncan's excitement at the prospect of becoming a father for the first time, lurked the fear that this additional responsibility would make his job a lot harder. Staying safe was an instinctive priority which became more important the day he married Vera. Now the need to stay safe had risen sharply and although caution was part of the equation of a dogfight, it wasn't a dominant part. Staying safe more or less equated to being risk-averse and no dogfight was ever won by the pilot who avoided taking risks. Risks were part and parcel of a fighter pilot's job and the only practical way of avoiding those risks would be to do the unthinkable - to give up flying. He knew he wasn't the first pilot to face this situation and he longed for someone to talk to but even if he did find a sympathetic ear, simply raising the subject could possibly be misconstrued as cowardice. For a while he questioned whether he'd have volunteered for escort duty on the upcoming bombing raid on the Ruhr had he known about the new baby. It served no purpose to dwell on that decision but now he had to decide if Vera's news was something that ought to make him reconsider and request to be stood down for the operation. He went round and round this in his mind before concluding that if he changed his mind this time, it would effectively ground him for at least nine months and after that, surely having a young baby would make him even more risk averse? This had become a watershed moment in his career as a wartime pilot and if he was going to change his mind about the bombing raid he'd have to do it first thing the next morning. He tried not to imagine the Squadron Leader's reaction. However, the more he thought about it the more he realised that it was his duty to fight on. The country was in dire peril of being invaded by the hated Nazis and he was needed to help his homeland and ultimately, his family. In the end it was not a difficult decision, he would lead the fighter escort on the bombing raid.

Without having to openly discuss the consequences for him of this new addition to their family, Vera knew what was going on in her husband's head. They would never get used to the regular goodbye where neither of them knew whether or not they would ever see each other again but this was the life she had openly and willingly signed up to. The unborn baby changed that by adding a new dimension to their circumstances but did it change the overall picture? She thought not. Best to leave things as they were unless of course Duncan needed to discuss it but it was their unspoken conversation which settled the issue between them and which also made her realise how close they were. In that silent discussion they had agreed that he would continue to be an active fighter pilot and she would continue to worry about him every minute that he was in the air.

While Duncan and Vera were celebrating the prospect of their first addition to the family, in Hannover Ruth was finding life increasingly difficult. Her mother's dementia seemed to be developing at an alarming rate and Ruth was worrying more and more about leaving her alone during the day while she was at work. She thought about asking if she could go onto part-time work but even if it had been agreed she doubted if they could make ends meet on half her current salary. It would mean moving to a smaller, less expensive apartment on the outskirts of the city and that would mean more time spent travelling and fewer shops within walking distance. Then there was the additional stress that a house move would place on her mother who would be thrust into new surroundings at a time when she was beginning to have difficulties navigating around their two bedroom flat. A typical day for Ruth now started at least thirty minutes earlier than previously as she had to lay out her mother's clothes and prepare her breakfast before leaving for work. That wasn't too much of a burden but what weighed her down most was the uncertainty about how her mother was faring during the day. Her greatest fear was that she would decide to go for a walk and be unable to find her way back. Despite this Ruth remained reluctant to lock her mother in while she was at work. She started preparing sandwiches for her mother to eat at lunchtime and to avoid the risk of lighting the gas to make a hot drink she also prepared a flask of coffee for her. Meanwhile, the war was making additional demands on the manufacturing company she worked for and employees were being asked to work extra hours. Sometimes Ruth didn't manage to get back to the apartment until late in the evening and this created anxiety which in turn increased the stress on Ruth who had to pretend to be cheerful and patient when in reality she was tired and hungry. Despite this they still enjoyed many happy moments, mostly when reminiscing about the old days when Ruth was young and they had been on holidays at the coast. She longed to be able to take her mother back there one day to relive those good times but the war made that increasingly unlikely. In the evenings after dinner they would often listen to the radio hoping that the war might come to an early end but as the weeks and months passed it began to look as if the war might last for many years. The London blitz was the main topic of news on the radio for weeks on end and it sounded like most of the city had been flattened.

'*Why do so many innocent people have to die?*' Asked her mother one night.

'*God knows.*' Replied Ruth '*This terrible bombing won't make the British submit, it will only make them more resolute and revengeful. There have been rumours of air raids on Berlin.*'

For Ruth and her mother, apart from the rationing, life hadn't been greatly affected so far but they both knew that before this war was over it was highly likely that things would change for the worse. The big worry in Germany was that the United States of America would enter the war on the side of the British as they had done in the First World War. Although officially neutral the US were already shipping huge quantities of food and arms to Britain.

Ruth had good days and bad days but the trend in her morale was gradually downwards. At times she felt a heavy cloak of hopelessness wrapped tightly around her. There didn't seem to be even the faintest glimmer of light at the end of the tunnel. At some point in the foreseeable future her mother would need full-time care and what would she do then? To add to all this was the ever-present worry that some day the fact that they were Jews would be discovered. This concealment was already a crime. Anti-Semitism was growing and almost every day there were more stories circulating about how the Jews in the city were being driven from their businesses and homes. To escape from all this, at night before she fell asleep Ruth tried to find peace by casting her mind back to the unforgettable evening that she and Duncan had spent together watching Romeo and Juliet at the ballet. But however memorable were the choreography and Prokofiev's brilliant music score it was all only a sideshow to what had happened between them. They had barely touched each other or spoken during the performance, yet by the time the final curtain fell and they looked into each other's eyes, each knew that their spirits had become inextricably entwined and would remain so until the end of time. This memory was by far her most precious possession. It was the imaginary engagement ring she never had, a priceless gemstone stored in a red velvet lined jewel box in her mind which she could open with great care to gaze at and remember. Although she tried and tried again to reconcile herself to the fact that she and Duncan would never meet again that flame would not be extinguished. So deep inside her heart she continued to cling to the possibility however remote, that they had a future together. She knew it was foolish but even the tiny, flickering hope that they might meet again one day was enough to keep her going.

During this time Frau Schneider could feel her mental powers eroding and although that brought the agony of indecision and distraction where she found it difficult to complete even the simplest of tasks, it was her awareness of the crippling effect she was having on Ruth that hurt her the most. She hated being a burden and despite her gradually failing memory and Ruth's efforts to disguise her worries, she was fully aware of the detrimental effect it was having on her daughter, the only person in the entire world who mattered to her. During the long days alone in the apartment she wondered at how over time their roles had become reversed. For so many years Ruth had been completely dependent on her for everything, both physical and emotional. That was a mother's role and Frau Schneider had been the best of mothers to her only child. She had wanted other children but they hadn't come along so while Ruth was growing up she received a hundred percent of her love and care. Things were so different now. Although the love she felt for Ruth had not dimmed in any way, her ability to translate that love into deeds had waned to the point where recently she had even lost the ability to prepare dinner. She was the child now and Ruth had to take care of her every need. It wasn't fair. Her daughter was the focus of all her love yet she could see the pain she was inflicting on her and she could see how her life had become narrowed down to the point where it only consisted of work and caring for her. With the time spent alone in the apartment when Ruth was at work these thoughts gnawed away at her and the pain she felt became almost unbearable. There seemed to be no way out.

A long way away in Paris, a German SS Officer called Johann Schmidt was settling into his well-appointed accommodation. He was there to play his part in ensuring that Hitler's orders on security, surveillance and terror were implemented in the recently occupied city. When France capitulated the French army laid down its arms and Paris was declared an open city but the French resistance movement continued to fight, wreaking havoc in the more densely parts of the city. Resistance snipers were targeting senior German officers and Himmler had ordered a crackdown where ten randomly chosen Parisians were to be publicly executed every time a German officer was shot. He was glad to learn that this strategy was yielding results and the number of assassinations had dropped dramatically in the days following his appointment. He was hoping that his time in Paris would not involve too much nastiness. As the son of a respected party member and having been a star pupil in the Hitler Youth, Johann was the model product of the German Nazi programme. His impeccable Aryan credentials ensured entry into the elitist Schutzstaffel where he rose swiftly through the ranks to his current rank as Hauptsturmführer. He seemed destined to rise further and this assignment to Paris was the ideal opportunity to shine. All he needed to do was to keep out of trouble. His job in Paris was to oversee the listing of all Jews in the city. This was a huge administrative task which initially relied on voluntary declaration by members of the Jewish community but then depended on finding and exposing those Jews who for obvious reasons wanted to keep their identity secret. This discovery process was a complicated business which he approached in several complementary ways. The obvious starting point was the register of births and deaths but when that avenue dried up, he was obliged to enlist the support of the Gestapo to pursue more direct methods. Rewards were offered to any Parisian who under the promise of anonymity would disclose that their friend, neighbour or work colleague was a Jew. However the promise of anonymity was soon dropped when the Resistance encouraged patriotic Parisians to anonymously reveal that scores of their acquaintances were Jews, thereby keeping the Gestapo busy chasing ghosts. When the policy of anonymity was discontinued the number of disclosures dried up to a trickle and the long process of searching out who was a Jew and who wasn't began. Johann kept a wall chart of the numbers and maintained a massive central file which would become the core information bank when the new laws pertaining to Jews would be enacted and when the expected resettlement programme started. As in Germany, the penalty for hiding one's Jewishness was imprisonment with the length and nature of the sentence depending almost entirely on the whim of the sentencing SS officer. All of Hauptsturmführer Schmidt's work was in anticipation that soon the laws pertaining to Jews in Germany would be enacted in all the occupied territories. These laws would exclude Jews from the army, press, commercial and industrial activities and the civil service and subsequently require the registration of Jewish businesses and the exclusion of Jews from any profession, commercial or industrial.

For a German SS Officer in France, life was good. The imposed 20:1 exchange rate between the Franc and the Deutschmark ruined the local Parisians financially but allowed the occupying forces to live the high life. Although tempting, this was not Hauptsturmführer Schmidt's natural style.

Certainly he enjoyed dining in fine restaurants and drinking the best French wines but he felt vaguely uncomfortable with the attention he received from the Parisian mademoiselles who professed a genuine interest in him as a person but who were obviously attracted to his relative wealth and status. When France fell almost two million French servicemen were shipped off to prisoner of war camps leaving a significant surplus of unattached French females. These girls knew the risks they were taking by fraternising with the enemy but for many of them it was a risk worth taking if it led to a better life for a few days or weeks and maybe a pair of nylon stockings which otherwise would have been far beyond their financial reach. Johann's discomfort had its roots in Hitler's Lebensborn programme where racially pure Aryan girls voluntarily slept with SS Officers who by definition were already vetted to be racially pure, in the hope they would become pregnant and help build the German master race. Like all of his brother SS Officers who were selected for the programme he had enjoyed his participation at the time but he felt vaguely disquieted that he had no way of knowing if he had fathered any children. But he was young then and losing his virginity in the service of the Führer was both doing his duty and fun. His discomfort didn't prevent him from socialising and having the occasional fling with a local Parisienne girl but he craved something more enduring and it was at those times that he remembered his chance encounter with Ruth and her mother on the banks of the Lien on that sunny summer day. Maybe he should have pursued her with more determination but there was something about her that had deterred him. Perhaps she had been afraid of the uniform and the reputation that went with it? In Germany the

SS were either respected or feared but mostly feared. Perhaps things would have been different if he'd been in plain clothes when he met her? Of course he'd never know so it was pointless to spend much time thinking about their encounter, however from time to time he did wonder from how Ruth and her mother were getting on.

On the afternoon before the bombing raid on the Ruhr Duncan kissed Vera goodbye and made his way to the camp for the briefing about the night raid on the heart of Germany's industrial might. In a few hours time he would be living on the edge of death somewhere over Germany in the middle of the night and only a few hours after that he would be back in the camp mess hall having bacon and eggs for breakfast. It was hard to come to terms with the fact that in the next twelve hours or so his existence would range from one hundred percent secure to something like a fifty-fifty chance he would get shot down and either die or spend the rest of the war in a POW camp. But he knew not to dwell on that. All that mattered was to remain totally focussed on the job he had to do that night which was to defend the bombers he was escorting by engaging and shooting down the enemy. There were many targets in the Ruhr but one prize that was specifically sought was the massive Krupp factory at Essen. It was believed to be the primary manufacturing facility for the tanks upon which the feared German Panzer Divisions depended. The pilots and crew were shown aerial photographs of the vast manufacturing complex and when questioned about the anti-aircraft defences, the only response they got was. *'You can expect heavy flak.'* It was a lengthier briefing than usual and although trying to maintain his concentration, he found himself automatically checking the left hand breast pocket of his uniform to make sure that the envelope containing Ruth's picture was safely inside where it had always been during each of his countless sorties. Every fighter pilot had his good luck charm and his was Ruth's picture with its message of love on the back. The old guilt was still there but he'd come to terms with it, believing that it would eventually fade and die away completely of its own accord and not because he had somehow forced her out of his mind. He'd never been in the air without her. It didn't escape him that their flight path to Essen would take them quite close past Hannover and he couldn't help wondering how Ruth and her mother were faring.

Before long he and his wing of Spitfires were in the air heading for the rendezvous with the flight of bombers which had assembled over Beachy Head. They took up their escort positions alongside the Wellington bombers and then like a flock of huge birds they headed across the Channel towards Germany. Maintaining strict radio silence they flew over the coast of Holland hoping that the raid would go undetected for as long as possible but soon the stabbing searchlights warned them that their presence had already been detected. This was inevitable. The noise of more than fifty bombers and twenty fighters would be enough to awaken even the most drowsy air defence crew. They crossed into German airspace and by then it was a straightforward task for the enemy air defence force to work out where the raid was heading and as expected the flak gradually intensified as they rumbled on through the night towards Essen and their primary target, the Krupp factory. Then suddenly a flight of Messerschmitt 109s appeared out of nowhere and once again he was engaged in the old familiar life-and-death airborne dance with the enemy. The detail of a dogfight was different every time but the overall formula remained the same - trying to get on the tail of the enemy and shaking the enemy off if he got on his tail. It was simple in theory but in practice it depended on his flying skills being superior to the enemy's and it also critically depended on the relative merits of the opposing fighters. It was here Duncan knew he had the edge. The Spitfire he was piloting was a superior fighter aircraft where it mattered most - turning. Agility was the critical parameter in a dogfight and although the German fighter could climb faster and dive faster than a Spitfire, that was of little consequence in the scrap he was now engaged in. Not only did he know he was in the better plane but he knew that the German pilot also knew it. In seconds he had the enemy in his sights and a short burst of fire from all eight of his Colt-Browning machine guns resulted in a plume of black smoke streaming from the doomed Me109. He didn't wait around to see if the pilot baled out. Then all hell broke loose as they approached the city of Essen. Despite batteries of ack-ack guns opening up and searchlights sweeping the skies the bombers stoically held their nerve and flew remorselessly on towards the target. Duncan's escorting fighters beat off yet another determined Me109 attack and followed the bombers into the cauldron of death. He lost count of the number of bombers which went down in flames and he could see that several of his colleagues had also been shot down and one or two had baled out. He shivered as he thought of the fate which awaited them. Meanwhile fires erupted from the huge Krupp industrial complex beneath them as they dropped their bombs and swept off into the relative safety of the darkness beyond the city limits. Then what remained of the raiders wheeled south and began the run for home. At this point he remembered the adage that more men died returning from missions than actually on the mission because of lack of concentration arising from the false belief that the worst was over. He wasn't sure if it was true or not but it served to remind him of the dangers of relaxing until he landed back at the airfield and there was the extra need to concentrate while he was over enemy territory.

Fifteen minutes into the return flight the low fuel warning light came on. Glancing at the dial to his horror he saw that he was almost out of fuel. At first he hoped the fuel gauge was faulty but instinctively he knew that was a forlorn hope. His mind raced. It was possibly an untimely mechanical failure but what seemed more likely was that a stray bullet had punctured one of his wing tanks. He was currently flying in formation with the Wellingtons at their cruising speed of 245 knots which was well below the Spitfire's top speed. Should he speed up in the hope that he could maybe reach the English Channel, or would he be better to maintain his current speed where the engine was consuming fuel at a significantly slower rate? At some point in his training they'd been shown a graph on precisely this question and as far as he could remember the most fuel-efficient speed was somewhere around 250 knots. A quick glance at the map gave him no cause for hope - he had no chance of getting to the Channel. It was time to break radio silence and let his colleagues know his dilemma.

'Hi guys, Duncan here, need to inform you that I'm fast running out of fuel. One of my tanks must have been punctured. It's pretty clear I will have to bale out but I've decided to stay

in the formation until the engine cuts and hope that maybe I can get as far as Holland.' He said, doing his best to sound calm. There was no need to point out the benefits of not landing on German soil. At least in Holland there was a chance he might get help from the Dutch. In Germany he would go straight to a prisoner of war camp.

'Roger that Duncan.' Came the flat reply. There was nothing more to say.

For another agonising half hour there was no sign that his plane was doomed. The huge Merlin engine roared reassuringly in the darkness, mechanically unaware of what was about to happen. His engine had performed faultlessly throughout all of his many sorties and through no fault of its own it was now destined to end in a fireball of destruction. Absent-mindedly he patted the side of his cockpit and said. *'Thanks for looking after me for so long. I'm going to miss you.'*

In the next few minutes he rehearsed the drill for baling out and then all he could do was to wait for that sickening moment when the engine stuttered and then stopped for the last time in its life. He didn't have long to wait. Minutes afterwards it happened as the mighty engine sucked the final few litres of fuel into its twelve thirsty cylinders. First a slight splutter, then a longer one and finally silence. He was flying at three thousand feet so he had plenty of time to make sure he followed the bailout procedure. During training each of the pilots had committed the procedure to memory and could recite it to the instructor at any moment when challenged to do so. He'd hoped he would never have to go through this procedure but now was the time. Reciting it out loud and in spite of his racing pulse he performed each action calmly and as carefully.

'Undo seat harness, unplug oxygen hose, pull out mike lead, reach up and release canopy, unlatch cockpit door, push stick forward, climb up out of seat and dive out behind trailing edge of wing, hoping to miss tail assembly on way out.' Seconds later he was surreally suspended under his shining white canopy, drifting gently through space and watching the death of his beloved Spitfire which gradually tipped up and went into a vertical dive. It must have been travelling at over four hundred miles per hour when it hit the ground and burst into an enormous fireball of total destruction. Duncan could still see the flames as he came down in the middle of a ploughed field and he could still faintly hear the rumble of the receding formation as it flew back towards England. *'Safe home.'* He said as he quickly collected his 'chute and ran for the cover of the nearby trees. What happened next depended entirely on whether he'd been spotted or assumed to have been killed in the plane crash. If it was the latter, then by the time the crash had been examined and it was discovered that there was nobody on board he might be able to hide somewhere. All would become clear very soon. If his parachute had been seen then a search party would be looking for him within minutes. Despite knowing that it was probably futile trying to evade capture he instinctively began searching for somewhere to hide both himself and his parachute. On reaching the trees he could see it was a conifer plantation, so dense that it took him fully twenty minutes to penetrate deep enough into the forest to feel safe, although he worried that in the process he might have left tell-tale shreds of his parachute snagged onto the tree branches that he'd had to fight his way through. When daylight came, if he hadn't been captured by then, he would have to make sure

that where he'd entered the forest wasn't signposted with white silk markers. That he could fix in the morning but there was absolutely nothing he could do about his footprints in the field which would lead any tracker directly to where he was hidden. Slumped against a tree and warm from his strenuous activity he took stock of his situation reckoning that if he wasn't discovered by noon the following day there was a chance it had been assumed he'd died in crash. But as he had no water and only the small tin of emergency pilot rations, he couldn't stay where he was for long. Assuming he wasn't discovered he'd have to come up with a plan during the day and then perhaps move on when darkness fell. Thankfully it was a dry night and still warm from his exertions he soon drifted off into a deep sleep.

On awakening it took him several minutes to work out where he was. Glancing at his luminous watch he saw it was already approaching noon so he must have slept for several hours. Beyond the confines of the forest it would be broad daylight yet here in its depths there was barely enough light to see. It gradually dawned on him that his parachute descent must have gone unnoticed otherwise he would have been able to hear the search party and more specifically their tracker dogs. It would only be a matter of time before the Germans discovered there were no human remains in his plane and would therefore start searching for the missing pilot. Presumably they would deduce that he'd baled out somewhere along the flightpath from the Essen raid but how far back would they search? As he considered his options he opened the tin of survival rations and consumed a small chocolate bar, chewing it slowly to make it last. Making a home run from so deep inside Germany was extremely improbable. He was dressed in flying overalls on top of his RAF uniform and even if he was able to dress as a local, he still had no identity papers. He was also aware of the important fact that remaining in uniform would ensure he was treated as a prisoner of war and to discard it would be to run the risk of being shot as a spy. Yet if he remained in his uniform he had virtually no chance of escaping detection. A quick scan of his flying overalls revealed it had only a single RAF insignia which he easily removed as he mulled over the hopelessness of his situation. For the present he had no other option but to wear what he had on and hope for the best. If at some point the opportunity arose to swap his clothes for something less obvious he could decide then but his immediate problem was what to do right now. Then a tiny germ of an idea sprung into his mind. When he came down he figured he must have been somewhere to the south of Hannover. He didn't remember seeing any lights but that was unsurprising as the Germans would presumably have had similar blackout restrictions to those in effect in Britain. Hiding in a city should give him more options than hiding in the countryside and of much more importance was the fact that he knew someone in Hannover - Ruth! If he could get to Ruth and her mother's apartment he could maybe hide there for a while and work out how to get across the border into Holland. Once there, if he could somehow contact the Dutch Resistance they might be able to smuggle him back to Britain. It was a very long shot but in that dark forest and with no viable alternative he began to think it was the best chance he had. There were so many unknowns that for the time being all he could do was to wait until darkness and then with the aid of his survival compass make his way across country in a northerly direction in the hope that he might eventually arrive at Hannover. With luck he could then find somewhere to hide just outside the city before making his way to her apartment. For a while it all seemed to make sense and then another thought forced its way to the surface. Even if he did make it to Ruth's apartment, wouldn't she be risking her life if she took him in? Ruth and her mother had no love for the Nazis so it was very unlikely that she would instinctively want to turn him in but it would be asking a lot for her to risk all in order to help him leave her, especially as he'd only just returned?

'First things first,' he said to himself, *'I need to get out of this forest and start heading towards Hannover. Any subsequent decisions only need to be faced if I get there without being picked up en route - and that's a big if.'*

Back in England there was a knock on Vera's door at 6am that morning. It was the knock she never wanted to hear. Slipping into her dressing gown she hurried downstairs and fearing the worst she opened the door to see the station Commanding Officer standing outside. Feeling slightly faint she heard him say the words she most dreaded hearing.

'I'm afraid Duncan didn't make it back from last night's raid Mrs Buchanan.' His words floated in slow motion across the short distance between them and his voice seemed to be coming from miles away. *'May I come in?'*

'Of course - please call me Vera.' She replied automatically, as she led him into the kitchen. *'Can I make you a cup of tea?'*

He sat down at the kitchen table while she busied herself filling the kettle and placing it on the gas stove.

'Vera,' he said softly. *'We're ninety-nine percent sure Duncan is alive. On the way back from the raid and still over Germany he radioed to say that he was losing fuel, probably from a stray bullet but that he would continue with the formation until the engine cut and then he'd bale out.'* He paused as she served him the tea and sat down opposite him. Her mind was still refusing to accept what he had just said, as if his words were being held at bay and not processed. She felt that as soon as she spoke it would somehow trigger the release of this awful news into the core of her mind and only then would it would become real. Like all wives and sweethearts of RAF pilots she had reluctantly tried to rehearse how to handle precisely what was now actually happening but it had been a worthless exercise. Nothing could have prepared her for the brutal reality that she might never see her husband again and suddenly she felt utterly naked and helpless. After a life-changing moment of silence she instinctively pulled her dressing gown more tightly across her chest and then said in a voice quavering with emotion. *'Thank you Sir. When will we know for sure he's alive?'*

This was by far the hardest part of a Squadron Leader's job in war time and no matter how many times he had to break the bad news to one of his boy's partners, it never became any easier and each time it was different. Sometimes there was an emotional breakdown with a torrent of anguished words and sometimes there was a stoical silence where the only communication was between their eyes, his deeply sympathetic and hers a mixture of disbelief, torment and sadness.

Drawing breath he quietly responded. *'If we presume that he was captured and taken to a prisoner of war camp, then the first notification we will get will be from the Red Cross. That could take a couple of weeks. There is also the possibility that he could evade capture for a while but it would be wrong to build your hopes that he might somehow make his way back to England. I'm afraid that is most unlikely, he came down well inside Germany.'*

Still feeling slightly faint but now more in control Vera sighed deeply and said. *'I guess there's not much more to say. Would you like another cup of tea?'*

'No thanks Vera, unfortunately I've some other calls to make.' He replied ominously. *'If you like I can arrange for one of the Women's Royal Air Force to come around and keep you company for a while? - I know what a shock this is for you and sometimes it's good to have someone to chat to.'*

'Thank you but I think I'd rather be on my own just now. Maybe you could leave a telephone number just in case I change my mind later?' She answered in a voice which was now almost completely under control.

He rose from the table, thanked her for the tea and just before leaving said. *'I'll let you know the minute we hear anything from the Red Cross. As I said earlier, we're ninety-nine percent sure that Duncan is alive so don't give up hope Vera. Your husband is not only a brilliant pilot, he's also a very resourceful young man.'*

She stared at the closed door for a while after he left while absent-mindedly stroking her stomach where already in her womb their child was growing. Then she bowed her head and spoke to the child. *'You'll have heard all that but I don't want you to worry. I know that your father is alive and one day I'm positive he will come back and do all the things that fathers do.*

He'll read you bedtime stories, take you to the swings, teach you to swim, help you with your homework and comfort you when you're unhappy. In the meantime I will be as strong as I can and do everything in my power to see that you stay safe and grow strong in there until the big day - your birthday.' That morning she made calls to her parents and to her friend Grace in Brighton both of whom suggested that she come and stay for a while but her instinct was to continue where she was for now and maybe do some visiting later. Although the news of Duncan's failure to return after the raid had been a terrible shock, after so many sorties she realised that perhaps in her subconscious mind she had always been preparing for precisely this outcome? She'd heard from others who'd lost their loved ones that somehow they'd known if their partner was dead or alive, now when this had happened to her she was convinced that Duncan was alive and this feeling wasn't just based on what the CO had told her about him baling out before his plane ran out of fuel. She knew he was alive. Later that day the local Anglican Minister paid her a courtesy visit.

'The camp informs the church in situations like this and I was wondering if there was any help that I could give you?' He said with well-practised sincerity.

'That's kind of you vicar but we're fine thanks.' She replied.

'Good, glad to hear you've got company. If you do need a chat or anything else I could help with, just get in touch - you know where to find me.' He said with a smile before smartly remounting his bicycle and riding away in the direction of the church, the spire of which she could see in the distance. For a while she thought it might have been polite to have invited him in but that could have been interpreted as the need for some

spiritual comfort and she didn't want that. He seemed to be a decent man who was obviously genuine in his offer of help but she was not a church-goer and she saw no reason to become one simply because she'd got bad news about her husband. It was only later that she remembered that when she'd said *'We're fine'* that he'd automatically assumed she had someone with her, when in fact she'd been referring to her unborn child which he knew nothing about. She smiled to herself as she realised that even though Duncan was far away and out of reach somewhere in Germany, she was not alone. Part of her husband was growing inside her and their unborn child connected them in a way that no letter or telephone call ever could.

When darkness fell, Duncan did his best to bury his parachute, harness, flight helmet and goggles. Although his flying overalls weren't typical wear for German farm labourers, they didn't shout *'Downed RAF pilot!'* either. Without question he needed to avoid contact with the locals and as he started to reverse cautiously out towards the edge of the forest he reminded himself of the one real positive he had should he unexpectedly encounter a local - he could speak German like a native. There was no moon and when he emerged from the dense undergrowth into the ploughed field he breathed the fresh air deeply. Even where he'd been, only a few metres inside the forest, the air had been heavy and uncomfortably still. Now he could feel a faint breeze on his cheek and it lifted his spirits. *'Things could be a lot worse.'* He muttered to himself, noticing his footprints from the previous night in the damp soil as he followed the edge of the forest west in the hope that he could soon start making his way northwards towards Hannover. Before long he came to a promising looking firebreak and for the next hour he followed it in a generally northerly direction. Thanks to almost total cloud cover he reckoned there would be approximately six hours of darkness before he'd have to find somewhere to hide again for the day. Six hours of travel over this sort of countryside equated to about about ten miles and surely by then hopefully he'd be approaching the outskirts of Hannover.

Towards dawn when the first faint light of the new day started to illuminate the eastern sky he stumbled across a long abandoned farm building in which he could hide for the day. Originally it had obviously been a barn as it still contained one or two pieces of rusting farm equipment and in one corner there were some ancient bales of rotting straw. Fortunately the upper hayloft was partially intact and with some difficulty he was able to climb up to where he could spend the day in relative safety. He found some dry straw in one corner and settled down to rest and eat a little more of his rapidly dwindling emergency rations. This appeared to be the ideal hideout and even if someone entered the barn, they would be very unlikely to discover him. Furthermore, if he was now nearing the outskirts of Hannover it would be possible to use this barn as a base to which he could return after a recce the following night. This became his new plan. Tomorrow night he would strike out towards the city and if he was unable to find somewhere safe to hide then he could return here. Content with his night's work he soon dozed off to sleep.

Daylight and the dawn chorus awakened him from a brief but deep sleep. He'd been dreaming of England and Vera and it took him a few minutes to re-register where he was. His ears perked up when heard the sound of distant car, giving him hope that he was in fact approaching the outskirts of Hannover. As time passed the noise of the traffic grew and it was clear to him that he must be relatively close to a busy road. This was good news. When darkness fell again he could make his way to the road and hopefully find a signpost which would give him a clue as to how far away he was from the city. Based on that he could decide either to return to the derelict barn or to press on into the city and find another place to hide during the day. His other alternative was to try to make it to Ruth's apartment but when he thought through her likely reaction on hearing a knock at the door in the middle of the night, he decided it might be better to try and intercept her on her walk either to or from from work and then decide along with her what to do. There were considerable risks involved in every alternative and eventually he concluded that being discovered moving around in the city in the middle of the night was probably more risky than mingling with the rush-hour crowds. So the plan he formed was to recce the route into the city the following night, return to the barn under the cover of darkness and then aim to intercept Ruth either on her way to or from work the following day. By then he'd be completely out of food anyway so one way or another he had to enter Hannover and test his ability to pass as a native by ordering a coffee with his emergency Deutschmarks at one of the roadside cafés on Ruth's way to work. He was also aware of the fact that he was beginning to look rather unkempt and in need of a shave so perhaps he ought to visit a barber shop as well as a café and maybe try to meet up with Ruth on her way home from work when he was looking a bit less scruffy? All the time he knew that if he was stopped by the police or the Gestapo and asked to show his identity papers he was doomed. He laughed to himself at the thought of trying to explain to a suspicious Gestapo officer that he'd lost his papers. They weren't known for being sympathetic and understanding. Absent-mindedly he felt for her photograph and took it out of its brown envelope. As he held it up in the dim light and looked at it once again his heart leapt. The magic that engulfed them on that summer evening a year ago flooded back and for the first time in many months he entered that room in his head that belonged to Ruth and which contained the precious memories of their time together. *'I wonder how she will react to seeing me again?'* He questioned silently. Then another thought occurred to him. *'What if they've moved away?'* He considered that for a while before realising that his current circumstances demanded that he takes one day at a time. All he needed for now was a plan for the next step and to think any further ahead was futile.

When Ruth closed the apartment door on the way to work that morning she was both relieved and worried at the same time. Relief came from getting time away from her mother who was gradually slipping into dementia and requiring increasing care almost on a daily basis and the worry which came from leaving her alone all day. It was always a relief to get home and find that everything was ok. She'd always be welcomed home with a cheerful smile and an offer of a cup of tea which, to her mother's delight Ruth always gratefully accepted. It made her mother feel that she could still contribute - that she was still of value. However the longer term outlook was grim and with no other choice Ruth was taking each day as it came and trying to make the best of the hand that she'd been dealt. She and her mother still managed a walk along the river bank at the weekends when the weather was good but apart from that and the occasional brief trip to the shops to buy food, Ruth never left the apartment. Her life had become a long dark tunnel with no light at the end and walls that were gradually closing in. In the office she rarely engaged in chitchat during breaks and at lunchtime, preferring to either work through her break or read. She was no longer pestered by her male colleagues in the office who had long given up trying to take her out on a date. Her instinct was to explain her situation to her colleagues and use her mother as her excuse but somehow it was too private, too personal to share with anyone and even if she had opened up what could anyone do to help? It was her duty to look after her mother and she would continue to do that to the best of her ability for as long as she could. In the meantime her colleagues could think what they liked.

The walk to work took nearly thirty minutes during which time she thought of many things. Although the streets were crowded it was a quiet time for her, a time in which she could think about the twists and turns of her life, make plans and occasionally dream. She had to ration the time she spent dreaming as it always led her into the same corrosive cul-de-sac of 'If it weren't for my mother, I could...' but this was a train of thought which only led to resentment and bitterness. It was during these brief dreams that once in a while she would open the door in her mind to where she kept her memories of Duncan and even a few minutes recalling those unforgettable times would lift her spirits. It didn't matter that she would almost certainly never see him again, no-one could take these precious memories away from her. Some people went through their entire lives without ever truly being in love and even if she never saw him again she had been lucky to have experienced the thrill of tumbling headlong over that edge and into love. She knew that one day these memories would eventually fade away and die but each time she revisited the 'Duncan room' it seemed to refresh the memories, perhaps even enhance them and so she was encouraged to spend more and more time living in that blissful moment which now seemed so distant from the realities of her current life. She paid little or no attention to what was happening in the war. It was a brutal conflict to which there could never be a happy ending and even if peace was negotiated it would not be a true peace, how could any occupied country accept vassaldom without continually dreaming of revenge? The more force used to suppress a nation the more hatred it would engender. Also and more worrying for Ruth, as time passed the conditions for Jews were growing steadily worse. Apart from the rationing and the fact that no Jew was allowed to hold a professional job, the hatred of Jews was being inculcated into every child that was growing up in Germany at that time and every day there were stories of the horrors being inflicted on the Jews in Poland. It was abundantly clear that as long as Adolf Hitler was in power Germany was not going to be a safe place for Jews to live. All the time she was haunted by the thought that one day she and her mother might be exposed as Jews. Their concealment of that fact was sufficient to send them both to jail, a thought that was too painful to consider.

On her way to work she passed a small café where on occasions, especially if it was raining, she would stop in for a quick cup of coffee. It was an attractive café, not too expensive and with friendly service. Over the years she'd got to know the owner and they'd gradually become friends and were now on first name terms. Even though it wasn't raining, on that morning for no particular reason she decided she'd time for a quick coffee so without thinking twice about it she pushed the door open and walked into the near-empty café.

'Guten tag Ruth.' Said the owner, a large, middle-aged man with a bald head, a small moustache and a welcoming smile. *'The usual?'*

'Yes thank you Hans. Your coffee is a great start to my day.' She replied as he turned to face the gleaming coffee machine.

'Anything to eat this morning?' He said, raising his voice to be heard over the hissing noise as he steamed the milk.

'You know how much I love your croissants but I don't want to put on weight.' It was her standard answer to his standard question.

'Ruth, my dear, you have the figure of a goddess and although I don't think the occasional croissant would make any difference you are right to look after yourself because as you are, you bring joy to everyone who meets you - and especially to me!' He said, turning to hand her the cup of coffee. She was used to his compliments which were always sincere, unthreatening and made with a twinkle in his eye. She knew he had children of his own, probably not much younger than her and he must worry about them as all parents do but the moreso in these dark days. *'What must it feel like to have your son go off to war when he is barely out of his teens?'* She thought.

'*Thank you for the coffee and the compliment Hans. I hope you have a good day.*' She said, flashing a smile at him that would keep him going until the next time she called in. As she turned to go he couldn't help thinking to himself that something wasn't quite right with her. He had known her for many years and recently he'd begun to feel that beneath her friendly and engaging exterior lay a sadness which she couldn't speak about. Of course it wasn't his place to question her and he would never cross that line unless she opened up to him. He watched her as she reached the door and stretched out her hand to open it but before she touched the handle, the door was opened by a young man who was entering the café. He immediately apologised and held the door open for Ruth who for some reason that Hans couldn't understand seemed frozen to the ground. He also saw the startled look on the young man's face and in an instant he realised that this relationship was special in some way yet not a word was spoken by either of them. Then the young man reached out and took Ruth's hand to lead her out of the café and the door swung closed. Strange, thought Hans as he absent-mindedly continued polishing a glass tumbler.

Outside on the busy pavement Ruth was shaking with emotion and struggling to keep control. Duncan put his arm around her shoulder and for a few seconds they walked in silence with the crowd. Then she turned her face towards him and as the flame of love burst into life in her heart she said. '*Duncan, I can't believe it is you.*'

He leant across and whispered softly in her ear. '*Sorry for the shock. We need to behave as normally as possible. I am an*

RAF pilot and I was shot down a few days ago near here. I couldn't think of anywhere else to go.'

Her mind raced and fighting back her impulse to embrace him she whispered back to him in a voice breathless with a mixture of emotion and fear. *'They will be searching for you and dressed like that, sooner or later someone will become suspicious and call the Gestapo. You must hide through the day and this evening after dark around 11pm come to our apartment block. It is too dangerous to use the main stairs - you might be seen by our neighbours - but there's a fire escape at the back which you can use. I will put a card behind the blackout blind against the window so you will know which is our flat. Tap quietly on the window and I'll let you in.'* He nodded, gave her a quick peck on the cheek and said *'Auf wiedersehen'.* Then in a few seconds he had disappeared into the throng. For the remainder of her walk to work she fought to control her emotions and by the time she arrived at the entrance to her office, although her heart was still beating fast she felt reasonably under control.

Meanwhile Duncan was on cloud nine. He couldn't believe his good fortune in bumping into Ruth at the first attempt, now he had to concentrate on avoiding detection during the day. He was starving and thirsty so without giving it much thought he made his way through the morning rush to the café where he'd so recently met Ruth. Apart from a few customers queuing up for coffee, the café was empty. He waited his turn, ordered a coffee and a cheese roll and carried it to one of the empty tables in the corner of the café. With time to kill he ate his breakfast slowly and watched through the café window as the morning rush hour gradually subsided. By the time he had finished it was relatively quiet outside and he realised that to remain much longer in the café would be to risk arousing suspicion. He was about to leave when the owner of the café started to move around the tables, wiping surfaces and collecting the used crockery and cutlery.

'*Morning.*' He said with a smile. '*It looks like it will be quite a nice day today.*'

Wanting to avoid unnecessary contact yet keen not to arouse suspicion by being too abrupt, Duncan glanced at this watch. '*Goodness, is it that time already? I must be off.*' He said as he pushed his chair back from the table and rose to leave the café. As he walked towards the door he passed Hans who looked up from the table he was polishing and said. '*I saw you earlier. You're obviously a friend of Ruth's.*' Thinking fast and keen to get out of the café as quickly as possible he replied. '*Yes. It's been several years since we last saw each other. Quite a coincidence. Ships passing in the night. You never know who you'll bump into, do you? Now I've a train to catch so I better get going. Thanks again.*' And with that he quickly exited the café and headed off in what he thought was the direction of the station. Reflecting on the exchange with the café owner he was very glad he'd said he'd a train to catch. It had been on the tip of his tongue to say he was late for work but that would have implied that he was a local, inviting questions about where he worked and why he'd never stopped into the café before on the way to work. However, he realised that saying he was rushing to catch a train could also have aroused suspicion as he wasn't carrying a bag and that might be considered a bit unusual. On reflection he felt it had not been such a good idea to go back to a café which was obviously used regularly by Ruth. As a result she would almost certainly be questioned about him the next time she dropped in for a cup of coffee on the way to work. Meanwhile all the time his pulse was racing at the thought of seeing Ruth that evening, but how to spend the hours between then and 11pm was his immediate problem.

At work Ruth was trying unsuccessfully to keep the lid on her swirling emotions. *'You seem very cheerful today Ruth. What's up?'* Said her manager when he was doing his rounds.

'Nothing that I can think of sir.' She replied before quickly changing the subject to a discussion about the production schedule she had been working on that week. But it rang alarm bells that despite her best efforts her colleagues clearly noticed her excitement. For the next couple of hours she concentrated fiercely on the task at hand but always she was aware of her bubbling emotions lying just beneath the surface. During her break she went over and over this seismic development in her life. There was so many questions, so much to decide and so many risks. How long would Duncan stay? Would he want to return to Britain as soon as possible? Would he want to take Ruth with him? Where could they go? And what about her mother? She knew that she and Duncan would have to work through all these questions and come up with a plan so there was no point in dwelling on them until they could discuss the options at length together but it didn't stop her thinking about it every time her concentration on the production schedule lapsed.

Duncan, meanwhile, was wrestling with the relative merits of hiding out of sight or in plain sight. Behaving furtively would invite suspicion so his number one priority was to act as normally as possible and that meant walking purposefully as though intent on getting somewhere. Any hint of aimlessness would attract unwanted attention either from considerate passers-by inquiring if he needed help, or in the worst case scenario from a plain-clothes member of the Gestapo. It was tempting to head for a library and secrete himself away in a quiet corner with his head buried in a book but even to remain there for any length of time would raise suspicions. He was a fit young man who by rights either ought to be working in an armaments factory helping the war effort or serving in the Wehrmacht. And then there was his flying suit and his unkempt appearance. Maybe he should risk a visit to a barber's shop for a shave? But almost by definition barbers were determined conversationalists and Duncan knew that the longer the conversation the more likely he was to trip up and raise suspicions. So far he hadn't obviously attracted any unusual attention but from time to time he imagined he was getting the occasional second glance. Finally an idea came to him, he would pass the day moving from public toilet to public toilet and spend up to an hour at a time in each. Then all he'd have to worry about was being noticed by the cleaners and he'd no idea how frequently they did their rounds but if the public toilets back home were anything to go by, it would be once a week at the most. Content with his plan,Duncan sought out the first of several public conveniences in which he planned to spend the day. Sitting on a toilet seat for most of the day he had plenty of time to consider his options and the one overriding decision he had to make before he met Ruth that night. Would he tell her he was married? If he did then it was asking an awful lot of Ruth to help him escape back to England. Not only would she be risking prison or worse by concealing a British airman but she would be helping the man she loved to leave her for ever. If he didn't tell her he was married, then why would he not want to stay with her and see out the war in Germany or alternatively, try to escape together to somewhere safe like Switzerland and start a new life together there? In either case he would be betraying one or other of the women he loved and that was the nub of his dilemma. He loved them both. There was also the problem of Ruth's mother. He knew that whatever he wanted to do, Ruth would want to look after her mother, either by staying in Hannover or by bringing her with them along whichever path they chose. In his heart he wanted to be honest with Ruth and tell her about Vera and their unborn child but in the final analysis he knew it would have to remain a secret. If he told her he would have no right to ask her to take any risks on his behalf. He would have to leave immediately and say goodbye to Ruth for ever. That would break his heart and probably Ruth's as well. As the day progressed he firmed up his decision to keep his marriage to Vera a secret and he accepted he would just have to live with the guilt of this deception. Would she suspect he had a hidden secret? Maybe, but he knew that if she ever asked him the direct question *'Are you married?'* He would have to be able to look into her eyes and tell her a blatant lie.

Through the day he moved between public toilets always moving in the general direction the square near the church where Ruth and her mother lived. A quick look around the back of the apartment block revealed the fire escape she'd told him about so now all he had to do was to kill another couple of hours until 11pm when she'd be expecting him to tap on the window. He returned to the nearest public conveniences and for the final time that day sat on a toilet behind the closed door and waited. During the evening rush hour a steady stream of people entered and left the public toilet but he felt safe. Evening commuters were invariably in a hurry and it was most unlikely that his continuously closed cubicle would be noticed. For a while he fretted about the possibility that the public toilets would be locked overnight but surely, he thought, whoever was locking up would be obliged to call out to anyone inside that they needed to leave immediately? The other concern he had was that by now it was inevitable that a search for the pilot of the downed Spitfire would be underway and word would have been distributed to the Gestapo to keep an extra watchful lookout for anyone who was behaving suspiciously. For the umpteenth time he blessed his fluency in German and after his brief exchanges with Hans the café owner he felt confident that he could pass himself off as a German citizen. Having blond hair and blue eyes also helped. What he really needed but couldn't possibly get was a set of identity papers.

When Ruth returned home that evening it was with some trepidation that she placed a small card behind the blackout curtain in her bedroom which backed onto the fire escape. There was something surreal about the situation and she fleetingly wondered if her encounter with Duncan had actually happened or if it had all been a figment of her imagination. Brief though their encounter had been, she quickly dismissed that thought but began to worry that there would be no tap on the window which would undoubtedly signal the bad news that he'd been discovered by the Gestapo. But there was nothing she could do about that, what worried her much more was what to do after she'd heard the tap the window at 11pm. In the meantime she prepared a large pot of goulash for dinner, knowing that Duncan would be ravenous if/when he arrived. Also, she would make sure her mother was tucked up in bed long before 11pm. Then she and Duncan would have time to come up with a plan during the night but between now and then it seemed pointless to think beyond his arrival.

'*Time for bed, Mother.*' She said at 9:30pm. Since the onset of dementia everything with her mother had been taking longer and longer. Even doing something as simple as going to bed had become a lengthy process which could take up to an hour and now Ruth also had to oversee everything. It would be difficult enough explaining Duncan's presence to her mother in the morning but by then at least they would have had time to talk and make plans. As she tucked her up in bed her mother said softly, '*is everything ok Ruth? You seem to be very nervous.*'

'*Everything's fine Mutter, it was a very busy day at work and perhaps I'm a bit more tired than usual - but there's nothing to worry about. Sleep well.*' She said as she kissed her mother goodnight before switching the light off and making sure the the door was closed tightly as she left. It worried her that despite her best efforts she was obviously unable to conceal her excitement. First it had been her work colleagues who had detected something was different and now, maybe less surprisingly her mother had also sensed her tension. As the minutes ticked by she felt her pulse quicken further. '*I think I'll have a drink,*' she said to herself before pouring a small glass of brandy and taking it to her bedroom to wait in the darkness for Duncan's knock on the window. It was a still night and shortly before 11pm she could hear footsteps ascending the fire escape from the courtyard below. Startled, she leapt to her feet and stood by the window while she waited with bated breath and thumping heart. Then it came - the tap-tap on the window. Fighting to control her emotions she pulled back the blackout curtain and there in the dim light she could see Duncan's outline against the night sky. It was him. He had come. It wasn't just a dream and in spite of everything she caught a tantalising glimpse of a better life, a life where there was hope not despair, a life where there was light instead of darkness, a life of love and happiness not hatred and sadness. She opened the window and greeted him, her voice ringing with urgency. *'Come in quickly Duncan. I'm so relieved you made it. I've been worried sick.'* Then without waiting for a reply she hugged him tightly and they kissed, the kiss they'd both regretted not having more than a year ago when they had said goodnight on her doorstep after the unforgettable evening at the ballet. It felt like a lifetime ago and so much had changed in the intervening year. Yet their love for each other had not changed and if anything it had grown stronger. With that kiss Duncan entered a parallel universe where the only fixed reference point was Ruth. So he clung to her like a drowning man clings to his buoyancy aid. She was his lifeline and he was hers. Soon they would have to decide what to do but for now they were lost in each other. It was a singularity in both of their lives. A moment when everything in the past was of no importance and only their future together mattered. He had a bowl of goulash, a shave and a hot shower and when he had dried off and was wrapped in a towel he said. *'Ruth, I can't put into words how much I love you. No matter what happens to me after this, I will alway remember this as the time where my life began.'*

Ruth felt her heartbeat surge as she moved across the room to embrace him again. Looking up at him she replied softly. *'And I love you too. Now is the time to get some rest, I must be off at 7:30am . We will make a plan tomorrow - there is so much to discuss.'*

'Where will I sleep?' Said Duncan.

'With me.' She replied unhesitatingly.

He awoke the next morning to be greeted by Ruth and a cup of coffee. She was in a hurry to leave so without wishing to be rude but keen to get to work on time she said in a hushed voice. *'Mother is having breakfast in the kitchen at the moment. I have told her you are here, hiding from the Germans. She remembers you fondly and will be happy to have your company during the day. Mother never leaves the apartment now - you will notice that her short term memory is failing. Actually she has dementia, which sounds terrible but apart from her memory and her ability to do some things that used to be second nature for her, she's fine. Please don't leave the apartment and also please stay away from the windows or keep the curtains drawn. We aren't really overlooked but it's better to be safe than sorry. I am sure that the Gestapo will be looking for you. Tonight we can talk more but now I must be off!'* She kissed him goodbye and once again he felt his pulse race. He heard the apartment door close as she left and he knew he would count the minutes until she returned. As he washed and got dressed his mind turned over the juxtaposition of their relative situations. For the first time since the crash he felt safe yet his safety had placed Ruth and her mother in dreadful peril. For him the consequence of being discovered by the Gestapo would be no more than a tough interrogation by the SS followed by internment in a prisoner of war camp for the duration of the war. For Ruth it would almost certainly be much, much worse. Harbouring an enemy pilot in time of war would be considered a very grave offence which on its own would receive a long prison sentence and she could even face execution. In addition, during the investigation the fact that she was Jewish would almost certainly emerge and that would seal her fate. By turning up in Hannover he had placed Ruth and her mother in the most awful danger and only by leaving them could that threat be lifted. Maybe he should leave immediately - before Ruth returned? He could write a note which explained he was unwilling to place them in such danger? Quickly concluding that this would be a bad idea, at least before discussing the options with Ruth that evening, he made his way to the kitchen where Ruth's mother was sitting at the table.

'Good morning Frau Schneider, it's nice to see you again.' He said as he took the seat opposite her across the table.

'Nice to see you too Duncan. It was quite a surprise when Ruth told me your story this morning. You look none the worse for your ordeal.' She replied. *'Will you be staying long?'*

Avoiding the question, Duncan asked her. *'How are you doing Frau Schneider - it's been more than a year since I was here, just days before the war started.'*

'Oh, this awful war Duncan. Why can't we resolve things without fighting? Men - they're the problem. If it was us women running the world there'd be no wars. What is it about men and fighting?' She asked rhetorically, her eyes staring into the distance. There was a long pause before she continued thoughtfully. *'As for how I'm doing? Not so well. Ruth might have told you that my memory isn't what it used to be and it's*

getting worse. She doesn't like me going out of the apartment on my own these days - scared I'll get lost. I don't think I'd get lost but she says all it will take is for me to get lost once and then what? Ruth worries about me a lot, I know that. What can I do? I am a burden and I'm becoming a bigger burden every day. Duncan, listen to me, being old is hard so you young ones have to make the most of your youth. You have brought Ruth back to life and it's over a year since I last saw her so happy. Promise me you won't leave her again?' She pleaded as she reached out to take his hand and squeeze it tightly.

Caught off-guard he replied impulsively rather than with forethought. *'Frau Schneider, more than anything I want to be with Ruth. These are difficult times and it is hard to know what's the right thing to do but you telling me that being here is making her happy means I will want to stay - for as long as it is safe...'* His voice trailed off as he thought about what he had just said.

They tidied up in silence, washing and drying the dishes and putting everything away. *'Ruth works hard and I like to try to keep the apartment as neat and tidy as possible. I used to prepare the evening meal but she's scared I'll burn myself on the gas or cut myself when I'm chopping vegetables. Maybe we could do that together Duncan? What do you think?'*

Duncan was deeply moved by Frau Schneider's awareness of the impact her deteriorating memory was having on her daughter and he felt for her frustration at not being able to relieve that burden. For a while he was able to avoid thinking about the longer term and concentrate only on the immediate future and how to make the most of this time. But the grim reality soon returned and when Frau Schneider retired to her room for a rest he reluctantly mulled over his situation and the deception which lay beneath it. He needed to sort some things out before Ruth came home. Then they could come up with a plan.

At work Ruth was trying to concentrate on her job but even the briefest lapse in concentration saw her thinking about Duncan and what future if any they might have together. She tried not to let herself think too far ahead but at times she couldn't help imagining them living happily somewhere in the country, perhaps with a couple of children and a dog. It was just a dream, a very remote dream, but it was the only dream she had so she clutched it tightly. Thankfully, her colleagues hadn't commented on her behaviour so she presumed the excitement which was bubbling inside her had gone unnoticed. But the companion for her excitement was the gnawing fear that Duncan's presence would be discovered. *'There's no excitement without fear.'* She reflected thoughtfully. There would be lots of both excitement and fear in the days, weeks and months ahead.

On her way home that evening she had reason to feel afraid. Passing the café she saw a notice in the window warning people to be on the lookout for a downed RAF pilot that had baled out somewhere on the outskirts of Hannover. The final sentence of the notice was a reminder that if anyone, for whatever reason, was found to be sheltering him then they would be 'dealt with severely' which she presumed implied a lengthy prison sentence or death. This presented Ruth with something of a dilemma. Breaking her habit of calling for a coffee on the way to work a couple of times a week might make the owner suspicious and it was unlikely that he would have forgotten the incident at the door of the café where she and Duncan had almost physically collided. Perhaps she was getting too jumpy she thought but it might be better if she avoided conversation with Hans until the situation blew over. That didn't mean stopping her visits to the café altogether but she thought it made sense to cut the frequency to once a week at most. She continued to analyse their situation until she arrived at the apartment but it seemed hopeless. All of the alternatives she could think of led nowhere, yet it was vital they develop a plan otherwise it would only be a question of time before they slipped up and the consequences of that for all three of them didn't bear thinking about. At the back of her mind she thought that perhaps if Duncan remained undiscovered for a while the Gestapo might eventually lose interest and perhaps shift their search elsewhere. But surely that was a forlorn hope?

Opening the door she was greeted by her mother while Duncan stayed out of sight in the back bedroom. When she closed and locked the door behind her Duncan emerged with a broad smile on his face. *'Welcome home Ruth. How was your day?'* he said, giving her a quick hug.

'Work was the same as usual. We're very busy at the moment and there's talk of the factory going onto three shifts. However, that shouldn't affect me as I work in the office.' She replied and then added. *'What's that I smell? Have you and mother cooked dinner?'*

'We have indeed, your mother and I have had a great time working in the kitchen together. I hope it's OK.' He looked across at her mother as he spoke and was rewarded with a smile which was no less beautiful than her daughter's. It was a happy moment in worrying times and all three of them treasured it.

After dinner they tidied up and Ruth bundled her mother off to bed as early as possible so they could have as much time together to talk. She put some coal on the fire and they sat together on the settee, feeling its comforting warmth on their faces. The coals glowed in the semi-darkness, casting dark shadows which flickered on the walls of the room. *'How nice it would be to have our home, somewhere far from this terrible war, maybe with one or even two sleeping children in the bedroom....'* The sentence faded into silence and she looked across at him. *'Sorry Duncan, I got a bit carried away there. Back to reality - we need to decide what to do.'* Ruth said emphatically before telling him about the notice in the café window. He greeted the news with silence as yet again he was flooded with guilt when he thought of the extreme danger his presence had placed Ruth and her mother in. The sooner he left the safer they would be but the more danger he would be in. The odds were heavily stacked against him being able to make a successful home-run. From where he was England could only be reached by travelling across Germany and then through one or more occupied countries before arriving at the coast from where he'd have to get on a boat back to Britain. The only other alternative would be to attempt the five hundred mile cross-country journey through Germany to the Swiss border and then somehow get across the frontier. Although he'd be safe in Switzerland the route back to England would then involve a perilous journey through southern France and across the Pyrenees into Spain.

'*Ruth,*' he said, putting his arm across her shoulders and squeezing her to him, '*the longer I stay with you and your mother, the more danger I put you in. Yet to leave now that I've only just found you again would - break my heart. Already you are taking a huge risk and if I am discovered the consequences for you and your mother would almost certainly be much worse for you than for me. So my head tells me I should leave immediately but my heart tells me otherwise.'*

'I know,' replied Ruth, *'what you say is true. If you were discovered it is almost guaranteed that the Gestapo would also discover that we are Jews. That would make our situation worse. By law we should have declared that we are Jews years ago so already we're guilty of concealing that.'* There was a long pause before she continued. *'I know I shouldn't think this way, but if it weren't for my mother I'd suggest that we try to get out of Germany together. I know this would be very difficult but it would be better than continuing indefinitely as we are with you hiding in our home. However this can't happen because there is no way that I would abandon my mother - you can understand that, can't you?'*

Duncan nodded in agreement and after a moment he said. *'Where would we go if it was just the two of us?'*

'Switzerland.' She said, turning to look directly into his eyes. *'We could be safe there, build a home and bring up a family. We'd be beyond the reach of this awful anti-Semitism that has swept across Germany and living in a neutral country that has not been at war for five hundred years. I've never been there but it is supposed to be the most beautiful country on earth. Do you think it would be possible for the three of us to make it there?'*

Duncan could see she didn't want to let go of this dream but he knew it wasn't realistic. It would be a long and dangerous journey to the Swiss border, followed by the real challenge of actually crossing the frontier which would probably involve climbing into the Alps and traversing a remote mountain pass in darkness. All of this was clearly beyond Frau Schneider's capabilities, so he let the question hang in the air unanswered for a while in the hope that he wouldn't have to point out the insurmountable difficulties involved. This dream could not come true. To break the silence he went over to the fire and put on another shovelful of coal. The fire smoked briefly as the new coal subdued the glowing embers and then fresh flames flickered through the smoke and the fire sprang back into life. He returned to snuggle up beside Ruth on the settee and then together they watched the burning coal and felt their love grow in the comforting warmth. How he wished he had a magic wand which he could wave over them and wish them far away. After some minutes Ruth said. *'You maybe don't want to talk about it but you must also be thinking of trying to get back to England? You are a fighter pilot in the RAF and surely it is your duty to try to return?'*

'Technically you're right Ruth…' Duncan replied. *'…but I honestly can't think about that at the moment. We've only just got back together. Do we have to make a decision now, why not just carry on the way we are for a while? Maybe the Gestapo will lose interest in trying to find me? That would mean we'd be safer and maybe an opportunity to escape to Switzerland might arise. I don't want to rush into anything at the moment, I think it's best if we lie low and wait to see if something crops up. However, if at any time you think it is becoming too dangerous for me to stay here, I will leave immediately and treasure what time we've had together.'*

There was another long pause before Ruth responded. *'I have never been in love before but now that I am in love I can see that common sense is the first casualty. Common sense tells me that sooner or later your presence here will be discovered. It will be an accident. Someone will see you at the window. A caller will knock on the door and when my mother answers it she will inadvertently give you away. Also, you will go crazy being cooped up in this small apartment all day, every day and eventually you'll take the risk of going out. I know you speak perfect German but you have no identity papers and even though we are in a large city, this is a small community and if you do go out there's a good chance that someone will notice you. Then the question will be - will they tell the Gestapo? You are a good man Duncan I know that, but for practically every single German but me and mother, you are the enemy. We're the only friends you have in this country. People with even the faintest suspicion will talk. Why did I have to fall in love with you?'* She turned her face towards him as she spoke and he answered her with a kiss. When they broke apart she continued. *'I think that somewhere we have a few of my father's clothes which might fit you. At the very least we can dress you to look a bit less like an RAF fighter pilot. However the big problem is your lack of identity papers. If for any reason you are stopped by the police, the Gestapo or the SS you will be asked to show them. If you can't show them - it's kaput. I need to think about this but in the meantime, let's take life day-by-day and enjoy being together. My mother loves having your company and it was wonderful to come home to a cooked meal this evening. Thankfully vegetables aren't rationed so we shouldn't be short of food. So that's the plan, right? We're going to lie low, take things on a day-by-day basis and see if a path ahead shows up? Now let's get to bed.'* Although it was phrased as a question there he could see that it was rhetorical, Ruth had made up her mind. Do nothing, hunker down and wait and see what turns up.

In Paris it was a very important day for Hauptsturmführer Johann Schmidt. The work he'd done on listing all the Parisienne Jews by systematically checking all birth certificates, marriage certificates and more importantly, all name change requests had ultimately ended up on the desk of the SS leader, Heinrich Himmler and had subsequently been adopted as the model to be used by the SS across Germany and in all occupied cities. Today was the day that Himmler would reward him with the his personal gift of an SS-Ehrenring in recognition of his contribution. Johann was always meticulous about his uniform but today he went to extreme lengths to make sure he impressed the SS leader, everything had to be perfect and it took him several hours before he was happy. There were others receiving decorations but when Himmler's party moved down the line of recipients he was the one with whom Himmler had the longest exchange. *'Congratulations Johann,'* He said. *'Your work here is recognised and we thank you for your contribution. You have a bright future in the SS and after this ceremony I want to talk to you about a career opportunity.'* Johann clicked his heels and saluted smartly as Himmler moved briskly further down the line. As his adjutant passed he stopped to tell him to attend Himmler's office directly after the ceremony. Tingling with excitement, Johann started speculating what his next job - presumably a promotion -

would be. He was on the fast track, that was clear. The ceremony closed with a rousing speech by Himmler and after they were dismissed he made his way to 87 Avenue Foch, the SS Headquarters in Paris. It was an imposing location and he felt ill-at-ease and self-conscious as he walked across the spacious foyer to the receptionist who sat behind a large Swastika drape.

'Johann Schmidt.' He announced courteously. *'I have been asked by Herr Himmler to attend his office.'*

'Yes, Herr Schmidt, he is expecting you.' She lifted the phone and briefly informed Himmler's office that Johann had arrived, then she said. *'Please follow me.'* She rose from behind the desk to lead him to Himmler's office down a long marble-floored corridor lined with artworks. Tempting though it was to stop and admire them his mind remained focused on the immense double doors at the end of the corridor which were flanked by two immaculately uniformed SS Officers. As Johann and the receptionist approached the guards swung open the vast oak doors and announced to the occupants the arrival of Hauptsturmführer Johann Schmidt. The room was enormous with a high, vaulted roof and it was filled with antique furniture. Several senior SS officers were standing around Himmler's desk behind which were two huge Swastika drapes. On hearing the announcement Himmler stood up and waited as Johann walked nervously across the room. He approached the desk, saluted and stood to attention while the attending officers discretely moved to the far side of the room and resumed their deliberations in hushed voices. Himmler smiled and his eyes twinkled behind the rimless eyeglasses. *'Hauptsturmführer Schmidt welcome and please stand at ease.'* He said as he

retook his seat behind the massive desk. *'Let me first congratulate you once again on the work you have done. It will be an enormous help in identifying and rounding up Jews in all the cities of greater Germany.'*

'Thank you Sir.' Replied Johann nervously and noting that he had not been invited to take a seat. This would clearly be a short interview so he resolved listen very carefully to what his leader had to say and only to respond when asked. Aware of Himmler's fearsome reputation for hiding his ruthlessness behind a facade of charm and quiet pseudo-friendliness, Johann avoided the temptation to be drawn into the belief that he and Himmler were having a conversation. He was here to listen and only if probed for an opinion would he do anything other than respond directly to Himmler's questions.

Then Himmler spoke again. *'Johann, since your days in the Hitler Youth we have been watching your progress with interest and although you are still young this latest work has convinced us that you have the potential to rise high the SS ranks. Up to now you have been working exclusively on administrative projects and it is time for you to cut your teeth in an operational role.'* He paused and took a sip from a glass of water while Johann kept his mouth firmly shut as he waited until Himmler spoke again. *'You know that the Schutzstaffel was formed originally as the Führer's personal body guard unit but since those early days we have become much more. Of course we will always be prepared to lay down our lives to protect the Führer but now we are the elite guard of the Nazi Reich, the Führer's executive force charged with carrying out all security-related duties without regard for legal restraint but uppermost in our role is our sacred responsibility for the purification of the German race.'* Again Himmler paused to sip from his glass of water and again Johann resisted the urge to respond. Then Himmler opened a drawer under the desk and pulled out a large white envelope emblazoned with the SS logo and handed it to Johann who continued to restrain from any response other than to thank Himmler. *'This is your next assignment Hauptsturmführer Schmidt.'* He said in a tone which obviously signalled that their brief meeting was over. He rose from his seat and extended his hand. They shook, Himmler nodded and said. *'Good luck. I'm sure we will meet again soon.'* Johann clicked his heels smartly as he stood to attention and saluted. *'Heil Hitler.'* He said.

With the unopened white envelope still clutched in his hand he about-turned and marched across the room. The great doors swung open as he approached them, the guards outside obviously having received a signal that the interview was terminated. As he exited the room the high-ranking SS officers rejoined Himmler around his desk to continue their meeting. The doors clunked shut behind him and he breathed deeply on the long walk down the art-filled corridor. The interview couldn't have gone much better he felt, especially at the very end when he'd been handed the envelope. Although he burned with curiosity about its contents this had obviously been a test of his loyalty. To have opened the envelope without Himmler's invitation to do so would have been a bad mistake perhaps hinting at a chink in the unquestioning loyalty that was integral to the SS ethos. Now he couldn't wait to return to his apartment and find out what Himmler had planned for him. He placed the envelope inside his tunic and quickly made his way through the streets of Paris back to the privacy of his rooms where he took off his jacket, poured himself a brandy, sat down on his settee and opened the envelope.

Back in Hannover they were taking things day-by-day and time passed with little to differentiate one day from the next. Ruth went to work while Duncan and her mother stayed indoors. Frau Schneider had her afternoon nap while he prepared dinner and then they waited until Ruth arrived back. The conversation was always the same. *'How was your day? What did you get up to? What's for dinner?'* Although dinner was almost always the same, a vegetable stew with dumplings and once in a while it contained their small ration of beef. A week passed before Ruth thought she should stop at Hans' café on the way to work for a coffee. He was very busy, which suited Ruth who wasn't keen to become engaged in a conversation which almost inevitably would have referred to the chance encounter she'd had with the man in the doorway of the café. They exchanged the usual pleasantries and she left hoping that as time passed he would forget about the day she met Duncan in his doorway. That evening around the dinner table for the first time Ruth decided to open up the discussion about their situation with her mother. She had a reason to do this. At work that day she'd decided that irrespective of what course of action they chose, Duncan would need papers and she suddenly remembered that her mother had once known a man who had assisted many Jews by forging visas to leave Germany in the years between the Nazis gaining power and the outbreak of war. Her connection with this man had been much earlier but Ruth remembered his name when it popped up in conversation about getting exit visas forged. If he was still around thought

Ruth, then maybe he could forge a set of identity papers for Duncan? She'd heard nothing of this man for years so he might well have been betrayed by one of his customers and arrested by the Gestapo, however with no other option available she chose to raise the subject over dinner.

'*Mutter,*' She said as they finished their meal. '*Somehow we need to think of a way to get a kennkarte for Duncan. At the moment he can't leave the apartment because if he was stopped by the police and was unable to produce his identity papers he'd be taken away. That would be bad for Duncan…*' she said, casting a quick glance across at him when she spoke '*…and for us, Mutter. I'm sure you know that we would be in serious trouble if it was ever discovered that we had sheltered a British RAF pilot.*'

Frau Schneider was fully aware that her short term memory was deteriorating but her reasoning powers remained relatively undiminished. '*I know this Ruth and Thank you for deciding to involve me in the discussion. It is not my place to give advice or even to comment because I am completely dependent on you but it is obvious even to me that we can't go on indefinitely like this. I want to help. My loyalty to Germany faded and died as I watched the rise of the Nazis and saw their treatment of us Jews so I am happy to help Duncan in whatever way I can - I just wish I knew how.*'

'*There may be a way, Mutter.*' Responded Ruth. '*At work today I remembered that you used to know a man who forged exit visas during the years immediately prior to the war. Such a person could easily forge a kennkarte for Duncan, don't you think?*'

Ruth's mother sighed a meaningful sigh. '*He was a very good friend at one time Ruth and I'll never forget his name - it was Jakub Kaufman.*'

There was something in the way her mother spoke that told her this was a deeper friendship than she'd realised at the time but it was not her place nor was it the time to probe. One day perhaps her mother might wish to elaborate but until then Ruth would not speak of it.

'*Do you know if he is still around Mutter?*' Said Ruth, again glancing across at Duncan who had remained silent throughout the conversation between them.

'*I have no idea. It is years since we last spoke. However, I remember his address and you could easily check if he was still lives there.*' She replied.

'*Thank you Mutter. This is something we can follow up on. Now let's have a cup of coffee and relax, I feel tired after my day at work. Things are very busy and we are planning to go onto three shifts in January. Thankfully this doesn't include the office staff - yet.*' Said Ruth, adeptly changing the subject. She needed to talk it over with Duncan before taking it any further and it was highly likely that her mother would have forgotten all about the conversation in the morning. When they'd finished their coffee Ruth's mother gave her daughter Herr Kaufman's address and went off to bed leaving her alone again with Duncan. They settled down in front of the fire as usual and then Ruth spoke. '*I hope you didn't mind that I brought this up with Mutter. I should probably have talked to you about it beforehand but it has been on my mind all day. At least it is worth following up don't you think?*'

'*Definitely.*' Replied Duncan enthusiastically. '*I will need a kennkarte irrespective of whatever course of action we decide on. Let's hope Herr Kaufman is still living in the same place and more important, he can be persuaded to forge a kennkarte for me. Forging identity papers is probably punishable by death and he would be taking a terrible risk. With a name like Jakub Kaufman he's probably a Jew which will only add to the risk. We shouldn't get our hopes up, he may no longer be in the business or if he is then his services won't come cheap.*'

'*Of course you're right but we have no alternative at the moment and as we've said over and over again, we can't go on like this definitely.*' Ruth replied with a hint of exasperation. '*We must do something. Tomorrow I will come home from work via Jakub's address and make discreet enquiries. The first step is to see if he is still living there and when we know that we can decide how best to approach him.*'

Sensing her tone Duncan gave her a squeeze and quickly responded, '*I totally agree that it's the best - correction - the only option we have available at the moment so we definitely need to follow it up. I may have sounded negative but I was only just trying to be realistic. Sorry.*'

'*That's Ok. I didn't mean to bite your head off. Maybe the stress of our situation is getting to me? Wouldn't it be lovely to be able to go away somewhere for the weekend, just the two of us?*' She said wistfully.

'*One day, Ruth, one day.*' He replied.

Duncan lay awake for a long time that night worrying about their situation and how slim the chances of a happy ending seemed. He was also feeling guilty about his wife Vera and their unborn child back in England. Should he try to get word to her that he was still alive or should he acknowledge that the chances of him ever getting back to England were so slim that it might be better if she gave up hope and tried to move on with her life on the assumption that he was probably dead? Everywhere he looked there was heartache and once again he wondered if it might be best for him to simply walk out of the apartment one day and take his chances, however remote, on somehow getting back to Britain? That would certainly remove the huge risk to Ruth and her mother but there was still the non-trivial matter that they were Jews and had been concealing that fact for several years. Finally, he reached the obvious conclusion that the top priority was to try to get a kennkarte which depended on whether or not Herr Kaufman was still in the forgery business. They could make a start on that tomorrow so trying to put all his problems aside he snuggled up beside the sleeping Ruth and escaped into a troubled sleep.

Over breakfast the following day Duncan was at pains to ensure Ruth took as few risks as possible on her scouting trip that evening. He recommended that knocking on his door was not a good idea, at least until all other avenues had been explored. It was possible that Jakub Kaufman's forgery business had been discovered by the Gestapo in which case he would almost certainly be dead. More important for them was the fact that whoever was now living in Kaufman's house would probably report any callers to the Gestapo who would be on the lookout for any of his clients, past or future. Duncan's preference was for her to get as accurate description of Herr Kaufman from her mother as possible and then find a café from which to observe the entrance to his home. She could even enquire after him in the café but before she did that she'd need a cast iron story about why she wanted to contact him. Meanwhile Ruth much preferred the direct approach of simply knocking on his door and using the relationship he had had with Frau Schneider to open up the conversation.

'Ruth,' said Duncan patiently. *'It's highly likely that at the very least the Gestapo suspect Herr Kaufman's involvement in forgery, even if they have insufficient evidence to convict him and in that case they wouldn't be relying on the current occupant to report any visitors, they would be watching themselves. If you can find a café with a view of his front door then you might be able to spot if there are any plain-clothes Gestapo watching the building. The café owner might easily be in the pay of the Gestapo.'* When he saw the look in Ruth's face he dried up and smiled. *'I guess all I'm really saying is be very careful.'* With that he left the table and returned to their room leaving Ruth and her mother alone to get a description Jakub Kaufman - at least how he looked thirteen years ago. During their discussion her mother confessed that they'd had a brief but intense affair. It was hard for her mother to open up to Ruth about this but if anything, sharing it probably brought them closer together. It was the heart that was leading Ruth to take these awful risks so how could she judge her mother for following her heart?

As she left for work Duncan gave her an extra strong bearhug. *'Please don't take any unnecessary risks Ruth. Take it slowly and if you get the slightest feel that things aren't right, follow your instinct and back off. I'll be thinking about you all the time. I love you.'*

'I love you too, Duncan.' She said before kissing him goodbye. He watched her disappear down the corridor and he was scared. Since arriving at the apartment they had minimised the risk by keeping him hidden in the apartment but attempting to contact Herr Kaufman in order to obtain a forged kennkarte would increase the risk significantly. It was obvious that Ruth understood this but equally she understood that the status quo could not continue. The possibility of acquiring a kennkarte for him definitely merited following up because without identity papers he could never safely leave the apartment. The only difference between them was that Ruth wanted to act immediately on this opportunity and he felt they should perhaps think about it for a while before acting. He worried that Ruth's enquiries might attract unwanted attention which could lead the Gestapo to the apartment. If they sat tight for a couple more weeks then maybe the search for the missing pilot would be replaced by some new and more important issue? They tidied breakfast away and as had become their habit he made Ruth's mother and himself another cup of coffee. Time dragged for him during the day but for Frau Schneider having Duncan around brought the apartment to life and gave her somebody to talk to. Aware that her short term memory was failing, she felt that being able to exercise it with Duncan would slow the process so she was always keen to engage him in conversation and that morning there was only one topic, Jakub Kaufman, and he was happy to let her talk. With a faraway look in her eyes she told him that they'd met in a park one Spring day many years ago. *'So much has changed since then Duncan, is it the same in England?'* She enquired but without expecting an answer she carried on. *'One day your life is all about the future, opportunities, travel, children etcetera and the next it's in the past - mostly memories and even they fade in time. I suppose we carry on living because we're afraid of dying but when life loses its purpose and you can no longer contribute then what's the point?'* She sighed deeply before continuing. *'We met in a park when all the Spring flowers were in bloom. There was a small lake with some seats on the shoreline and I'd often go there just to sit quietly and think. On this particular day the sun was warm and I remember a soft wind brushing my cheeks and filling my senses with the smell of the wild flowers. I was miles away and I barely noticed that a gentleman had sat down at the other end of the bench. When I became aware of his presence I remember thinking it was odd that he'd chosen to sit on the same bench as me because there were several empty benches nearby.'* Feeling he knew what was coming, Duncan listened intently as she continued with her tale - a tale she had probably never told before. *'We started talking, first it was about the usual stuff - the weather, the flowers, the view and so on, but then our conversation became more personal. Normally I'd expect to be suspicious of a man's intentions when he started asking those sorts of questions but on this occasion for some reason that I can't describe it seemed completely natural. Before long we were sharing our problems. Funny that, isn't it? We're often happier to talk to a stranger about personal matters.'* She paused again and looking directly into Duncan's eyes, said. *'I guess that's what I'm doing now, isn't it? All I can say Duncan is that something happened between us which I'd never experienced before and have never experienced since. We fell in love, head-over-heels in love.'* Again she paused, sighed deeply and stared down at the table before continuing quietly. *'We became secret lovers. It was a doomed relationship - I think we both knew that from the start and when it ended it wasn't because we'd fallen out of love, it was because we'd no real choice. We were both married with children and to run away together and start a new life would have been the most selfish thing in the world. So one day several months after we'd met we returned to the bench by the lake and closed that chapter of our lives, sad that it had ended, but happy that it had happened. The memories of our relationship are very precious to me Duncan, I'm sure you understand that?'*

He felt humbled that she had told him this deeply personal story. *'Frau Schneider, you probably know that Ruth and I fell head-over-heels in love within hours of when we first caught sight of each other. Like for you, it was the most magical experience of my life.'* Then realising just how private these memories were to her he added. *'If you want me to keep what you've told me a secret, I will?'*

'Thank you Duncan,' She replied *'Do you think I should tell Ruth or should I continue to pretend that we were just good friends?'*

Her question tweaked his conscience. Being 'just good friends' was something he was all too familiar with. For a fleeting moment he considered revealing his secret to her but even as the words were forming he bit his lip and held back. Maybe things would be different in thirteen years time, he thought? *'Frau Schneider, only you can decide that.'* he said, *'Ruth might be upset that you've kept this secret from her for so long. But would anything be gained by telling her? I don't think so. However, it is up to you and I will never tell anyone about our conversation. Thank you for sharing it with me, it is a beautiful story and perhaps the more private it is the more precious it becomes.'*

'Thank you for listening Duncan. I hope that some good comes out of this old relationship and who knows, Jakub might still be around and wouldn't it be wonderful if he could get you a kennkarte?' She said as she rose from the table, *'I think it's time for my nap.'*

That evening after work Ruth caught a bus across the city to the address where she hoped to find Jakub Kaufman the forger. She had no fixed plan as this was intended purely as a scouting expedition but if the opportunity arose, she was determined to make as much progress as possible, provided it wasn't too risky. It would be a balancing act. Enquiring too enthusiastically would invite suspicion, yet to make any progress at all she would have to ask some questions. Her greatest fear was that because he was a Jew his home would be under surveillance. Furthermore, if he was suspected of being a forger then anyone enquiring after him would immediately fall under suspicion. She alighted from the bus a couple of stops away from the address and walked down the busy pavement in the late afternoon sunshine wondering if there was any chance at all of meeting Herr Kaufman without having to knock on his front door. It seemed highly unlikely that she would spot him in the crowd as the description she'd received from her mother was thirteen years out of date. Even if she did see someone who resembled her mother's description, what then? He didn't know who she was so any direct approach would be very awkward indeed, especially in public. Fortunately she soon arrived at a street-side café only a hundred metres from the address where she hoped to find Herr Kaufman. Once inside she ordered a coffee and sat at a table in the corner of the café quietly considering her options. Another chance encounter like the one she'd had with Duncan seemed highly unlikely, however she couldn't help carefully examining all the older men who came and went while she was sipping her coffee. None matched her mother's description so when she'd finished her drink she carried the cup and saucer back to the barista and left to rejoin the throng. Feeling frustrated at not having made any progress she resisted the temptation to go directly to the apartment. Better to discuss that with Duncan first she thought but she was beginning to realise there was no other practical alternative. Finally she caught a bus back to the apartment thinking it had almost certainly been a wasted trip but as she was going through the door it suddenly hit her, why not simply write him a letter? That evening they composed the letter to Jakub Kaufman. It took several attempts before they were happy but finally it was done. They sealed the envelope, affixed a stamp and left it on the table to be posted the following day. *'At least we're doing something.'* Said Ruth. *'In a few days we should know if he still lives there and even if he's moved away let's hope that the current occupant will forward our letter to him. Now all we can do is wait.'*

Back in England the London blitz continued with massive destruction over a period of two terrible months of nightly carnage. In mid-November the Luftwaffe signalled a widening of their bombing targets with a devastating raid on Coventry in which the famous cathedral was almost totally destroyed. Other cities were also targeted with indiscriminate bombing of urban areas causing thousands of casualties but it failed to crush the spirit of the country which under the inspired leadership of Winston Churchill became ever more determined to fight on to the bitter end. During those dark months Britain stood alone against the might of Germany.

As her pregnancy advanced Vera decided to remain in their flat near the airfield rather than return to live with her parents above the pub. She enjoyed having her own space and new circle of friends and although she got on well with her parents, she was reluctant to return there and the inevitable prospect of serving behind the bar again. Duncan's colleagues occasionally called in to see her and they were always optimistic about his prospects, reminding her of his fluency in German which would certainly be helping him to remain undetected. One of Duncan's closest colleague started to call in on a semi-regular basis when his schedule allowed and his optimism and cheerfulness helped to keep her spirits up. Her friend Grace came up from Brighton to stay with her for a week and when the weather was kind they took long walks together and talked about anything but the war. One evening they went to the cinema to see Henry Fonda in the film of Steinbeck's Pullitzer Prize winning novel *'The Grapes of Wrath'*. It left them both stunned at the terrible hardships ordinary families had to endure as they tried to eke out a living when everything seemed to be conspiring against them. Wartime life in England was hard, but nothing like what the Joads had to endure. Throughout all this time Vera was convinced that no news was good news so that was the mantra she clung to. Until she heard otherwise she would remain optimistic that her husband was still alive. On one or two evenings a week she helped out in the officer's mess on a part time basis and although she'd had enough of bar tending, she enjoyed the company of the pilots and they enjoyed hers. Often it was her welcoming smile in the mess that more than anything reminded them why they were risking their lives. So she lived her life taking one day at a time. The future looked so uncertain that to do otherwise could only result in the heartbreak of unfulfilled dreams. But the one dream she never let go of was the dream that one day Duncan would return to her. Letting go of that dream would only lead to breakdown and despair. But sometimes at night for no apparent reason she would find herself crying and for a while she'd flirt dangerously with self-pity but the thought of her unborn child always helped lift her spirits and renew her determination that come what may, she and her baby would be fine.

Late one afternoon at the Schneider's apartment, two weeks after she'd posted to letter to Jakub Kaufman they received a reply. Ruth opened the envelope nervously and read it out to Duncan and her mother. It was a short letter.

'My dear Ruth, it was so nice to receive your letter which came as a complete surprise. It has been a very long time since I last saw you and your mother but my memories of those happy times are still fresh. You were in your early teens then and now you will be a young lady - beautiful I'm sure, like your mother.' Ruth glanced across at her mother and smiled broadly before continuing. *'Not much has changed in my life since then. I retired from work a few years ago and now I fill my days with reading, some writing and painting. It hasn't been an easy time for us Jews but I'm managing and always hoping that things will get better.'* Again Ruth paused and looked up at her mother

with raised eyebrows. *'It seems he's having a hard time Mutter.'* She said as she started reading again. *'There is a small park near here and when the weather is fine I always try to get out for a walk. If you wished we could meet there sometime. I usually head out to the park after lunch and if it's not too cold at the weekend I'll be there between 2pm and 3pm. You can't miss the park, it's just around the corner from this address. It would be nice to see you. Yours sincerely, Jakub. PS. I'll be wearing a hat and long black coat and these days I have to use a walking stick.'*

Noticing the faraway look in her mother's eyes, Ruth said. *'You can come with me if you like Mutter? It would be an outing for us.'*

Ruth was thinking ahead. It would be better if their first meeting was purely convivial and only if they felt comfortable with how they got on would it be safe to open up a discussion about the kennkarte. Ruth was still worried that his apartment might be watched so she was pleased he'd suggested the park where their meeting would look entirely coincidental. In fact she wondered if it might never be necessary to visit his house which would be the safest option. That evening she and Duncan had something concrete to discuss at last. He was relieved that Ruth had suggested that she and her mother would meet with Jakub because he felt sure that if he was going to take the risk of forging a kennkarte, it would be because of the affair he'd had with Ruth's mother. Of course Ruth didn't know the full story of their relationship and he'd promised not to tell her but maybe after meeting Jakub at the weekend she might disclose her long-held secret. He hoped so. When the weekend came around the weather was fair so on the Saturday Ruth and her mother caught the bus to the other side of the city and as had been arranged, they met up with Jakub in the park. Ruth approached the only person she could see that resembled the description he'd given and was in the process of introducing herself when her mother interrupted and with obvious delight and said. *'Jakub, how very nice to see you again.'*

'And you too, Helena. You are looking as lovely as ever.' He replied, taking her hand and kissing it lightly on the back.

'Ever the gentleman, Jakub. You too are looking well.' She said.

Even with this brief exchange Ruth realised that there was more to their relationship than she'd realised. The communication that had taken just place between them was more than verbal and she made a mental note to interrogate her mother about this later. Ruth and her mother took up station on either side of him and then for the next half hour they strolled around the park together apparently without a care in the world. Ruth barely contributed to the conversation and she felt her presence was inhibiting them but by the end of their walk it was clear that the flame there'd been between them definitely hadn't died, indeed it was blossoming in front of her eyes. It had been many months since she'd seen her mother so animated and engaged. If nothing else came of the visit other than this renewed friendship, then it had been well worth it. As they came to say goodbye, Jakub leant forward and spoke quietly to Ruth. *'Ruth, thank you for bringing us together again after all these years. I would like to meet again and maybe have a meal together but please tell me why you decided to get in touch with me?'*

Ruth was slightly taken aback. Continuing to shake his hand and thinking fast she answered. *'Herr Kaufman, you are right, there is a reason which we've not discussed. Perhaps I could meet you again before too long - here in the park would be perfect - and we can discuss it. Next time I'd like to meet you alone and afterwards we can see how best to move things forward.'*

'I'm intrigued. Same time same place next Saturday, would that suit you?' He said before kissing them both lightly on the cheek and bidding them goodbye.

The bus journey back to their apartment took almost forty-five minutes and when they were settled Ruth turned to her mother, raised her eyebrows and smiled as she said. *'I think it's time you told me exactly what went on between you two, Mutter.'*

Back at the apartment there was a mood of cautious optimism for the first time since Duncan had arrived. The meeting with Jakub had gone really well but the next meeting would be the critical one. Ruth would have to open up about Duncan and then Jakub would have to make the risky decision whether to help or not. Ruth was not sure if he knew that she and her mother were Jews - she suspected that her mother would have told him but that also would have to be revealed. He would be much more likely to trust her if he knew that they were also Jews but should she tell him that they were concealing this from the authorities?

Another week passed before Ruth set off again to meet Jakub Kaufman. So much was riding on whether or not he would undertake the task of forging a kennkarte for Duncan. No matter how hard she tried there seemed to be no safe way of broaching the subject. She would have to tell him all before he needed to even respond to the question of forging the identity papers. If he refused to help for whatever reason, she would have nothing on him but he would hold their lives in his hand and furthermore, there was probably a substantial reward for any information leading to the capture of the RAF pilot. She was pretty sure that he would want to help but if he was caught forging a kennkarte for one of Germany's enemies it would mean certain death.

As before, they met in the park and after the usual pleasantries Jakub looked directly at her and said. *'You must want something from me. How about telling me what you need and let's see if I can help.'*

He seemed so sincere that almost before she realised it, she launched into the whole story starting with them falling in love just before the war broke out. By the time she'd finished she was utterly drained and she daren't think how she would respond if he said he couldn't help. It hadn't even occurred to her that perhaps he no longer had the skill or the equipment to do what she asked. They walked on for a short while in silence and then he put his arm around her and gently squeezed her to him. Then he spoke in a voice so soft that she could barely hear him. *'My dear Ruth, your story of falling in love reminds me so much of what happened between your mother and me. Before we knew what was happening to us we were so deeply in love that we were unable to pull back and it was a long time before we had the courage and strength to do the right thing and part company. At the time it was almost unbearably painful for us both but we knew there was no future for us together. I thought the pain would ease with the passage of time, but I was wrong.*

I still ache with love for your mother and seeing her last week brought everything back to me as if it was only yesterday that we parted. She seemed pleased to see me too, so who knows, maybe we do have a future together? So it is for her that I will help you. Also, I loathe the Nazis and all they stand for so I am happy to do what I can to assist in their downfall by helping one of their enemies.' There was a hard bitterness in his voice as he spoke. Then he was quiet for a while and she felt sure he could feel her heart thumping. She could barely control her relief but before she could think of how to respond he spoke again. *'It is many years since I did any of this kind of work - it became too dangerous - but I still have what I need to do this job. Actually, a Kennkarte is one of the easiest documents to forge but I will need to take a photograph so Duncan will have to come to my apartment, there is no other way. You and he will also have to decide on his name, personal details etc - look at your own Kennkarte and you'll see what's needed. I probably don't have to tell you how dangerous this is for us all so it is absolutely vital that we don't create any suspicion. Duncan is obviously a very capable young man but one slip, just one, and we will all be executed. It is important that nobody sees him at my door so it's best that he and I meet here in the park next Saturday morning at say 10am and we can walk together to the apartment. In that way if we meet any of my neighbours in the building I will think of a story to tell them. OK?'*

'Thank you so much Jakub. I know the risk you are taking and I will always be in your debt.' She said as she turned towards him and shook his hand warmly before they parted and went their separate ways. The long bus ride back to the

apartment passed quickly, her head whirling with the glimmer of light she could see at the end of the tunnel. She couldn't wait to tell Duncan that Jakub would forge a kennkarte for him and she was also looking forward to relating to her mother what Jakub had said about her. It would be a very faint light at the end of her mother's tunnel too, something for her to look forward to and dream about during the long and lonely hours she spent in the apartment. By the time Ruth arrived home she was exhausted both emotionally and physically. Over dinner she told them both about her meeting with Jakub and they were all in bed asleep by 9:30pm.

Time dragged for Duncan as he prepared himself for his first outing since he arrived at Ruth's apartment weeks ago. It would be great just to get out of the small flat and breathe the fresh air again but it would also be a tense time with the constant threat that he might get picked up in a random check by the police or the Gestapo. If that happened his plan was simply to try and make a run for it and hide somewhere. Obviously he couldn't return to Ruth's apartment, that would be far too dangerous and to try to make it to Jakub's home would place him in terrible danger. These were the only two people in Germany who could hide him and he couldn't contemplate putting either of them in such danger so he'd just have to hope for the best. But his chances of avoiding capture would then be wafer thin. He also worried about the inevitable interrogation he would receive if he was captured. There would be pressure put on him to reveal who had been sheltering him and that would mean torture which somehow he would have to endure. He'd rather die than betray Ruth or Jakub he swore. If he was lucky he would end up in a POW camp for RAF officers where the Red Cross would be notified and word would eventually reach Vera and his parents that he was still alive. Then he'd be faced with the choice of trying to escape or sitting out the war.

When Saturday morning eventually arrived he said goodbye to Ruth and her mother, giving a bearhug to Ruth which had her squealing in pretend pain. After making sure the coast was clear he climbed out of the bedroom window onto the fire escape and quickly descended to the secluded courtyard. When he looked back up to the apartment he saw Ruth's anxious face pressed against the window so he waved briefly, blew her a kiss and then hurried out into the busy street with his mind firmly focused on behaving as normally as possible. The very last thing he wanted was to be noticed. Meanwhile, Ruth stayed at the window with her forehead pressed against the glass and her eyes tightly shut but still the tears came. The stark reality was that she might never see him again. It was a bright but chilly morning as he walked briskly towards the bus stop and he was just beginning to relax a little when he realised his route would take him past the café where he had met Ruth. An abrupt change in direction or a hurried crossing of the busy road would attract attention so he increased his pace a little and tried to join other pedestrians so he wouldn't stand out. Then, for the second time at that exact spot he almost collided with someone who chose that precise moment to open the café door. It was Hans, the café owner.

'I'm so sorry.' He said, obviously flustered by the near collision.

'No problem.' Duncan replied hastily but in the brief eye-contact which took place between them he was sure that the café owner had recognised him. Not daring to look back he

increased his pace and three strides later he was past the café door and gone but for the rest of the journey to the park his mind was spinning as he wondered what Hans made of their brief interaction. For a while he started imagining he was being followed before finally putting that down to paranoia. Even if Hans had recognised him and he'd become suspicious, there was no way that a tail could have been put in place so quickly. Nevertheless, in his agitated state he decided it might be safer to get off the bus at an earlier stop and take a circuitous route to the park. By the time he arrived at the park it was busy. Families were out with their children making the most of the bright winter sunshine but amidst the throng it was easy for him to find Herr Kaufman who on being addressed by Duncan feigned surprise. *'What a pleasant coincidence to see you again young man.'* He said, being careful not to use Duncan's name. *'Let's walk together and catch up, shall we? It's been so long since we last saw each other I'm afraid I've forgotten your name, old age is no friend of the memory, I'm afraid.'*

'My name is Horst Muller, Herr Kaufman and it is very nice to meet you again.' Said Duncan as they turned and strolled to the edge of the park in the direction of Jakub's apartment. They chatted casually as they walked, trying to behave as naturally as possible so as not to attract attention. It was highly unlikely that they were being observed but it was taking an unnecessary risk to assume they weren't.

'Would you care to come back to my apartment for a cup of coffee, Horst? We have a lot to catch up on.' Said Jakub, who was obviously well-practiced in behaving normally in these circumstances. Duncan accepted graciously and in a few minutes they were in Jakub's kitchen waiting for the kettle to

boil. As he made the coffee Jakub said. *'As far as I could tell we were not observed by any of my neighbours in the apartment block. I have hardly any visitors these days so if we'd been seen they might have become curious. However, if you do accidentally bump into any inquisitive neighbours when you leave, tell them you are my nephew. Obviously avoid going into any unnecessary details but if for any reason you feel obliged to go into any details, tell them your name - Horst Muller - and that you live in Hamburg but you just happened to be visiting Hannover on business. OK?'* Duncan nodded agreement and over coffee and gave Jakub the details that he and Ruth had chosen for the kennkarte. Jakub carefully wrote them down and then took Duncan through to his bedroom where he had already set up his camera and a backcloth for the photograph. As he fussed with the lighting and the camera settings he said, *'when you have your kennkarte, what do you intend to do?'*

'We haven't decided yet Jakub.' He replied, not wishing to get into a discussion about the alternatives. He also thought that even if they had a plan it was probably better that Jakub remained in ignorance of it. For now all possible plans depended on him having a set of identity papers. When his photograph had been taken Duncan enquired cautiously about how long it would take before the identity papers were ready. *'No more than a couple of days.'* Jakub replied. *'Perhaps it would be best if Ruth and her mother met me again in the park next Saturday morning and I can give it to them?'*

'Perfect,' Replied Duncan. *'I'll better get going now. I can't thank you enough for this. At least with this I'll have a better chance of staying out of a prisoner of war camp.'*

They shook hands and after Jakub had checked that the coast was clear Duncan slipped out of the apartment and mingled with the afternoon shoppers who were going about their business. He caught the bus and settled down for the journey across town through the heavy afternoon traffic. Now they really could make plans for the future and he began to dream of escaping to Switzerland with Ruth as they had discussed and maybe living there until the war ended. But there would be no easy way out for him, the closer he got to freedom the more difficult would be his choice between the two women he loved. Here in Germany, it was simple. He was with Ruth and she was his priority. She had taken an extraordinary risk by sheltering him and although falling in love was not an equation, he knew that he had an obligation to look after her and her mother to the best of his ability. Difficult though it was to think about, in reality this meant helping them to escape from Germany and the constant threat which hung over them that they would be identified as Jews and guilty of having tried to conceal this from the authorities. By the time the bus arrived at his stop, he had put out of his mind any thoughts he might have had of trying to escape on his own back to England. After all that she'd done, to do so would be the ultimate betrayal. He descended from the bus and crossed the busy road to avoid having to walk past the café again. The last thing he needed was another close encounter with Hans. Nearing the apartment block he became aware of a minor disturbance near the entrance. Three official looking black vehicles were parked outside and then, to his horror he saw Ruth and her mother were being bundled unceremoniously into one of the waiting cars. Doors were slammed, engines revved and in seconds the small convoy had swept out of sight around the corner and peace returned. It was suddenly as if nothing had ever happened. Stunned and with his mouth agape he stood frozen to the spot. What should he do? One thing was certain, it would be suicide for him to go up to the apartment. Maybe it was Hans the café owner who had tipped off the Gestapo that Ruth had possibly been sheltering the RAF pilot? In which case they would be expecting him to return to the apartment at some point. Surely, if that was the case they would maintain a watch on the apartment and wait until he showed up? There could well be a Gestapo agent in the Schneider apartment waiting for him right now? Maybe it was nothing to do with him and that somehow the Gestapo had discovered that Ruth and her mother were Jews and had been concealing the fact for years? If that was the case it was a just horrible coincidence this this discovery should be made while they were sheltering him. Whatever the reason for their arrest, he desperately hoped it was nothing to do with him. That would mean certain death.

For a while he wandered aimlessly, unable to come to terms with his dramatic new circumstances and certain of only one thing, that it would be a very bad idea to return to the apartment. In any event there was nothing of any importance for him there anyway. His RAF uniform and flying suit had long since been destroyed and the only remaining proof of his real identity was his dog-tag which he continued to wear around his neck. Only a forensic search would indicate that he'd been living in the apartment but amidst his confused thoughts it dawned on him that this was no longer about him. It was Ruth and her mother who had been taken into custody and their prospects were bleak. But although he seemed utterly powerless to help them, deep inside he felt the beginnings of a new and steely resolve. He would not abandon them. Come what may he would do his utmost to secure their freedom but for that to be anything other than a hopeless dream he now had to urgently decide what he should do? Within seconds he realised he had only one alternative, he would have to throw himself on the mercy of Jakub Kaufman and so with a heavy heart he caught the bus back across town and made his way to Jakub's apartment where he tapped lightly on the door. Jakub opened it and without saying a word ushered him quickly inside and then shut the door as quietly as possible.

'What in god's name are you doing?' He said, his voice tense with fear.

'It is very bad news I'm afraid. I arrived back at Ruth's apartment to see them being taken away by the Gestapo. Maybe they had been exposed as Jews who were concealing their identity or maybe they were suspected of harbouring me? I don't know but I had nowhere else to turn other than you - tell me if I must go and I'll leave immediately but please, I beg you, let me stay at least until you've finished my kennkarte and then I promise I'll go away and you'll never see me again.' He said, trying desperately to control the awful fear that was rising inside him. His fate was hanging in the balance. If Jakub told him to leave, he had no idea where to go or what to do. His situation was next to hopeless.

'You give me little choice Duncan,' He replied shaking his head from side to side, *'I'll have to work through the night to finish the kennkarte and tomorrow, the minute you have these papers you become Horst Muller and you will leave. If you get caught and reveal under torture you how you came by a*

kennkarte, I will be executed. Remember that. They will also pressurise you to say who has been sheltering you. Ruth and her mother are already destined for a prison sentence but if you reveal that they helped you they also will be executed. You are carrying a heavy load Duncan but at least with these identity papers and your fluency in German you have a chance. Now I must get on with my work. There's the kitchen, please make some coffee and then it's best you don't interrupt me. You can sleep on the settee over there, if you can manage to sleep....'

Jakub wasn't angry but it was clear that he was deeply worried, so Duncan didn't respond but retired to the kitchen to make the coffee. When it was ready he carried a mug through to where Jakub was engrossed in his work.

'Jakub, one question if I may - do you have any idea where will they be imprisoned?' He said, apologetically.

'First they will be taken to the Gestapo Headquarters in Hannover for interrogation...' Duncan's flesh crawled when he heard the word 'interrogation' which meant only one thing - torture. The thought of Ruth being mistreated in any way was unbearable to him. Jakub interrupted his thoughts and continued, *'...then most probably, they will serve their sentence in Ravensbruck, a women's prison-camp north of Berlin. We hear that this is where almost all female prisoners from this area are sent now, whether they are political prisoners, Jews, common criminals, prostitutes or any other group which the Nazis consider impure.'*

Duncan returned to the sitting room and slumped onto the settee. Twelve hours earlier he had been full of hope and optimism, now he was in the depths of despair and with no idea what to do. However one thing had already crystallised in his heart, no matter how hopeless his prospects he knew he could never abandon Ruth and her mother. Somehow he had to try to free them otherwise he knew he could not go on living. It would be better to die trying.

For Ruth and her mother this was the day they had dreaded since the Nazis passed the Nuremberg Laws in 1935 forbidding Jews from from being German citizens and making illegal all sexual relationships and marriages between Jews and Aryans. An Aryan of so-called 'German blood' was defined as a person with four non-Jewish German grandparents. After these draconian laws were passed it became a serious crime to conceal one's Jewish heritage. Whether one practiced the faith or not was of no consequence so converting to Christianity was no help. When the knock came on the door they knew instantly it was not Duncan returning from his meeting with Jakub. Even if Duncan had come to the apartment door, which was very unlikely as he preferred to use the fire escape, he would have knocked lightly. This was a loud, insistent and determined knock, quickly followed by a shout. *'Open the door immediately or we will break it down!'*

Terrified, Ruth pushed her mother into the kitchen and closed the door before hurrying to the door of the apartment. *'I'm coming.'* She cried, shaking with fear as she unlocked and opened the door. In the corridor outside the apartment stood three Gestapo agents dressed in their regulation long black leather coats. They looked at Ruth for a few seconds, apparently savouring her terror and then the leader spoke. *'You and your mother must come with us. We know you are Jews and we know you have been concealing it for five years. This is*

a serious crime for which you both will be severely punished.'
When he'd finished, one of his henchmen brushed past Ruth
and found her mother cowering in the kitchen. He dragged her
to the doorway where both she and Ruth were bundled out of
the apartment and down the stairs towards the waiting
transport. Despite the commotion all the apartment doors they
passed remained shut. There was little doubt that the
inhabitants of the apartment block knew exactly what was
happening but nobody wanted to become involved. The
Schneiders had been good neighbours for many years but now
they were utterly alone. Powerless to resist they were shoved
into the back of one of the cars and driven off and in those few
minutes their lives had changed for ever. As she collected her
thoughts on the way to Gestapo headquarters she was thankful
that at least no mention had been made of harbouring an enemy
of the Third Reich. That carried an automatic death sentence
and the execution would be carried out after the inevitable
period of interrogation. It seemed obvious to Ruth that finally
the Germans must have initiated a programme of checking birth
and marriage certificates and as a result the thing they had
dreaded for so long had now come to pass. On arrival at
Gestapo HQ they were marched to a spacious cell in the
basement which was already occupied by several mixed group
of Jews all of whom appeared to have been apprehended that
day and apparently all for the same crime of concealment.
Some were slumped against the walls weeping silently while
others prayed. Most couples were clinging tightly together as if
they already knew that they would soon be separated. For a
while all eyes were turned towards the new arrivals and even in
the half-light the fear, pity and sadness in those eyes conveyed

more clearly than words their awful anguish and despair. Although barely a word was spoken the contagious sounds of fear filled the room. Throughout the rest of that day and into the night more and more Jews were flung into the cell. Ruth tried unsuccessfully to console her mother whose sobbing continued for hours until at last exhaustion overcame her and she fell asleep with her head resting in Ruth's lap. For a while she turned over their arrest in her head - it had nothing to do with Duncan but he wouldn't know that. It had been fortunate for them all that the Gestapo had arrived before he'd returned from his meeting with Jakub but when he did arrive back at the empty apartment, what would he think? What would he do? It wouldn't take long for him to realise that they'd been taken by the Gestapo so he might assume they'd been apprehended for sheltering him? He might even turn himself in and claim he had held them hostage? That would be the worst of all scenarios but for now she could do nothing but wait and hope, although there was little to be hopeful about. It was a long sleepless night for Ruth as she cradled her sleeping mother in her arms. At dawn the doors of the cell were opened and the guards began shouting orders. *'Men, on that side of the cell and women on this side - now, immediately!'* With no alternative most submissively obeyed leaving only a few couples clinging to each other. They were brutally beaten by the guards and then dragged to opposite sides of the cell. *'Women, follow me.'* Shouted the officer in charge and they were led from the cell along a long corridor to the rear courtyard of the Gestapo headquarters and loaded onto a line of waiting trucks. *'What will happen to us Ruth?'* Asked her mother with a voice filled with anxiety and fear. *'They will be taking us to prison Mutter but try not to worry, we will be together.'* Replied Ruth as she braced herself for the trials which lay ahead. It was the depths of winter and the temperature inside the open-backed truck was well below freezing. They only had the clothes they were arrested in so all they could do was huddle up to keep warm. Fortunately they were not sitting at the rear of the truck which was open to the elements. The convoy set off and rumbled through the empty city streets in the pre-dawn darkness and shortly afterwards arrived at the station where they were unceremoniously herded into cattle trucks and locked inside. Packed tightly together at least there was a collective warmth for all except those who were against the walls of carriage. *'Where are they taking us?'* Cried a distraught young woman, her voice filled with anguish and fear. *'Does it matter?'* Replied· someone standing nearby. Then another voice said. *'They'll be taking us to Ravensbruck. It's a large prison camp for women somewhere near Berlin.'* Adding as an afterthought. *'I don't think it's only for Jews…'* The train lurched violently as it got underway and the standing occupants of the carriage were crammed tightly against each other until the speed steadied and then they stood for more than five hours until the train pulled into a station on the outskirts of Berlin. Once again they were loaded onto open-backed trucks and three hours later, as darkness was falling, they arrived at the entrance to Ravensbruck concentration camp.

The recently appointed camp commandant of Ravensbruck, Hauptsturmführer Johann Schmidt was finishing his lunch and taking stock before the next influx of Jews which were scheduled to arrive just before dark that day. Since he'd arrived he had changed little, his plan being to spend these first few weeks observing and taking notes before drawing up and launching his own regime. There were clear SS guidelines on how concentration camps were to be run but within these rules he had a lot of flexibility to run the prison as he saw fit. During his time in occupied Paris he had made his name by developing a systematic approach to the identification of Jews and as a result of that work he'd been appointed camp commandant of Ravensbruck by Heinrich Himmler, Reichsführer of the Schutzstaffel, who had overall responsibility for all concentration camps in Germany and the occupied territories. Himmler had the ear of the Führer and was one of the most powerful men in Nazi Germany. Johann's colleagues joked that as his blue-eyed-boy he was destined for the very highest echelons of the SS. His work in Paris had been on the staff of the commander of the SS in Paris and it had separated him from the more brutal aspects of the SS. This appointment at Ravensbruck was Johann's first operational role and any progression though the ranks from here would depend on how he handled this camp. In many ways he was fortunate to have been assigned Ravensbruck which was widely understood to be one of Himmler's favourite camps being located in rich forested countryside close enough to drive there and back from Berlin in a day. Furthermore, it was rumoured to be close to one of Himmler's lifelong associates whom he enjoyed visiting. Consequently the camp and was assured of regular visits from the SS leader and so he was preparing himself accordingly, imagining being asked directly by Himmler, '*What makes you think you are in control of this camp Hauptsturmführer Schmidt?*'

He'd already rehearsed his reply, *'I'm glad you asked me this sir, I have given the matter a lot of thought and if you have a few minutes to spare I will take you through the camp's management system which ensures the efficient running of the prison and of course operates within the strict SS guidelines.'* He'd decided that a little modesty wouldn't hurt so he thought he should suggest that Himmler's input would be hugely valued. Although he'd only been at the camp for a short while he had already concluded that there was plenty of room to improve how it was run and maybe to do so with less blatant brutality. He dreamt briefly that his as yet undeveloped Camp Management System might be adopted across all concentration camps and if that happened it would certainly lead to promotion beyond the camp Commandant level and perhaps even onto Himmler's personal staff. Aware that he was getting ahead of himself he shut off the dream for now and concentrated ensuring his uniform was immaculate, his jackboots perfectly polished and his SS Cap sitting at precisely the correct angle. He needed to look the part and glancing at himself in the mirror he was impressed. He braced himself for the shipment of the Jews from Hannover and when his adjutant informed him that the prisoners were ready for his inspection he strode out into the garden of his lodge and through the gates into the prison, saluting the guards as he passed.

The prisoners were lined up in two widely spaced rows and it was immediately obvious that they'd been standing there for quite some time because almost all were shivering violently. Strategically placed around the parade ground were guards holding back vicious looking Alsatian dogs which snarled and barked at the two shivering ranks of defenceless women. It was all part of the terror and as he walked slowly down the front rank of prisoners he knew he was a key player in that terror. Jews were sub-human and he was part of the elite. They would fear him just by his presence but aside from the fear he hoped there might also be an element of respect, sadly however, he knew it was only fear they felt. This didn't worry him unduly and he felt only pride that his very presence had them quaking in their shoes. Was it really necessary for the frequent acts of extreme violence which were meted out at random by the SS guards and the prisoner Kapos? Every SS Officer knew that terror was an important weapon which needed to be used by the SS in order to subjugate the prisoners but it seemed to him that when it was used indiscriminately it was wasted, like firing loose rounds of ammunition into the sky. However, he had to be careful not to create the impression that he was 'soft'. He wanted to be feared and respected rather than feared and despised. It gave him a feeling of satisfaction to know that the Jews in front of him had been uncovered by the process he'd developed in Paris and for which he'd been given a highly-prized SS-Ehrenring¹ which he wore on the third finger of his left hand. Subconsciously he rubbed it with his left thumb and it reminded him that he was special, it also reminded him that he had to uphold the ethos of the SS throughout the prisoner induction process despite feeling that it was unnecessarily humiliating. Darkness had fallen by the time he started to inspect the second row and the parade ground was now illuminated by harsh spotlights which cast black shadows in multiple directions from each of the exhausted and terrified women standing in the line. He took his time, looking directly into the eyes of each woman, trying to determine what they were thinking. Almost without exception he sensed fear but most women kept their heads bowed and chose not to make eye contact. The last thing any of them wanted to do was to be marked out as a trouble-maker and the way a prisoner looked at the Kommandant could easily be misinterpreted. He was halfway down the line when he came to Ruth and her mother. Both were shivering uncontrollably but as he drew level with Ruth she looked up and in a flash she recognised him as the courteous SS Officer she and her mother had met in the park all those months ago. His heart skipped a beat when he simultaneously recognised her and felt that tug which he'd first experienced when they'd first met. She was breathtakingly beautiful and fighting to suppress any response that might have been noticed by his accompanying guards he quickly moved on to her mother who was standing alongside Ruth. She looked old and very frail but she looked him straight in the eye, not a defiant look but a look which made him feel uncomfortable without being able to determine exactly why. Ruth watched in horror, fearing that her mother would make a remark but the moment passed and Hauptsturmführer Schmidt moved on leaving Ruth wondering if indeed the Kommandant had recognised her and what it might mean if he had. At the end of the inspection he mounted a platform in front of the parade and made a short speech.

'Welcome to Ravensbruck where you will serve out your sentences. In this camp obedience is the most important thing for you to remember. It is everything. You will do precisely what you are told when you are told and in the way you've been told. If you don't you will be punished and if you disobey orders repeatedly you will be punished severely. Tomorrow *your Kapo will explain the hut rules but now you will be shaved and given your camp clothes and blankets. Morning parade is at 6am. Make sure you do not keep me waiting.'* He then nodded to his deputy and walked back to his lodge, still trying to control his emotions at seeing Ruth again. In the intervening months in Paris he had often thought of her, revisiting the fond memories of their encounter in the park in Hannover. Meeting her again under these circumstances was incredibly confusing for him. Not only was she a Jew but the fact that she was in this camp with her mother was almost certainly down to him. It would have been his research methodology which exposed them. Also, he was fully aware that any form of relationship between an SS Officer and a Jew was illegal and subject to the most severe punishment. But despite this he still felt attracted to her and even after the trauma of the past couple of days her stunning beauty still shone through. He went to bed that night troubled by the thought of her humiliation in the process he had deliberately chosen not to watch but which was supervised by all of his SS staff. One after another the women had their heads shaved and then, after being stripped naked, all of their body hair was removed. The final part of the process was a choking de-lousing spray which stung their eyes and covered them in white dust. Only then were they given their blue and white striped prison clothes and taken to the newly constructed hut which was to house them for the duration of their sentence. It was a procedure designed to strip them of their dignity and in this regard without exception it was successful.

Johann did not sleep well that night. In Paris he had been remote from the Jews he was helping to track down whereas here at Ravensbruck he was in direct contact with them. He had grown up with the belief that the Jews were a sub-human species who were responsible for all the financial woes that Germany had gone through since the end of the Great War. As a pure-blooded Aryan he firmly believed he was a member of the master race, destined to be part of the ruling elite in Germany in a Reich that would last for a thousand years. Since he'd joined the SS he had been trained to be completely dispassionate, holding loyalty only to Himmler and the Führer. The SS were above the law and he could never be tried in a civil court, even executing a Jew in cold blood was not considered a crime by the SS. To them the Jews were vermin and they needed to be wiped off the face of the earth. From his early days in the Hitler Youth movement his Christian beliefs had been supplanted by a new set of rules. None of this was he calling into question however a tiny worm was turning in his head. Was being a Jew just an unfortunate accident of birth and a label which thereafter was attached to an otherwise genetically identical species, or was a Jew genuinely sub-human and inferior? He'd been brought up to believe the latter but the foundations of this belief no longer seemed quite so secure. He couldn't stop thinking about Ruth who was the first and only Jew he had ever encountered on a personal level. When they'd first met in that park in Hannover and before he knew she was a Jew, he could easily have fallen in love with her. If she'd kept the fact she was Jewish a secret and they had fallen in love, got married and had a family, would he have ever discovered her secret? He found it very difficult to believe that she was in any way evil and sub-human, indeed he was finding it difficult to think she was any different from him. He smiled an ironic smile to himself as the symmetry of the situation occurred to him, Ruth probably thought that all SS Officers were evil and sub-human. Were there really any absolute truths when it came to matters of the heart, or was it all simply a matter of perspective? By morning he had made up his mind to run a personal experiment. He would take Ruth into his lodge as a house maid and see if over time she would reveal the evil and sub-human characteristics he'd been brought up to believe defined all Jews.

Back in Jakub's apartment in Hannover, Duncan woke up with a start. For a minute he didn't know where he was and then it all came flooding back to him. The terrible sight of Ruth and her mother being taken away by the Gestapo would haunt him until the day he died. He could see from the crack under his door that there was still a light on in Jakub's room where he had obviously been working through the night on his kennkarte. Today he would have to leave the safety of the apartment and make his way across Germany to Ravensbruck. He had no idea what he would do when he got there or even if he would get there but at least he'd chosen a moment of courage rather than a lifetime of guilt. It was mid-morning before Jakub emerged from his room holding the forged kennkarte on which he'd been working non-stop for the previous eighteen hours.

'Here it is Horst Muller. You are no longer Duncan Bucanan. You are a motor mechanic from Hamburg and the rest of your personal details are in the Kennkarte. Now you must leave immediately. I will make sure the coast is clear because I don't want anyone to see you leaving my apartment. This is the first forging I have done in years but back then I

suspected the Gestapo had got wind of my activities - that was why I stopped doing it. This was for Helena. When we met again I had hoped that maybe we could have had a future together but now I know this can never happen. Helena is old and will not be fit enough to work in a labour camp so I fear for her life. The SS consider Jews to be sub-human and if we're too old to work, then...' His voice tailed off into a deep sigh full of sadness. *'And here is some money.'* He added, passing Duncan an envelope stuffed with notes, *'you will need it.'*

'I know you didn't have to help me Jakub and I know the risk you have taken, all I can do is to thank you from the bottom of my heart and promise you that I will never betray you. Of course you will say that nobody knows how they will behave under torture - and you'd be right - but if I am taken, I will destroy - even eat - this identity card and hope that my RAF dog-tag will save me from execution.' Said Duncan as he pocketed his new identity card and the envelope full of money and headed for the door of the apartment.

'Before you go Horst, let's have a coffee together and we can part as friends.' Replied Jakub. *'Please don't worry about me, the Gestapo will never take me alive. I have not much to live for these days anyway.'*

Jakub checked to make sure that the corridor was empty and the two men then shook hands and parted company. He was out in the street before he realised he'd not actually told Jakub that he planned to go to Ravensbruck with the crazy idea of trying to rescue Ruth. In his heart he'd already given up on the idea of also rescuing her mother. It was never a realistic possibility but after Jakub's ominous comment, he suspected that Ruth's mother would probably be executed within days, if not hours, of their arrival at the camp. Once outside the apartment block he walked briskly for nearly an hour to get to the train station where he bought a ticket to Berlin. As he stepped onto the train he thought how the Gestapo would be much more likely to check on trains leaving Berlin rather than those going towards the capital. He was Daniel, heading straight into the lion's den. Shortly after leaving Hannover station there was a routine identity check. The plain-clothes officer glanced briefly at his kennkarte and then at him before handing it back with a grunt. *'You're a long way from Hamburg.'* He said, not waiting for a response before moving further up the carriage to continue his checking. As the train rattled east through Saxony towards Berlin, Duncan had plenty of time to mull over his 'moment of courage' and the more he thought about it the more it seemed like a suicide mission. It was impossible to make a detailed plan but there was always hope, however slim, that a way forward might emerge the closer he got to his destination. He characterised it like aiming for the dartboard not the bullseye. For now he would take one step at a time and his immediate objective was to get to the village of Ravensbruck, find somewhere to stay and then learn as much as possible about the camp. Only then could he start planning a rescue mission. Even saying 'rescue mission' to himself seemed outrageous but despite the terrible odds against succeeding the longer he sat with his decision the more comfortable it felt. His identity papers were checked again on the train out of Berlin but as with the previous inspection it was purely perfunctory. Jakub was obviously a master forger and he marvelled once again at his good fortune to meet him. From time to time he worried that Ruth's abduction by the Gestapo might in some way endanger

Jakub but the more he thought about it the less likely it seemed. However the only way he could establish that beyond doubt would be to discover that Ruth was alive in the camp. If the Gestapo had suspected her of shielding a British pilot she'd be either dead now or worse, still under interrogation in Gestapo HQ in Hannover. So his first step on arriving in the village of Ravensbruck would be somehow find out if she was a prisoner in the camp.

It was getting dark when he stepped down from the train in Ravensbruck. After a few minutes walk he came to a lively looking bar in the centre of the village which was obviously the main gathering point for the locals. He was faced with an immediate choice, did he go in and hide in the crowded bar or should he be more discreet and find somewhere quieter? With his new found confidence in the identity papers he chose the former and moving past the crowded tables he made his way to the bar where he ordered a beer and some food. *'Come far?'* Queried the barman, more out of habit and interest.

'Just come up from Berlin. I'm on my way north to Hamburg but as I've got a few days in hand I thought I'd spend them here - it seems like a nice place.' He replied noting that his appearance in the bar seemed to have gone virtually unnoticed.

'We like it. Nice to have the lake nearby.' The barman said as he was pulling the beer. *'If you're looking for somewhere to stay while you're here, we've got a room upstairs - if you want?'*

Feeling that his luck had taken a turn for the better, he responded. *'Sounds ideal. Not sure how long I'll stay but two or three nights at least - would that be OK?'*

'Sure.' He said. 'When you've finished your food I'll show you the room. I see you travel light,' He added, noting that his customer only carried a small shoulder bag.

Duncan carried his beer and sandwich to a deserted table in the corner and once again blessed the day he had learnt German. It was still important for him not engage in a complicated conversation with anyone but as far as day-to-day exchanges were concerned, his grammar and accent were perfect. He went to bed that night and slept like a log until the first rays of the dawn beamed through a crack in the blackout curtains. He'd already decided on his story - he was a keen fisherman and he thought he'd check out the lake, if the prospects looked good then he might invest in some fishing tackle and test his luck. With that as his cover he ought to be able to get a first sight of the camp which lay on the opposite side of the Schwedtsee from the village. The owner of the bar served him a simple breakfast and coffee and made an innocent enquiry about what he did for a living. 'I'm a motor mechanic,' He said 'I fix cars.'

In Ravensbruck after the humiliation of being shaved in public Ruth couldn't wait to get to the hut where she was allocated a bunk and advised by the stern Kapo to get some sleep because rappel was at 5:30am and anybody who was late would be punished. But she couldn't sleep. Although her mother had been spared the shaving process she had been taken away with the other older women to be 'looked after' and in her heart Ruth knew what this meant. As they were dragged apart, her mother squeezed her hand tightly and said. 'I'm not afraid, Ruth. You must survive this horror and live.' Then she was gone. This was a labour camp and anyone who couldn't work was surplus to requirements and both Ruth and her mother knew that they would never see each other again.

The following morning at 5am Ruth was rudely awakened by the Kapo of the Jewish hut and along with the rest of the hut occupants was bundled outside into the freezing cold and lined up on the parade ground with the rest of the camp inmates. It was a bitterly cold and windless morning with the eastern sky glowing pink and stars twinkling brightly in the frosty air. They stood in their lines for an hour waiting for the count to commence as here and there prisoners moaned and shuffled their feet to try to stay warm. Any movement was disallowed so when an inmate was spotted moving they were immediately beaten across the back by roving Kapos who shouted. *'There must be no movement, absolutely none and until everything is completely motionless the count will not start.'* Eventually, when it did commence another hour had passed before it was completed to the satisfaction of the senior Kapo. Then, racked with cold they were marched back to the relative warmth of the hut where the next hour was taken up with a detailed lesson on the hut rules starting with how to fold the blanket and finishing with a grizzly description of what punishments awaited the slightest non-compliance. Like most of her fellow inmates Ruth made up her mind to keep as low a profile as possible. She could see that already the hut Kapo had singled out several potential troublemakers who had done nothing but look at her the wrong way. Making eye contact was risky for fear of accidentally communicating the thoughts that were swirling inside her head and she decided to make eye contact with any of the camp hierarchy only if she was specifically ordered to do so. Breakfast consisted solely of weak ersatz coffee which at least was warm. Despite her frozen hands Ruth downed it immediately while others cradled the metal mug in their hands to warm them, she knew that ultimately the coffee would warm her more effectively from inside. Then they were herded outside to start digging over the frozen ground. Women judged to be slackers were viciously beaten to the ground and trying to assist a fellow inmate to her feet resulted in the helper also being beaten to the ground. The brutality was beyond Ruth's comprehension and she worked hard, mainly to keep warm, but by midday she was totally exhausted. The combination of shock, losing her mother and the emotional turmoil of trying to adjust to camp life brought her to the brink of breakdown but that was a path to nowhere other than a beating so she hung on grimly. Back in their apartment in Hannover she had learnt to take life one day at a time, here it was just about surviving the next hour and not thinking beyond that. The weak soup and two potatoes revived her a little but like most of her colleagues she was near collapse when they were taken back to the hut. As they entered they saw one poor woman was left standing in the courtyard. It was punishment for allegedly being a regular slacker. She remained upright and motionless, without food or drink until just before lights out. By the time the Kapo finally shoved her through the door of the hut and she'd fallen to the floor the evening meal of ersatz coffee and a hunk of bread had been finished and tidied away. Nobody dared to lend her a hand so she crawled painfully down past the tiered bunks and climbed slowly into her bed shivering uncontrollably. Already, after only a single day, Ruth could feel the last vestiges of their collective humanity draining away. The system was working.

They had begun the descent towards self-preservation. Soon the only rule would be dog-eat-dog.

The following morning the process was repeated although by then the inmates knew that the sooner they were standing in their lines, the sooner they would get their morning coffee so the count proceeded faster and without any of the previous day's hitches. The camp Kommandant put in a brief appearance to oversee the operation. Ruth tried to avoid looking at him, sticking as best she could to her policy of not making eye contact with any of the camp officers however, having recognised him she couldn't resist glancing up. To her horror she could see that he was looking directly at her. Her head was shaven like all the other thousand or so women and each of them wore identical blue and white striped clothing yet he was looking at her. There was now no doubt in her mind that he had recognised her on the parade when they first arrived at the camp. She lowered her gaze immediately but felt sure that a connection had been made. When she next dared to glance back up at the stage he had gone. The parade was dismissed and they returned to the huts for breakfast where the queue for coffee inched forward slowly and by the time it was Ruth's turn, the coffee was barely lukewarm. She had just turned to go back to her bunk when the Kapo called out her number. *'You - wait in the hut.'* Alarmed at being singled out she waited anxiously until the hut emptied. *'Come with me.'* the Kapo said, giving Ruth no clue what what was in store. They walked across the parade ground and out of the prison compound, through the main camp gates and past a small cluster of buildings which obviously housed the SS Guards. At the rear of this community and set back into the trees was a larger more elegant lodge which Ruth assumed were Kommandant's quarters. He must have ordered her to be brought to him and for reasons she chose not think about. She was led up the steps to the front door which was opened for them by a man in SS uniform, presumably the Kommandant's adjutant who took her down a long corridor to a door with an engraved brass plate which confirmed her suspicions. It simply said 'Kommandant'.

'Come in Ruth.' Said the smartly dressed SS Officer who was sitting behind the desk opposite the door. Carefully choosing not make eye contact she stepped inside the office and stood looking at the floor a few metres from the desk.

'That will be all Klaus.' He said, signalling to his adjutant that he was no longer required.

'But sir…' Responded the adjutant, clearly astonished that the Kommandant was asking to be left alone with a Jewish girl.

'It's OK Klaus. You could perhaps organise for some coffee please.' Said the Kommandant, waiting for the door to close before adding. *'Ruth, you may sit down.'*

Now alone together she looked up and made eye contact as she sat down in front of him. It was impossible to read his face so she remained silent and impassive, being careful not to look either resentful or insolent but without even a hint of a smile.

'You recognise me, don't you? We met a long time ago in a park in Hannover on a beautiful day when you were out for a walk with your mother.' He said in a voice which was neither friendly nor in any way aggressive.

'I remember you….' and then adding after a lengthy pause during which he nodded to signal that she should continue, *'you were very courteous.'* The words left her lips before she had time to think of how they might be received. She'd been in the

camp - his camp - for only two days but during that time her mother had been taken away from her and probably been executed and she had had to endure humiliation beyond any previous experience or even imagination, yet here she was paying him a compliment.

'*Thank you,*' He responded with a faint smile.

Finding his steady gaze disturbing, Ruth dropped her eyes and looked at the empty desk, waiting anxiously for whatever he was planning. She could feel his gaze as if it were physical contact and despite the comfortable warmth of his spacious and well-appointed office, she shivered involuntarily. Before he could continue the door opened and his adjutant came in with a tray containing a pot of what smelt like real coffee, a small jug of milk a sugar bowl and two cups.

'*Thank you Klaus,*' He said. '*That will be all for now.*' as his adjutant clicked his heels and left the room again.

When the door had closed he spoke to Ruth again. '*Ruth, I will come to the point. I need a housemaid and I thought you might be interested? If you want to do this job you will stay here in the servant's wing with the rest of the staff and work under the supervision of my adjutant, who you have just met. What do you say?*'

Guarding her natural instinct to immediately clutch at what seemed to be a gift from heaven, she looked steadily at him for a couple of seconds before replying. '*Thank you Herr Kommandant, I am grateful and I will do my best to justify your decision to offer this job to me. When do you want me to start?*' She said trying desperately to remain calm while her heart thumping so loudly she felt certain he could hear it.

'You will start now. I probably don't need to tell you that any misdemeanours of any description or complaints from my staff and you will be returned immediately to your hut.' He said politely and not waiting for a response he lent forward and rang the bell on his desk. Within seconds the door to the office opened and his adjutant entered. *'Klaus, this prisoner is to be my housemaid. Please take her to the servants' quarters and see that she has a shower and some more appropriate clothes. Her name is Ruth.'*

Back in the village of Ravensbruck, Duncan was sitting at the bar having a beer before dinner having spent the day scouting around the lake. It had been a totally wasted day. After making his way down to a small park on the western shore of the lake he could see that it was ringed with dense forest and the only manmade object that was visible was a tall chimney which stood above the trees on the far side of the lake. He assumed that it was part of the concentration camp but beyond that he had gained no knowledge about the camp. He sipped his beer and contemplated his dilemma. He was less than a mile as the crow flies from the camp which he assumed housed Ruth and her mother and he had absolutely no idea what to do next. Noticing his faraway gaze the barman said. *'A penny for your thoughts?'*

'Sorry, I was miles away, dreaming of being somewhere by a beach in the sun,' He lied, wondering how he could shift the conversation to the concentration camp without arousing suspicion.

'Had any more thoughts about fishing?' Continued the barman, making conversation.

'Not made up my mind yet. I spent some time down at the edge of the lake today but it seemed too shallow and it didn't seem easy to get to the lakeside at many other spots around the shore.' Then almost before he realised he was saying it, he asked. *'I saw a large chimney at the opposite side of the lake, is that a factory or something?'*

The barman continued polishing a beer glass and casually said. *'Oh no. That's the women's prison camp, it was opened back in 1938 and it's been growing ever since, at least that's what I've heard. In the early days it provided a lot of employment for the locals but not anymore unfortunately. Rumour has it that there is now a small mens' camp next to the main camp and they're using the prisoners to do the construction - mainly building huts to accommodate more prisoners. I think all the drains, electricity etcetera were installed at the outset so the work that's required now isn't particularly skilled. Makes sense, I suppose. Better having the prisoners doing something useful than breaking rocks or whatever is defined as hard labour these days.'*

At that point a couple of locals came into the bar and ordered drinks, bringing the barman's conversation with Duncan to an end, which was timely because something the barman had just said planted a seed of an idea in his head. The male convicts who were doing construction work in the women's prison might have limited contact with the female inmates. Naturally the guards would be trying to minimise any communications with the inmates but it was a possibility. If he was sent to prison then maybe, just maybe he could get himself onto a construction team. Then it might be possible to establish conclusively whether Ruth and her mother actually were in the camp after which would come the especially tricky part of trying to come up with an escape plan. However, the first part of the plan was straightforward, becoming a convict would not be difficult, all he would have to do would be to pretend to be drunk and then start mocking the Führer. Alternatively he could put a brick through a store window and get caught stealing. He finished his beer and ordered dinner which he ate as usual on his own in a quiet corner of the bar while all the time thinking about this rather drastic plan. It was certainly a daring idea but the more he thought about it the less attractive it became. He didn't sleep much that night, his thought processes constantly ending up in dead end after dead end. Most of the following day he spent sitting on a bench looking across the lake towards the treelined shore which concealed the concentration camp. He was hoping for inspiration but none came. The next day and the day after that went much the same way, it was a very long shot of a plan - get arrested for an offence with a short custodial sentence in the men's prison adjacent to Ravensbruck concentration camp. It was virtually hopeless but he reluctantly decided that having made the tough decision of preferring to die trying, rather than living with the guilt of not trying, unless an alternative presented itself overnight, the following day he would try to engineer a prison sentence. Burglary was a straightforward criminal offence and it seemed to be a better bet than the political crime of disparaging Hitler. He went to bed that night feeling like a condemned man.

Less than a mile away across the lake Ruth had spent her first two days learning the ropes. The rest of the Kommandant's staff were extremely wary of her because in spite of being a Jew it was apparent she was getting special treatment. So they were careful not to follow their instincts and treat her as they would treat all Jews - with disdain. One of her duties was to take the Kommandant his midday meal on a tray. Although she was now being well fed compared to her old inmates in the Jewish hut, his lunch was a feast and it always included a pichet of French wine. Habitually he ate alone, instinctively understanding that it was a mistake for the commanding officer to be too close to any of his subordinates. She carefully placed the tray on his desk and turned to leave when he said *'Ruth, I would like to talk with you for a while. Please stay.'*

'Of course, Herr Kommandant.' She said as she sat down in the chair he gestured towards, noting that he had said he wanted to talk 'with her', as distinct from 'to her' and more unusually, he had said 'please' rather than simply ordering her to stay.

'I want to ask you a question, a difficult question, and I would like you to answer it truthfully and not give me the answer which you think I want to hear. You have my word that no matter how you answer you will not be punished and your job here will still be secure. Do you understand?' He was choosing his words with great care and he spoke slowly as though he'd had doubts about whether to ask the question or not.

Beginning to realise that he might be feeling more uncomfortable than she was, she replied quietly. *'I understand. Thank you. I will try to answer you as honestly as I can.'*

He breathed deeply and lent forward with his hands clasped together on the desk and then he posed the question that had been on his mind since the minute he had spotted her in the line-up of new prisoners only a few days ago. *'Do you hate me Ruth?'* He said intently as he looked directly into her eyes.

Ruth's mind raced. Whilst she believed his sincerity it was clear to her that despite his protests to the contrary, if her answer upset him then her future as a housemaid to the Kommandant would inevitably be less secure. Should she ignore what he'd said about being totally honest and try and please him with her answer? What would a pleasing answer be? Was this the first move in a perilous relationship he might be embarking on, risking his career by breaking the most important of all SS taboos, no sexual relations with Jewish women? Finally she realised that if she tried to be clever, he was smart enough to spot it and so she replied with what was in her heart. *'Herr Kommandant, I hardly know you. How could I hate you without having seen you do something that merited hatred?'* He continued to look at her impassively, nodding to encourage her to continue. So,taking a deep breath she walked to the edge of the precipice and said in a voice much calmer than she felt. *'Please do not think me bold to ask you the same question, do you hate me?'* For a while she felt she would tumble over the edge and then he smiled at her, tapped his desk and stood up. Walking with his hands clasped behind his back he went over to the window and looked out. *'You see this is what I am trying to understand. Since I was a boy I was taught that all Jews were evil and sub-human yet in all my life you are the only Jew I have ever actually talked with. First we met in the park in Hannover but then I didn't know you were Jewish. Now you are here as my prisoner, guilty of concealment, facing an indefinite confinement and the circumstances of this meeting could hardly be more different and now I know you are a Jew every instinct I have is to despise you. How can this be? The circumstances have changed but have you changed because I now know you are a Jew? What if we had had a relationship in Hannover and all the time we were together the fact that you were a Jew remained a secret, why should the relationship change because of a label that you are a Jew? Or maybe there something I would have seen about you over time that would have led me to discover that you were, as I have been brought up to believe, evil and sub-human?'* He turned to look at Ruth again and shrugged his shoulders. Then he asked again. *'Do you hate me Ruth?'*

'I am not a practicing Jew, in fact I am an atheist. So in my case you are right to call being a Jew a label for that is all it is, an accident of birth. However, because I have this label I have been brought up to fear the SS, I suppose you could say I've been taught to hate the SS for what they have done to thousands of innocent German Jews like me. But if you were not wearing that uniform I would have have no reason to hate you, yet like you I am forced challenge the feelings that have been drilled into me. You are the first SS Officer I have ever talked with, so there is a kind of symmetry here but only if we are both without the labels, me the Jew and you the SS Officer. But with these labels attached to us there is no symmetry other than perhaps the symmetry of mutual hatred.' She looked away from him, not realising that she was wringing her hands slowly.

'Is something wrong?' He said, noticing she had become ill-at-ease.

'Herr Kommandant, I am very scared that I may have said too much. If I have offended you please forgive me. Honesty can be a painful master.'

He could see the fear in her dark brown eyes and he was deeply moved by her plight and her vulnerability. He had colleagues who would have thought nothing of pressing a pistol to her temple and pulling the trigger. *'Please don't be frightened.'* He said, *'I meant what I said. This conversation will stay between you and me. I won't discuss it with anyone and I am asking you to do likewise.'* She nodded and stopped wringing her hands as he continued *'please don't worry. I asked you to be honest and you have been. You've given me lots to think about. I have a week's leave starting tomorrow so I will be away, my father died and I am driving down to our family home in Konstanz in the far south of Germany. It is a long way and I will spend most of the time travelling but when I am away you will serve my deputy as you have served me, OK?'*

Ruth nodded in agreement, suppressing the urge to ask him what had happened to her mother. She knew that nothing he could say or do would bring her back, so she said nothing and quietly wondered if when he was telling her about his father's death he had sensed the unasked question which had been on the tip of her tongue. *'What did you do with my mother?'* She left him to eat his lunch in private and returned to the kitchen to help with the cleaning and the preparations for dinner. It had been an extraordinary discussion with the Kommandant and the length of time she'd spent alone with him in his office drew some comments.

'What took you so long, Ruth? What were you talking about?' Said one of her prison colleagues wearing the purple triangle of the Jehovah's Witnesses who had been imprisoned for refusing to perform military service, join Nazi organisations

or give allegiance to the Hitler regime. The camp guards relished the task of trying to break the resolve of the Jehovah's Witnesses, subjecting their hut leaders to months of torture, solitary confinement and near starvation in the camp's notorious Bunker. But despite this they had earned the reputation for being the most honest and best behaved hut in Ravensbruck. Ruth, who wore the yellow triangle of the Jews, envied the strength of her colleague's faith but was amazed at what she understood to be the core of that faith, believing that only one hundred and forty-four thousand select believers would go to heaven and the rest of the followers who obey God would live forever in an Earthly paradise. Like most of the inmates in Ravensbruck, since her arrival she'd had time to think about religion and whether she believed in an afterlife and heaven and although the thought was tempting and she could see how the Jehovah's Witnesses were sustained by their faith, her atheism only became stronger. Many of her close neighbours in the hut could be heard praying for the strength to endure the terrible privations they were suffering. To her it seemed strange that these same people didn't hold the deity from whom they were seeking help, accountable for their plight in the first place. The SS tried without success to get Jehovah's Witnesses to abandon their faith, yet for the Jews it was different. Many of the Jews in her hut had never practiced their faith, but because of the accident of birth they were henceforth labelled as Jews and no amount of renouncing their faith made any difference. Being Jewish was considered by the Nazis as more of a culture rather than a religion. The Jews were a race apart.

'He was asking me what was for dinner.' She lied.

Johann finished his lunch and then went to his bedroom to finalise his packing for the long drive down to the south of Germany the following day. He had planned an early start and when he'd finished packing his suitcase, he carried it down to the garage and put it in the car along with the spare fuel which he would need for the long drive. Better to make sure he had enough petrol to get to Konstanz without having to fill up en route, fuel was in short supply throughout Germany and although as a senior SS Officer he should have little difficulty in obtaining it in any of the towns he would pass through he thought it better to set off with a full tank and enough extra petrol to get him to his destination. It had been a while since he'd used his small staff car, an Opel Kadett and on a whim he decided he ought to run the engine for a while to see that everything was working properly. Despite being unused for several weeks the car obligingly started almost immediately but after only a few minutes running the engine started to overheat alarmingly. Frustrated and angry he turned off the engine and sat fuming in the car as he tried to decide what to do, finally concluding that he'd give his adjutant the problem.

'I'll get onto it straightaway, Herr Kommondant.' He said enthusiastically and happy to be entrusted with this important task. He was a regular in the village bar and short of alternative ideas he called the barman to ask for help. He introduced himself on the phone and then having explained the problem, finished off by saying, *'...so you see, somehow I need to get the car fixed for the Kommandant or else I will be in trouble. Can you help?'*

'Leave it with me and I will call you back shortly,' He replied as the germ of an idea occurred to him.

As on previous evenings, Duncan appeared in the bar and ordered his usual beer. He'd not had a good day, most of which had once again been spent by the lakeside looking across at the line of trees which hid the camp on the far shore. Despite racking his brain he kept coming back to the idea of breaking the law and getting sent to the men's camp to serve out his sentence. Once inside he hoped he could get selected for the work detail which was building huts in the women's prison and after that he'd just have to see how the landscape unfolded. Although this plan seemed hopeless, if it enabled him to see Ruth and let her know he was doing everything possible to be with her, he would have achieved a lot. More than anything he wanted her to know that he was nearby, trying to help in whatever way he could. Every time he thought of her it renewed his determination to die trying to save her rather than live with the guilt of abandoning her and after all, she had already risked her life for him. He carried his beer to the usual table in the corner and sat down. It was early and the bar was still quiet so the barman was taking the opportunity to wipe over the tables, empty ashtrays and collect the empty glasses. When he finished he walked over to Duncan's table and said. *'Hi Horst, I don't want to interrupt your thinking but have you got a minute?'*

'Of course.' He replied, gesturing to a seat opposite him across the table. *'Please join me.'*

The barman took a seat and said. *'I remember you told me you were a motor mechanic, right? Well I've just had a call from the camp across the lake and the Kommandant's car is overheating and apparently he needs it for a long journey tomorrow. If you think you might be able to fix it and you want the work I'll give them a call.'*

Struggling to control his racing pulse Duncan replied as casually as he could,. *'Sure, I'd welcome the opportunity to earn some money and I've still got a day to spare so, tell them I'm happy to help if I can.'*

'Ok,' Said the barman and without further comment went off to telephone the camp. Five minutes later he returned. *'I've told them that you're a motorcar mechanic and you're willing to help. The Kommandant wants to be off early tomorrow morning so you've got about twelve hours to fix whatever the problem is. I was going to ask you about timing but they were very insistent and a car is on the way here now - They'll be here in a few minutes. They want you to work overnight if necessary and they'll happily pay you at twice your normal daily rate - that's provided you can fix it, of course. One thing, if you've not worked with the SS before be very careful. Keep your opinions to yourself.'*

Duncan just had time to collect his coat before he heard the sound of a car stopping outside the bar. The door swung open and an SS officer strode into the near empty room. *'I am here to collect the motor mechanic, Horst Muller.'* Duncan raised his hand to acknowledge the officer and said. *'I'm Horst Muller,'* and then followed the officer out to the waiting Mercedes, the engine of which was still running. Duncan was shown into the rear seat of the car and the officer got in beside him and ordered. *'OK, back to the camp as fast as you can.'* As they sped away from the town around the north side of the lake Duncan was tempted to ask why the Kommandant had not decided to take the car they were in on his long trip but he took the barman's advice and kept silent. The car they were in was probably not for private use. It was a large three axle convertible Mercedes which would be used to collect visiting dignitaries from the station. Ravensbruck wasn't far from Berlin and would have had more than its fair share of visits from the top brass. A few minutes later they pulled up outside a substantial lodge which was obviously the living quarters for the camp Kommandant. Duncan was taken straight to the garage where he was introduced to Hauptsturmführer Schmidt.

'Hauptsturmführer, this is Horst Muller, a motor mechanic from Hamburg who just happened to be staying in the village. He is aware of your deadline and has agreed to work continuously on the car until it is fixed.' The Kommandant shook Duncan's hand, dismissed his adjutant and said. *'Horst, thank you. I have to leave first thing in the morning to get to my father's funeral and it is too late to make any alternative arrangement. It is a long drive to Konstanz and I need to be sure the car can make it.'* He then continued to explain the overheating issue and for a while the two men discussed the likely causes. It was Duncan's first encounter with the Schutzstaffel and he was relieved to find that the Kommandant was not the fearsome stereotype SS Officer that he'd been expecting. Although dressed in his uniform, both his tunic and shirt were open and despite his obvious worry about the car, he seemed quite relaxed. *'You should be able to find all the tools you need in the garage. If you need any help my adjutant is available. I'll also come back and see how you are getting on from time to time. Would you perhaps like some coffee and a sandwich?'*

'That would be great, Herr Schmidt, also would it be possible to borrow a boiler suit to protect my clothes?' He replied.

'But of course, my adjutant will get one for you immediately. Now I will let you get on with the job. Good luck!' The Kommandant nodded courteously and left the garage. A few minutes later the adjutant returned with an SS emblazoned boiler suit and then Duncan found himself alone with the car, barely able to believe his good fortune. Although as yet he had no plan of how to pursue his own objective, here he was in Ravensbruck as an invitee of the camp Kommandant, doing him a massive favour which, assuming he could fix the car, would leave the Kommandant indebted to him. He might even offer him a job! It took an effort to force himself back to the here and now and concentrate on the problem with the engine. Fixing the car was his number one priority and he pushed his other agenda to the back of his mind. A half an hour into the job and he was pretty sure that the problem was fixable but would take most of the night as it involved removing the cylinder head to replace the gasket. He summoned the adjutant and dispatched him to find a replacement gasket if possible, or failing that find some gasket material with which he could repair the damaged one. Nothing could have prepared him for what happened next. He had his head buried in the engine when the door opened behind him and a voice said. 'Your coffee and sandwich, sir.'

Without looking up from his work he pointed to a table on the other side of the car and said. 'Ah, thank you, I could do with some coffee. Put it over there please.'

She carried the tray of food around the back of the car, placed it on the table and then turning to face him said. *'Will that be all sir?'*

Glancing over the top of the car's engine their eyes met and the world stood still. There was a stunned silence as they both realised that to release their emotions and drop their guard in any way would place them in mortal danger, so thinking fast he said. *'Thank you.... I'm sorry, I don't know your name. My name is Horst Muller and as you can see I'm trying to fix the Kommandant's car so he can get away first thing tomorrow morning.'* He widened his eyes as he spoke, desperately trying to communicate the importance of hiding the fact that they knew each other. Even though they were alone, for all they knew the adjutant or even the Kommandant might burst into the garage to check on progress at any minute.

'My name is Ruth,' She said, embracing him with her eyes.

'Then Ruth, perhaps you could bring me some more coffee in a couple of hours time - around 2am - if that would be possible?' He asked, still desperately trying to control his emotions and attempting to communicate only with his eyes.

'Of course, Herr Muller.' She replied, her heart racing wildly as she reeled from the shock of meeting the man she loved when she'd lost hope of ever seeing him again. Since her arrest the only thing other than their plight that she'd thought about had been Duncan. But in all those thoughts never once did she allow herself to hope that she would ever see him again. Now he was here and it could have been no accident. He must be here to try and rescue her!

As he worked on the engine, an idea was beginning to form in Duncan's head. It seemed too good to be true that the

Kommandant was intending to drive all the way south to Konstanz which lay on the German/Swiss border. Superficially it seemed outrageous but what if he and Ruth could somehow kidnap the Kommandant and travel with him? Being in an SS emblazoned car with a senior SS Officer at the wheel would practically guarantee they would not get challenged. How they would get across the border into Switzerland was another matter but there would be plenty of time to think about that on the twelve hour drive south. Also, there was little point in worrying about crossing the border when they had yet to successfully escape from the camp.

By the time he'd arranged for the resupply of coffee he'd worked out the bones of a plan which he needed to communicate to Ruth as accurately and in as few words as possible. It depended on his recent good fortune continuing for at least another two throws of the dice. Hopefully in the morning by the time the Kommandant was ready to leave, there would be an occasion when Duncan, Ruth and the Kommandant were alone in the garage together. He would overpower the German, grab the Luger which was always worn on his hip as part of the SS uniform and then instruct him to drive off with both him and Ruth in the car. Overpowering the Kommandant shouldn't be too difficult as the assault would come as a complete surprise to him but it would have to be quick and quiet and somehow they would have to leave Ravensbruck as if everything was normal. Ruth could crouch down in the rear of the car between the front and rear seats and the guards at the gate would assume that the Kommandant was dropping the motor mechanic, clad in SS overalls, back in the village before heading on the long drive south. It was essential they didn't arouse any suspicion. There would be no chance of getting away if the alarm was raised shortly after they'd driven out of the camp. Time passed quickly and at 2am when Ruth appeared with the fresh coffee he explained the plan to her in hushed tones.

'Maybe you could intercept the Kommandant on the way to the garage, offering to bring a flask of coffee for the journey? But somehow you and I need to be alone in the garage with the Kommandant immediately prior to departure.' He said urgently.

'I should be able to do that. If I keep my ears peeled I should be able to hear him. The minute he leaves his room every morning he expects to be attended to so it will not seem unusual if I am fussing over him immediately prior to his departure.' She whispered back to him before adding as an afterthought. *'He has been kind to me, although they have killed my mother.'*

At this Duncan was shocked. The sad news about her mother wasn't a surprise, but what did bring him up short was the fact that he'd not even considered including her mother in the escape plan. He grimaced and said. *'Oh God, Ruth. I am so sorry.'*

'It's OK.' She said, and then turned to leave.

For the next four hours he worked furiously on the engine, finally tightening up the last nut as the time approached 6am, half an hour before the Kommandant's planned departure time. Closing the engine cover he fired up the engine and left it running to see if it settled at the normal temperature. After ten minutes it steadied and he breathed a sigh of relief - it looked as though he'd successfully diagnosed the problem and fixed it.

He blessed the time he'd spent with his ground staff servicing the Spitfire's Merlin engine. Disturbed by the noise of the engine and anxious to be off, Hauptsturmführer Schmidt appeared at the door of the garage.

'So Herr Muller, is it fixed? - I am ready to leave now if it is.' He asked, his voice both friendly and hopeful.

'Yes Sir, I believe it is. I have replaced the cylinder head gasket and run the engine for ten minutes or so and the temperature has remained steady so I think it is fixed.' Said Duncan wiping his oily hands on a rag as he spoke. He'd already sensed the Kommandant's desire to get going as soon as possible but he knew he'd have to stall him until Ruth arrived. *'I was thinking that it might be best if I accompanied you at least as far as the village just to be certain I didn't miss something?'* He enquired, still wiping his hands and looking over the Kommandant's shoulder at the open door behind him, praying that Ruth would appear.

'Why yes of course, that is a good idea. You must be very tired?' He said.

'Actually I'm fine now,' He replied with great conviction as he had just spotted Ruth hurrying towards the garage door.

At the sound of her footsteps the Kommandant swung around, at first alarmed but then on seeing Ruth he welcomed her through the door. *'Ruth, how kind of you. I see you have a flask of coffee and some food for us. This is perfect as I want to be away as soon as possible. I've already loaded my suitcase so...'* He was in mid-sentence when he felt Duncan grab him from behind, forcing his arm up his back and holding his other hand tightly over his mouth.

'Quick,' Hissed Duncan. *'Grab his gun!'*

Ruth dived across the space between them and before the Kommandant could wrestle himself free she unclipped his holster and grabbed his Luger P80. Pointing it directly at the German's head she said in a steely voice. *'If you make any noise I will shoot you.'* At this he stopped struggling. Duncan released his grip and moved swiftly around to Ruth who gratefully handed him the Luger.

'Hauptsturmführer Schmidt, please get into the driver's seat.' Said Duncan, *'I will sit beside you with the gun pointed at your heart and I want you to drive out of the camp as normal and start on the road to Konstanz. We mean you no harm but if you try at any stage to communicate with anyone, I will shoot you. Ruth and I have absolutely nothing to lose so believe me, although I will not enjoy killing you I will do so without any hesitation. One false move by you is all it will take. Do you understand?'*

'I do.' Replied the Kommandant, still shocked by what had just happened.

Ruth piled into the back of the car and crouched down over the transmission tunnel as they drove out of the garage towards the camp entrance. The guard spotted the car approaching and recognising it was the Kommandant's he immediately raised the barrier and saluted smartly as they swept out of the camp.

'It's Ok Ruth, you can sit up now.' Said Duncan, barely able to believe they had pulled off such a daring escape. They drove through the village of Ravensbruck as the first rays of dawn were lightening the eastern sky. Nothing stirred, the road was empty and for the first time since he'd parachute landed in Germany he dared to hope that they might escape into Switzerland. But his recent experience had taught him that just

when things seem to be going well is when they are most likely to go wrong so he pushed the hope of escaping to Switzerland beyond the horizon and concentrated as hard as he could on the present. There was silence in the car for a long time before finally the Kommandant spoke. *'Who are you, Horst Muller? Why do you want to get to Switzerland and why is Ruth with us?'*

There seemed little point in hiding his true identity so he glanced briefly back at Ruth and then replied. *'I am a British RAF Spitfire pilot and I was shot down near Hannover almost four months ago. It will be no surprise to you that I'm trying to get back to Britain and going via Switzerland seemed like my best bet. My name is Duncan Buchanan although, as you point out, my kennkarte says I'm called Horst Muller.'*

'Duncan, you have done well to evade the Gestapo for so long. I think you must be a very resourceful man and you have my congratulations.' He said, almost admiringly. *'And my second question - why is Ruth with us? Oh, and please call me Johann, I think we know each other well enough now to be on first name terms.'*

'It's quite a long story Johann but we're going to be in the car for at least twelve hours so I may as well take you through it.' Said Duncan, already realising that this man was not the stereotypical SS officer. There was an unmistakable hint of humanity about his behaviour which seemed at odds with the fearful image projected by this most elite group of the German armed forces. He then went on to relate the story of how he had met Ruth in the days leading up to the outbreak of war and how they had fallen in love. Occasionally during the telling of this story he would glance quickly back to Ruth who had positioned

herself in the middle of the back seat where she could not only see the road but also Johann's eyes in the rearview mirror. He was also occasionally glancing back at her.

'Through a friend, Ruth helped me get the kennkarte without which by now I would almost certainly be behind barbed wire in a POW camp. I suspect that this could be why she and her mother were apprehended by the Gestapo. Anyway, when they were taken by the Gestapo I swore I would try to rescue them - no matter what the cost - and here we now are, you on your way to your father's funeral and us on our way to the Swiss border and maybe freedom. Sadly Ruth's mother is not with us but I understand that she was one of your camp's victims although we do not know this for sure.'

Johann looked into the rear view mirror and addressed his comments to Ruth. *'Your mother is dead, Ruth. Here with you and Duncan, it seems rather pathetic for me to say that she was killed because one of the camp rules is that if a person is unfit for work because of age, handicaps or illnesses, mental and physical then they are of no use and are disposed of. I have some flexibility in the running of the camp, but not as regards this.'* He paused for a few second and sighed deeply, *'but I am very sorry Ruth. I too have just lost my father.'*

Ruth winced at this but she drew back from pointing out the different circumstances. Death of one's parent always causes grief irrespective of how they died. She didn't think their circumstances were equivalent but to some extent he did, so it seemed pointless to argue with him as he was undeniably upset by the loss of his father.

Johann then continued. *'However, I can put your mind at ease regarding your apprehension by the Gestapo. I developed a new process of investigation which was rolled out across all German cities and it has resulted in the successful apprehension of thousands of Jews who had been concealing their identity. Ruth and her mother were picked up as part of this process.'* Wishing he hadn't claimed ownership of this new system, for which he had received not only the SS-Ehrenring from Heinrich Himmler himself but also the promotion to camp Kommandant at Ravensbruck, he continued, *'it had nothing to do with your kennkarte Duncan, although I could understand you thinking that.'*

Duncan breathed a huge sigh of relief. This had been troubling him since the he'd encountered Hans, the owner of the café where he had bumped into Ruth when he'd first arrived in Hannover. He'd been on his way to meet Jakub Kaufman and he was sure that Hans had recognised him. *'Thank you for telling us this Johann, it is a load off my mind.'* He said gratefully. *'Up to now I've always felt I could have been responsible.'*

'I already guessed this,' interjected Ruth from the back seat. *'I felt certain you weren't responsible. What I didn't know was that he was the architect of the programme which uncovered the fact that we were Jews.'* Referring to Johann who remained silent and impassive. Right then he preferred not to be reminded of this. At the time he'd done the work he had been remote and disassociated from the heart-breaking realities that resulted from it. Now that he had become personally involved it made him feel distinctly uncomfortable.

For a while there was silence in the car as they drove on through the rolling countryside on mostly empty roads. Apart from the occasional military convoy there was not the slightest hint that Europe was engulfed in war. Everything seemed to be continuing as normal but of course it wasn't. Most homes they passed had said goodbye to one or more of their conscripted sons who were now taking part in that unseen war. They were three hours into the trip when it suddenly hit Duncan that back at the camp, by now Ruth would definitely have been missed.

'Johann, you Germans are well known for having procedures and processes for everything, what is the procedure when one of the camp inmates disappears - as Ruth has done?' He said, suddenly worried and angry with himself for not thinking about this earlier. Not waiting for Johann to respond, he looked back at Ruth and said. *'Did anybody see you when you came to the garage this morning?'*

'I don't think so but it's hard to be certain.' She replied, suddenly aware of the consequences if she had been spotted.

Duncan turned again to Johann. *'So what is the procedure, Johann?'*

'There have been no escapees from Ravensbruck during the short time that I've been Kommandant so I've not had to do anything more than skim over the procedure when I was trying to familiarise myself with the general running of the camp. As with most camps, Ravensbruck is surrounded by forest so the procedure assumes that the escapee will initially try to hide in the forest somewhere until the hue and cry dies down. Normally a search party with dogs would be expected to find the escapee within two days and if not the search might be extended for a further couple of days at most. Our camps are very difficult to escape from and it's winter so a prisoner would be unlikely to survive more than one night out, two at the most.'

'So Johann, let's hope your colleagues follow the procedure and concentrate their search for Ruth in the forest. By the time they give up on that, hopefully we'll be safe in Switzerland.' Said Duncan, feeling somewhat relieved and then adding a question, 'would they ever suspect that Ruth might be in the car with you?'

Johann considered his answer carefully before replying. 'When I took Ruth on as my housemaid it raised a lot of eyebrows. She is a Jew who has only just arrived at the camp, so by no measure could she be judged to have earned this position. I don't have to explain to anyone why I choose a particular person as a member of my staff but inevitably people had their suspicions about Ruth and I suppose there will have been rumours flying around. However, it was only after a few days that my adjutant commented on how well-suited she was to the job, so it appears as if my choice was vindicated. Nevertheless I suppose it was obvious to the rest of my staff that Ruth was a favourite. I tried not to openly show this but it was a fact - Ruth is a favourite...in fact she is more than a favourite.' After this he sighed deeply again before turning to look Duncan squarely in the face for a couple of seconds. 'You see, when I first met Ruth in the park I didn't know she was a Jew and if circumstances had been different...' He quickly glanced at Ruth in the rear view mirror before continuing deliberately and strongly, '...I would have pursued her to the ends of the Earth. You must understand, for my whole life I've been told that the Jews are responsible for all Germany's past and present woes, they are vermin, evil, sub-human and have no place in Germany. Until I met Ruth and her mother I had never even spoken to a Jew - at least not knowingly. So my *opinion of the Jews was only what had been planted in my head by my parents and the Hitler Youth movement. It was what I was brought up to believe but now, having got to know Ruth - slightly - already I can see that even if some Jews are as I was taught, not all are. So now I think that maybe Jews are just like the rest of us - there are good Jews and bad Jews. I'm sure that the label SS carries a similar stigma. Not all SS officers are happy to put a gun to the temple of a Jew and pull the trigger - yet that is probably what most people think. A couple of days ago Ruth and I had a conversation about these labels - her label and my label - and I am left wondering how well our labels fit? Ruth told me she has never been a practicing Jew and now that I am at the sharp end of the SS operation I am wondering if the SS label is a good fit for me...and if it had not been for our labels, would our lives have developed very differently?'* At this he shrugged his shoulders. *'There, I've said it out loud. I owe this to Ruth.'*

After he'd spoken there was a long silence and then out of the blue Ruth said. *'Johann, why don't you come to Switzerland with us? I don't think you were ever meant to be in the Schutzstaffel.'*

He gave her a long look in the rearview mirror before replying. *'I have thought about this,'* He said in a voice filled with sadness. *'But I must attend my father's funeral in two days time. When I'm there I will have time to reflect on your observation Ruth - an observation which I value.'* It was a much abbreviated answer which hid his true feelings. He had been deeply attracted to Ruth since their first meeting in Hannover shortly after the outbreak of war and barely a day had since gone by without thinking about her. Then, incredibly, she had appeared in the parade ground of Ravensbruck and his heart had almost stopped beating when he recognised her. In that instant his world had turned upside down. Since then she had never been out of his thoughts and despite the attention he knew her appointment as his housemaid would attract, he'd gone ahead with it. There was no doubt that some of his colleagues suspected his motives but as Kommandant none of his SS staff would dare question the appointment. He wanted to be close to her and help her but when he had authorised the gassing of her mother he knew that the last chance of being with Ruth had gone. She could never forgive him and it was the end of his dream. Then suddenly, everything changed and he'd been abducted by Ruth's lover, a British RAF pilot who had risked all to try to rescue her from Ravensbruck. As a committed SS officer it was anathema to assist the enemy in any way but by helping Ruth escape to freedom in Switzerland he couldn't avoid also helping an RAF pilot escape back to Britain. The dichotomy was pulling him apart. He was being forced to chose between the two most important things in his life, his oath to the Führer and his love for Ruth. Again he caught Ruth's eye in the rearview mirror, how had this Jewish girl captured his heart? In a flash he saw through the fog of his misplaced loyalty. It was an epiphany. She had already seen in him what he had now understood. It was his upbringing alone that had determined what he believed and until now he had never thought of challenging those beliefs. But when faced with the life decisions of the heart he knew he had been deceived. Along with millions of other Germans he had been swept along by the tide of Nazism and its rancid propaganda about the Jews. Ruth had shown him how untrue it all was and now he could see clearly that doing his SS duty and thwarting their escape would destroy the only person he had ever loved. For a brief moment he tried to imagine what his life would be like if he did thwart their escape. Could he really return to his job as Kommandant of a concentration camp and continue to enforce its brutal regime on defenceless women, most of whom were there simply because they believed something different from him? It seemed so obvious now that his current beliefs were only what he had been told to believe as he was growing up. Planted as seeds by his parents and then nurtured by the Hitler Youth, the Nazi Party and the SS, these seeds had grown unchecked and unchallenged inside him until now. The central tenants of his life were choking the life out of him like ivy chokes the life out of a tree. For the first time he was challenging his core beliefs and he knew with absolute certainty that for the rest of his life the deepest truths that would guide him would be based on love, not hate. How could he obey Hitler's orders and carry on sanctioning the gassings, the cruel and inhuman punishments and the barbaric medical experiments in Ravensbruck?

His mind made up he cleared his throat and said resolutely. *'I will help you both to escape but I am doing this for you, Ruth. Duncan, you do not need to hold the gun on me any longer. I know the area around Konstanz well, it was where I grew up until the age of fourteen when I was sent away to join the Hitler Youth. Between Lake Konstanz and the Zellersee the River Danube narrows to less than one hundred metres, in fact it is more of a strait between the two lakes than a flowing river. The border runs down the middle of this strait. On the south side is the Swiss village of Gottlieben and I think your best chance is if I drop you off near to the northern shore and then under cover of darkness you should be able to get across to Switzerland. When I was young there were always small boats around on both sides of the strait so maybe you'll be able to steal one. Also, there is a good chance that the strait is frozen. The winter has been very cold in that area and if it is frozen then to get to safety would only require a sprint for fifty metres. The border will almost certainly be patrolled, I have no idea how heavily but the German border guards will not shoot at you once you are more than halfway across.'*

Duncan looked across at the Kommandant and then back at Ruth who smiled and nodded at which point he uncocked the Luger and laid it in the glove compartment and said. *'You are a very courageous man Johann and I respect you for making such a difficult decision. We'll take you advice.'*

'You have been up all night Duncan, We need to fill up the car so when we've done that I suggest you try to get some sleep. We are still a couple of hours from Konstanz so you have time for a decent nap. You will need to have your wits about you for the crossing.' Johann said.

They emptied the cans of petrol into the car and when they set off again Duncan glanced back at Ruth who smiled calmly and said. *'It's OK, you can trust Johann. Try to get some sleep.'* He didn't need any more persuasion and within seconds his head drooped forwards and he fell into a deep sleep. Johann then spoke quietly to Ruth. *'Would you really have shot me if I had cried out for help this morning when Duncan jumped on me?'*

'Honestly, I don't know. I'm sure that I meant it at the time but could I have pulled the trigger and killed you in cold

blood? I don't think so.' She said, *'but I'm very glad I didn't get put to the test - not just because we couldn't have escaped without you but because I believe that beneath that uniform - that label - you are a man of integrity and decency who has been caught up in an evil organisation and it is only a question of time until you have to face the difficult decision to leave the SS. Could you do that, leave the SS?'*

'If I thought you and I could be together then it is an easy decision, I would come to Switzerland with you and start a new life but I know that can't happen. You and Duncan are in love and I could never ask you to leave him. Also, I authorised the killing of your mother and how could you ever forgive me for that? More than anything Ruth, I want you to be happy but your path to happiness is not with me it is with Duncan. You are correct when you say that it is decision time for me and before you ask me, I don't think I can ever go back to Ravensbruck.' There was a profound resignation in his voice as he forced a smile. *'But you've no need to feel sorry for me Ruth. You have helped me more than you can possibly imagine. How do they say it? - better to have loved and lost than never to have loved at all.'*

For a long time nothing was said as they drove into the gathering darkness under a cold star-filled sky. Then as they neared the northern fringes of the city of Konstanz Johann poked Duncan who woke up with a start. *'In a short while I'm going to drop you off at a lane which runs south-southwest to the edge of the Danube, immediately opposite Gottlieben. I can't remember exactly how far it is down to the shoreline but it can't be much more than a kilometre. There are no buildings along the lane but it is possible that the border guards use it so you will have to be careful. If you hurry you should be at the shore in fifteen minutes. I hope for your sake there isn't a full moon tonight.'*

When they reached the junction with the lane Johann pulled over and stopped the car on the deserted highway. He got out swiftly and opened the back door for Ruth who gracefully as ever stepped out to face him. *'Thank you Johann - for everything.'* She said, *'I hope you have a happy life.'* He smiled at her and nodded before reaching out to shake her hand. Sweeping it to one side she warmly embraced him and then quickly turned away to walk around the car and join Duncan.

'Farewell Duncan,' He said with a wave. *'You are a brave man and also a lucky man. Look after Ruth and in less than an hour you both could be in Switzerland. I hope you make it.'* He then climbed back into the car and quickly drove off leaving the couple less than a mile from the Swiss border and freedom. With no time to waste they jogged off down the lane in the darkness, happy to generate some warmth in their legs after the long car journey. It was bitterly cold, the flanking hedges were covered in hoar frost and whatever pools of water there may have been were frozen solid. It would have been easy to fall and sprain an ankle so Duncan cut back on their pace, eventually deciding that it was safer to walk quickly rather than to continue running. Then in the distance they saw the loom of what appeared to be a searchlight sweep across the night sky.

'That searchlight looks as if it is on the river bank at the end of this lane so we'll need to take to the fields. It is obviously patrolling the river.' Said Duncan breathlessly and squeezing Ruth's hand. She looked at him and in the starlight he could see how scared she was. *'We'll be fine Ruth. In this weather there's*

a good chance the river will be frozen and if it is we should be able to time our sprint between the searchlight sweeps. There's bound to be some trees along the riverbank where we can hide. It looks like there is only the one searchlight in which case we ought to be able to get across between sweeps.' He said, trying to sound as positive as possible but secretly very worried about what they would do if the river wasn't frozen over. As they forced their way through the hedge he was trying to suppress the thought that the river might only be frozen along the shoreline in which case any boat they might be able to steal would have to be dragged across the ice to the open stretch of the river. It might also be stuck fast in the ice. Either scenario did not bode well for them but until they reached the river bank there was no point in worrying about it. Grateful for the almost total darkness they stumbled across the frozen field as fast as they could towards a clump of trees a hundred yards or so from the searchlight tower. Then they saw the light again. *'Damn it,'* cursed Duncan, *'I should have timed it - we need to know if it is a regular sweep of the river or if it's random. Being Germany, I would expect it to be on a fixed period.'* Then adding as an afterthought. *'we need to be as quiet as possible now. Sound will travel on a still night like this.'*

They quickly came to the trees and although it turned out to be only a narrow strip lining the riverbank, it was quite dense and provided good cover for them. Then they saw the searchlight again and from their hiding place in the trees they could see it sweep from right to left down the centre of the river. After the sweep passed they could see a few lights from the village on the opposite bank of the river, only a hundred yards away but by far the most perilous hundred yards that either of them had ever faced. They could almost touch safety but to reach for it prematurely would lead to certain disaster. Now was the time for maximum concentration. *'Ruth, we mustn't rush this. I know we're freezing but it's vital we take the time to think this through. First, we need to see if the river is actually frozen all the way across. We're less than a hundred yards from the end of the lane and if the river is frozen, then we might be able to see footprints when the searchlight sweeps across. If we can't, then we may have to take the risk.'*

'I know, Duncan.' She said bravely through chattering teeth. They were both freezing cold and by dawn they could be in serious danger of hypothermia, thought Duncan. During the next hour they timed the searchlight which was a regular fifteen second sweep every minute. The sweeps were in alternate directions and they could see from the irregular speed that it was a manual searchlight being hand steered.

'We need to time our run so that we set off immediately after the searchlight passes our position on its sweep to the left. That should give us over a minute to get beyond half way - remember, the border with Switzerland runs down the centre of the river. Ruth, that's only fifty yards to run! We can do it!'

His enthusiasm did little to assuage Ruth's fear. *'What if it isn't frozen hard enough and we go through the ice?'* She replied now shivering uncontrollably. He put his arms around her to comfort her but also to share some of his warmth and after a few minutes her shivering subsided.

'We'll run as fast as we can and if the ice starts to creak we will have to go down on all fours to spread the load. I'll hold your hand but it's best stay as far apart as possible but whatever happens, don't let go of my hand. I don't see any

boats and even if we did find one I honestly think our best bet is to make a run for it. Just think Ruth, in a few minutes time we could be in Switzerland.' He could see that they now had no choice. Another couple of hours in the open and they would be virtually immobilised by the numbing cold. Already he felt his own speech beginning to slur which was a sure sign that hypothermia was near. Bracing himself for one final supreme effort he squeezed Ruth hard and said. *'Ruth, I love you with all my heart. Since you and your mother were arrested by the Gestapo I have lived on the edge of despair and you have been though hell, yet here we are on the brink of safety. All we need is one last big effort - and for our luck to hold.'*

They readied themselves at the very edge of the trees where a rock-strewn beach no more than ten yards wide led to the frozen edge of the river. The searchlight swept past them illuminating the ice right up to where the river widened out into the Zeller See, it then turned and retraced its path back to the main bridge across the river to Konstanz which was the only part of Germany on the south side of the Rhine. Duncan confirmed the timings and said. *'OK Ruth, the second that the searchlight passes us on the way back we go, alright?'*

'I'm as ready as I'll ever be, Duncan and whatever happens I love you too.' She said, squeezing his hand tightly, *'I won't let go Duncan, I'll never let go.'*

Crouched low at the edge of the beach and no longer aware of the cold they held their breath as the illuminated patch on the ice moved past them and widened as the angle changed. Then It turned and a few seconds later it passed them moving slowly in the opposite direction. The second the darkness returned they stood up and raced across the beach towards the iced-up river.

Ten strides into their sprint and right on the edge of the ice Ruth tripped over a boulder and howled in pain as she crashed onto the beach. Struggling to her feet she hissed. *'Duncan, it's my ankle!'* Hauling her to her feet he grabbed her around the waist and slung her arm over his shoulder. Then they ran as fast as they could out onto the ice. They were only a couple of strides from the edge of the beach when the searchlight abruptly stopped its transit towards the bridge and began tracking back towards the couple as they half-ran, half-stumbled out towards the centre of the river. The guards had heard Ruth's cry of pain.

'Ruth, we're nearly halfway, another few strides and we'll be in Switzerland!' He pleaded but she was already going as fast as she could. The next second they were caught in the searchlight and a voice shouted. *'Halt right where you are or we will shoot!'*

'Keep running,' Yelled Duncan, dragging her along with all his strength. A burst of gunfire split the night and Ruth slumped to the ice. *'Five more paces and we're safe,'* he cried out, desperately hauling her across the ice with every ounce of his remaining strength. The searchlight stayed locked onto them as he redoubled his effort, each stride taking them closer to safety but the machine gun on the tower had them in its sights and it could spray them with death in an instant. But they were already across the imaginary frontier and the German gun remained silent. Duncan kept hauling desperately until they reached the beach on the Swiss side of the river where they remained in the beam of the searchlight. Just as Johann had said, they did not open fire once they'd crossed the frontier. Duncan and Ruth were safe in Switzerland.

He gently pulled Ruth towards him and held her close, her head resting on his heaving chest. She was still alive but he could see the trail of blood she'd left behind on the ice. *'Ruth, Ruth, we're safe. We made it to Switzerland. We're free now.'* He cried out in desperation. *'Please hang on, please don't leave me.'* He begged as he felt the tears welling up in his eyes. She looked up at him with sad but loving eyes and tried to speak. He had to lean forward to hear her whisper in his ear the Hebrew words he'd first heard her whisper to him as they said goodbye on the unforgettable night when they fell in love.

'Ani ohevet otkha.' Were the last words she spoke and he was still sobbing uncontrollably when one of the villagers who had been disturbed by the gunfire came across and put his arm around him.

'You're safe now. This is Switzerland.' He said but Duncan didn't hear him. He was lost in his grief.

Three days later, after a brief burial service, Duncan stood alone by her grave looking out across the Danube into Germany. Their luck had run out right on the final step of their epic adventure. For a while he wished he'd died with her but in his heart he knew that Ruth would not have wanted that. He drew some comfort from the fact that she had died in freedom and wrapped in the arms of the man she loved. Then his thoughts were interrupted by the sound of a single gunshot coming from the direction of Konstanz. *'I wonder what that was about?'* He said to himself, not really caring.

When Johann arrived at his family home he was warmly greeted by his mother and his two sisters. Although the mood was sad, it was generally agreed that to die prematurely with a massive heart-attack was a much better way to go that to slowly fade away into the oblivion of dementia. But all Johann could think about was Ruth and Duncan and whether they'd made it safely to Switzerland. Since dropping them off he'd had plenty of time to reflect on what he'd done and the longer he lived with the decision to help them, the more convinced he became that he'd done the right thing. But not knowing their fate gnawed away at him until one morning he went to the local Gestapo HQ and discreetly enquired about refugee crossings into Switzerland.

'There are very few attempts now since we started patrolling the river around the clock. However there was a pair of refugees that tried to cross just a couple of nights ago. They shot the girl but the man made it across into Switzerland dragging the dead girl across the ice.' Said the Gestapo officer, oblivious to Johann's thinly concealed shock. For a while afterwards he wandered aimlessly in the streets of Konstanz before heading to the bridge from which he could see all the way down the Danube to the Zeller See. Somewhere on that icy river the girl he loved more than life itself had been killed. He took a deep breath, raised his Luger to his temple and pulled the trigger.

Three months later after a dangerous journey through Vichy France and across the Pyrenees into Spain, Duncan disembarked from the steamer which had taken him from Lisbon to Southampton where finally he set foot again on English soil. Later the same day he knocked on his front door to be greeted by his loving wife and the year-old daughter whom he'd never met. They hugged, kissed and cried with joy to be reunited.

'I knew you'd come back, Duncan, I never gave up hope.'
Said Vera as she shut the door behind him. Meanwhile Duncan was shutting another door in his head. He had carefully swept up all the precious memories of his adventure with Ruth and locked them safely away in a secret room in his mind that only he would ever visit - a room called 'Ruth'.

THE END

[1] Himmler's personal gift - unofficially called the Totenkopfring (Death's Head Ring)

Printed by Amazon Italia Logistica S.r.l.
Torrazza Piemonte (TO), Italy